ngwriter and musician Viv Albertine was the guitarist in
t-punk band The Slits and was a key player in British
nter-culture. She went on to gain a BA (Hons) in Filmmaking
l worked as a director in film and television. Her first solo
um *The Vermilion Border* was released in 2012, and her
moir, *Clothes, Clothes, Clothes. Music, Music, Music. Boys,*
ys, Boys was a *Sunday Times*, *Mojo*, Rough Trade and *NME*
ok of the Year, as well as being shortlisted for the National
ok Awards.

rther praise for *To Throw Away Unopened*:

ven more compelling and breathtakingly candid that its
edecessor.' Stuart Maconie

self-portrait that reveals where her strength of character comes
m . . . Thoughtful, funny, fearful, lonesome and honest, willing
offer up the best and worst of herself.' *Sunday Express*

ome of these revelations are exclusive to her. But often she is
t exposing universal truths . . . Albertine's prose is blunt-cut,
her thoughts are nuanced. Each emotional outburst is
ospectively unpicked with exhilarating precision.'
Daily Tele

'It is driven by a relentless honesty about herself and the dysfunctional family dynamic she was born into, which she lays bare with an almost forensic eye . . . Her conversational style of writing is lullingly deceptive, allowing the revelations, when they come, to explode like well-placed time bombs in the narrative.'
Observer

'Her eye-watering honesty, about everything from sex and shitting to the people who make and unmake us, is the engine of this book. It's a declaration of both love and war . . . Excavating the lives of her parents this musician has re-evaluated not just herself but also the triangulated relationships between people connected by blood. Past traumas drop deep anchors, abutting the present-day reality of a life, but Albertine has made compelling art out of what lies beneath, and is heading for a new horizon.'
Irish Times

'*To Throw Away Unopened* is, if anything, even more searing than the earlier memoir . . . It is about class, poverty, violence, housing, anger, divorce, loneliness and love . . . It involves an astonishing amount of liquid being thrown, in ways that make you want to stand up and scream with joy. Albertine will just not back down, and why the hell should she? . . . It is a profoundly feminist book in that it never backs down from recognising the reality of Albertine's life and opportunities, nor those of her mother and daughter. It sugarcoats nothing . . . Albertine is a magnificent writer . . . I vote Viv Albertine for Minister of Culture.' *The Wire*

'An uncompromisingly honest and often brutal narrative in which she carries a candle into the shadowy corners of her life that most would shy away from . . . As with her first book, Albertine's writing is direct and unaffected, a world away from irony and pretension.' *Loud and Quiet*

'A brave, uncompromising exploration of what makes a person who they are.' *Stylist*

'Furious and funny. The honesty of it makes you gasp.' *Uncut*

'I don't know any other writer who's even half this honest – it's this unsparing frankness that gives the book its lush power. Reading it I felt I was really out there on the ledge with her, feeling emboldened, and like both of us were a little less alone.' Lauren Elkin

'Not only Viv's memoir but, told in her direct, generous voice, a moving account of how generations of women in her family have hacked their lives so they can step outside the norm.' Joanna Walsh

by the same author

Clothes, Clothes, Clothes. Music, Music, Music. Boys, Boys, Boys

Viv Albertine

To Throw Away Unopened

FABER & FABER

First published in 2018
by Faber & Faber Limited
Bloomsbury House
74–77 Great Russell Street
London WC1B 3DA

This paperback edition published in 2019

Typeset by Faber & Faber Limited
Printed and bound by CPI Group (UK) Ltd, Croydon, CR0 4YY

A CIP record for this book
is available from the British Library

ISBN 978–0–571–32622–8

10 9 8 7 6 5 4 3 2 1

For Kathleen and Lucien

Some names and identifying details
have been changed.

I

To be an artist is a guarantee to your fellow humans that the wear + tear of living will not let you become a murderer.

Louise Bourgeois, diary entry, 27 August 1984

1 Next morning, there I was, perched on the edge of my kitchen chair making a list as if nothing had happened. The wooden seat cut into the crease at the top of my thighs but I stayed put, chin in hand, elbow digging into the table, for about two hours. They're a typical middle-class Hackney-dweller's table and chairs – 1950s, Ercol. I bought them from Stella Blunt's in Broadway Market. Don't bother looking for the shop now though, it's shut down. Shops and bars pop up and shut down every week in Hackney.

Hackney Wild*

The first time I saw the Hackney house, a fat brown rat was squatting on the doorstep, snout tilted skywards, sniffing the kebab-and-spliff-scented air. I helped my mother out of the car and we huddled together on the pavement to stare at the rat, who, with an unblinking eye, stared back at us. We were North Londoners, the rat was an East Londoner. I felt it had the upper hand. I glanced up at the front door. It was coated in an orangey-brown varnish, with a 'No Junk Mail' sticker peeling off the letterbox. I thought that by the time I looked back down at the pavement the rat would have scarpered, but it was still there, staring. Perhaps it was stoned. If it had been a human, even a big

* Hackney Wild – a sourdough loaf made at E5 Bakehouse, London, E8

muscly bloke, I would have lifted my arm, jangled my keys at it and said 'Excuse me,' in a forceful tone. You can't do that to a rat. The stand-off ended when I emitted a piercing, delayed-shock, half-choked scream. Ratty seemed to understand this form of communication and, with a streak of greasy brown fur, vanished under a pile of house bricks stacked up in next door's front yard. My mother spent the next half an hour reassuring me. 'Are you sure it was a rat, dear? Don't be daft. You imagined it.'

> . . . trying to make out, like most mothers, that things are what they're not.
> Virginia Woolf, *Mrs Dalloway*, 1925

Mum was ninety-three when we encountered the rat and she knew she was on her way out. After fifty-eight years of parenting me, her volatile, unpredictable daughter, who never did anything at the same time as other people's children – no milestones ticked off as other parents were ticking off university, job, marriage, house, car, children, grandchildren – she wanted to know before she died that I at least had a home, any home, even this one, next door to a rat.

Christos, the owner of the Hackney house, showed us around. When we arrived on the top floor he pointed out of the back window, across a large paved yard, and said, 'That one on the corner, Magnus lives there, he's an artist.' (Magnus turned out to be my first ever boyfriend from school – he helped me pass my GCSE art exam and I gave him crabs. I found out his number and texted him. *Hi Magnus, it's Viv, please contact me urgently.* I wanted to ask him if I'd fit in there. He thought that was funny. *We haven't been in touch for thirty years,* he texted back, *and now I need to contact you urgently!?*) 'Then there's Jenny,' continued Christos. 'She's a war photographer; Jo's a light artist, Kaffe's a sound artist, and right next door,' he tapped on the glass to focus my attention, 'is Gustav Metzger. You know, who started the auto-destructive art movement and was in Fluxus.' (Gustav died on 1 March 2017.) The house was in a group of ten live/work units, and you had to be a practising artist to buy there. I liked the idea of living in a community. My daughter Vida and I were at a vulnerable stage in life, straight out of a divorce, my ex-husband, Vida's father, moving out of London and starting a new family, and my mother dying. Not the right time to be insular. I wasn't convinced about the house though. The corrugated-iron and fibreglass roof had green slime in the gullies – which you could see from the inside when you looked up – and the facade was plastered with rice-pudding-textured, Germolene-pink render.

Half an hour later Mum and I were back on the street. A soiled disposable nappy gaped up at us from the pavement. Neither of us mentioned it but we both lifted our feet up higher than necessary as we stepped off the kerb and headed towards my car. I slid into the driver's seat and set off for the home that I would soon be leaving, a double-fronted mews house in Camden Town.

2 I can still picture myself hunched over the kitchen table, even though it was four years ago. But I see my body from behind, like I'm looking at someone else. I wrote down everything I had to do in an exercise book. I can still remember the main points: register death; call the council; email gas and electricity companies; freeze bank account; choose flowers. Oh, and find a minister. It had to be a woman. I couldn't bear a bloke getting it wrong or sounding all pompous, that would've killed her twice over. I thought I might as well make the calls straight away. I knew I wouldn't be able to sleep.

Architects' Row

I had so many stressful experiences in the Camden mews house, you'd think I'd have been only too pleased to leave it (seven years of infertility treatment, thirteen operations, eleven IVF attempts, one miscarriage, one ectopic pregnancy, my gall bladder removed, one dose of cancer and one divorce, for starters). The property was built in 1988 and designed by Scottish architects Madigan and Donald. The rooms were decorated with Charles Rennie Mackintosh black ladder motifs and had elegant Japanese flourishes like sliding screens instead of doors. The day we moved in one of the removal men muttered out of the side of his mouth that it looked like a Chinese restaurant. The rest of the team sniggered. I over-tipped them to show they hadn't upset me. On the ground floor, ceiling-height frosted-glass doors slid apart to reveal a wide, reclaimed-beech-floored living room and a semicircle of windows opening onto a tiny minimalist tropical garden. The hallway was dominated by a concrete column studded with tiny chocolate and caramel-coloured chips of stone. It towered up through the entire house like a giant unfurling ice-cream cone. It was a statement house. 'Architects' Row', the postmen called our street. Groups of architecture students wandered past our kitchen window every day, stopping outside the front door to make notes on the house opposite, which was one of Norman Foster and Richard Rogers's first buildings.

I loved arriving at our solid Anthracite Grey front door and slotting my Banham key into the locks. That's when I knew I'd left my council-flat-and-free-school-meals past behind me for good. Whenever I had a spare moment I'd stand at the triangular window upstairs, look out over the rooftops and chimney pots towards BT Tower and think, *This is London*. But I couldn't afford to live there, especially after the divorce. Most of our neighbours were lawyers and architects, had a couple of cars, one German, one French, and went on three holidays a year. I was an unemployed single mother with a second-hand red Skoda.

3 I wrote the list in my neatest handwriting and if you'd heard my voice when I made the phone calls, you would have been amazed, it was so confident, cheerful almost. Something wasn't right though, because when I looked out of the window, even though it was a clear day, I couldn't see anything. I knew the tip of the Shard was out there: I'd seen it hundreds of times. There's a yellow brick warehouse in the distance and a railway line on top of the arches over to the right, but all I could see was a fuzzy white mist.

Purple

I was so excited when I brought my three-day-old daughter home from hospital to the Camden house that I knocked on the door opposite and asked my neighbour to take a picture of the three of us: Vida, Hubby and me, on the doorstep. I wouldn't cross the threshold until this momentous event had been documented. In the photograph I'm grinning into the camera, Vida's frowning with a woolly hat pulled too low over her eyes and Hubby looks bewildered. Funny to think that three months later I would be diagnosed with possibly terminal cervical cancer. That it was in me then, as I smiled into the camera, no knowledge and no fear in my eyes.

The cancer treatment lasted five months. As soon as it was finished and I could stand, I went out and bought a lilac vest, a violet cardigan, an aubergine skirt and a purple fleece and wore them every day. My instinct was to follow the colour purple wherever it led me. I even bought a purple car and drove around town in a little purple bubble. I'm drawn to purple (and turquoise) whenever I'm ill or in trouble. I think my intuition was particularly acute at that time because I had strong maternal instincts. I didn't question why all I could think of was colour, but apart from my baby, that was all I could get excited about. One of Vida's first words was 'purple'. I didn't realise how often I said it until she pointed at a parked car and called out, 'Purple!' Mum and I used to call purple 'Purps' when I was young, like it was an old friend. Prince understands, so does Alice Walker. She uses the colour as a motif throughout her book *The Color Purple* to signify good things and the enjoyment of life.

The author Maggie Nelson documents her attractions to the colour blue in her book *Bluets* (2009) and describes how she is drawn to blue during difficult times in her life. Reading Nelson's observations on the link between colour and illness was enlightening and comforting. She also writes about the philosopher Johann Wolfgang von Goethe, who was in a disturbed state of mind when he developed his Theory of Colours – 'Goethe is not alone in turning to color at a particularly fraught moment' – and notes that Derek Jarman and Ludwig Wittgenstein both wrote books on colour while they were dying.* A woman approached me once at a reading after I discussed my love of purple. She was a painter and said that while her young son was very ill all her paintings were purple. I remember confessing to my sister, Pascale, when she called me from her home in Canada, that there was nothing in

* Johann Wolfgang von Goethe, *Theory of Colours*, published in 1840 in English. Derek Jarman, *Chroma: A Book of Colour*, 1994. Ludwig Wittgenstein, *Remarks on Colour*, published in 1979 in English (I've only read Derek's book)

this world apart from my baby that I could get excited about. I didn't care about anything or anyone. I was frightened. She said, 'Try and think of something, anything that interests you,' and all I could answer was, 'Colour.' Not a coloured object, just colour.

By the time the cancer treatment was over we were a week into December. I was determined that despite my exhaustion, Vida's first Christmas was going to be perfect. I lay in bed every day, still reeling from the chemotherapy, dreaming up a colour scheme. I decided all our decorations, wrapping paper and ribbons would be purple. We bought a ten-foot Christmas tree from the local garden centre and stood it in front of the curved window. I strapped Vida into her pushchair and headed off to the shops, a woman possessed, looking for purple, mauve and lilac decorations, arriving home every evening laden with boxes of Christmas balls, reams of wrapping paper and yards of purple ribbon. The tree filled a third of the room and was so tall that the hairy green tip bent over and brushed the ceiling. When I finished decorating it I stood back to admire the end result but was disappointed. It looked more like a shop-window display than a Christmas tree in a home.

I thought I'd pulled the whole perfect-Christmas thing off until halfway through cooking lunch on Christmas Day, I threw back my head, opened my mouth so wide I practically unhinged my jaw, bared my teeth and screamed at the ceiling as if I was being murdered, no doubt curdling all the (organic) bread sauces being stirred up and down our middle-class mews. Then I stabbed my best ceramic saucepan – the one I was about to parboil the potatoes in – with a carving knife. As the saucepan shattered all over the hob I remember wishing it had been a person (but

I couldn't think who it should be) because then I'd have been carted off to prison and wouldn't have to pretend to be capable of looking after myself and being married and acting normally any more. I wasn't strong enough after the treatment to pretend that. All I had enough energy for was loving my baby and thinking about colour.

That night I lay awake mulling over the events of the day – opening the presents, eating the turkey, the meltdown in the kitchen – when it occurred to me we'd forgotten to film any of it. To record *Baby's First Christmas* (without the meltdown obviously), the beautiful home she lived in and how big and purple her first Christmas tree was, was all part of the day's plan.

I stayed awake for hours feeling like a failure. At 3 a.m. I woke my husband and blamed him. He didn't respond, so I telephoned my mother and cried. I could call Mum any time during the night because she was a night bird (no good calling her in the mornings though). Between us we cooked up the idea of staging Christmas all over again on Boxing Day.

On Boxing Day morning I retrieved all the packaging from the bin, rewrapped the presents and put Vida in her red 'Baby's First Christmas' T-shirt again – luckily it wasn't too stained. Mum and Pascale came over to our house and we started filming. We all looked surprised as we opened our presents for the second time and smiled as we chomped through the roast potatoes, vegetables and cold leftover turkey (can't tell on film). Then we clinked our glasses and yelled 'Merry Christmas' at each other. I only got away with the whole charade because of the cancer: for a while there, everyone thought I was going to die (milked it).

Fake Christmas was much better than Real Christmas, there was less pressure and it was funny that we were all in on the conspiracy. I made everyone swear they'd never let Vida know it wasn't her real first Christmas we'd recorded, but eventually I relaxed and told her all about it. Fake Christmas is part of her history now, along with the drama of Mum's Last Night.

4 I closed my eyes. Inside my head I could see a dark-brownish-red field, like dried blood, pierced with thousands of tiny bright lights. When I pushed the heel of my hand into my eyelids the red field bloomed yellowish and the lights shot sparks. I knew if I didn't concentrate, I'd go under. But then I reminded myself, *No, you can't go under. Your next of kin is now your little girl.*

Roast Potatoes

Before I was married I'd always rather see Mum at Christmas (just the two of us, baggy clothes, roast potatoes and a lentil bake – heaven) than anyone else. She wasn't sentimental about it, in fact she was quite happy to stay at home on her own, but I felt it was my duty to see her and anyway, I liked to. When Mum's last Christmas rolled around in 2013 she was ninety-four and so ill and tired that she couldn't face leaving her flat. I invited her over anyway, but she said, 'Don't worry about me, Vivvy, I'll be fine at home, you go ahead and do

your own thing.' I had to confess that this was Vida's year
to spend Christmas with her dad and I was on my own, so
please would she come. (Fifty-nine years old and no one to
rustle up for Christmas Day. Dragging my ninety-four-year-
old mother out when all she wanted was to spend the day in
bed. Embarrassing.) Even though we both had flu I collected
Mum on Christmas Day, drove across town, hoisted her up the
stairs and parked her on the sofa. After a few seconds her head
drooped, her jaw dropped and she was asleep with an untouched
dry Martini and lemonade on the coffee table in front of her.
Meanwhile, I got on with undercooking the turkey. Halfway
through the afternoon Mum's head jerked up like the dormouse
in *Alice in Wonderland* and she barked, 'Don't forget to cut a
cross in the bottom of the sprouts!'

'People don't do that any more,' I snapped. 'I know what I'm
doing.' She looked hurt, but when I peeked over a second later,
she'd nodded off again. I cocked up the meal: the sprouts were
hard and I had to throw away the turkey – it was raw in the
middle. We were both too ill to enjoy the rest, even the roast
potatoes. And we were an eight-roast-potatoes-each family.
Skinny as Mum was, she'd always had a good appetite, so when
she couldn't eat her roast potatoes I knew the end must be nigh.

Apart from the exchange about the sprouts we had a lovely
three days together, not a cross word. Then Vida came back
and things livened up. We opened our presents and Mum put a
polka-dot shower cap on her head and let us take pictures of her
in it, which was most unlike her, she liked to be a bit dignified
about things. This was another indication that she knew she was
dying. Other signs to look out for are when an elderly person
starts giving away their things – usually about two or three

years before they die – and if they insist, rather aggressively, on returning anything they've borrowed or get annoyed if you give them gifts – they don't want any more clutter.

I'd forgotten about the roast potato and shower cap signals when I got the phone call. The trouble with having an elderly parent is that you have to treat every phone call, every fall and every Christmas like it's the last one, because when you're in the middle of something important – and when there have been so many calls, falls and hospital trips that you've become inured to them – it will be the last one.

5 After writing lists and making calls for a couple of hours I thought I'd better check on Vida, so I went downstairs to my bedroom. The kitchen's on the top floor: we swapped the rooms round as upstairs has a higher ceiling and gets more light. I was acutely aware of everything I did that morning, every move and every sensation was heightened, like I was on drugs. I registered the cold from the flat, grey lino through my socks and gripped the handrail so tight going downstairs that my palms sweated and the veins on the back of my hands stood up in snaky blue rivulets. I was afraid I might fall, even though I went up and down those stairs twenty times a day. I watched my feet, thinking, *I must not slip, I must not slip, I'm all she has left.* When I reached the bedroom door I stopped and listened before pushing the handle down, not because I thought it would squeak and wake Vida – I knew it wouldn't, it's made by Hewi, German engineering – but to hear if she was crying. Vida was fifteen at the time but she looked like a baby, curled up asleep in

the king-sized bed. I studied her face for a while, fascinated by her eyes, which are green, darting from side to side under closed violet lids.

Dirty Old Town*

After my divorce I went to a financial adviser to see if there was any way Vida and I could afford to stay in the Camden mews house, but he said, 'The only way you're going to survive financially is if you take in lodgers or sell the house and downsize.' He was right. The place had so many light bulbs I couldn't afford to pay the electricity bills. Every tread on the staircase had two lights and they pockmarked all the ceilings – 'builder's acne', it's called.

I was twelve when my mother sat my sister Pascale and me down during her own divorce and asked us whether we'd rather have lodgers or move to a council flat now that our father had gone. The word 'lodger' frightened me. I imagined leering old men in dirty raincoats; something I'd seen in a TV programme starring Tony Hancock put me off the word. So I said, 'Move to a council flat.' There's a fine line between including your children in big decisions and burdening them so that they go through life thinking they messed up the family's fortunes.

After her divorce, Mum, Pascale and I moved from our semi-detached house in Woodberry Crescent, Muswell Hill, to a tiny, dilapidated, two-bedroomed council house next to the

* Ewan MacColl, 1949

Victorian gasworks in Turnpike Lane. One of the three giant gas holders that loomed over our street was the famous Hornsey Gas Holder No. 1, built by Samuel Cutler in 1892. Until it was demolished in 2016, it was Britain's oldest surviving example of a gas holder constructed with 'a lattice of helical girders and vertical guides . . . a truly geodesic cylinder'.* I didn't appreciate the elegance of Hornsey No. 1 when I lived in its shadow. All I knew was that coming home from school I was frightened to turn the corner into Clarendon Road. It looked like a Lowry painting in winter.

* Colin Marr, www.pmra.co.uk

6 Vida was so sound asleep that she had no idea I'd slipped off and had been upstairs writing and making phone calls for two hours. I climbed back in beside her and edged under the quilt. I didn't want to risk waking her up by getting right under the covers. I lay on my back and stared at the ceiling, listening to her breathe. I used to listen to her breathe every night when she was a baby, every inhalation and every exhalation. If I thought she paused for too long in between breaths, I'd lean over her cot and huff into her ear a few times to remind her what she had to do. It occurred to me as I was lying there, eyes stuck open, thinking about Vida as a baby, that if I let what had happened last night into my head slowly, one word at a time, I might not feel so guilty about how I'd behaved.

Dreaming on a Bus*

I kept thinking about the ointment-pink Hackney house, how it was near the shops, the park, a cinema and a theatre, and how warm tungsten light from the windows of a Turkish restaurant lit up the corner of the street – like the diner in Edward Hopper's *Nighthawks* – which meant walking home at night would be safer. As soon as you cleared the restaurant you could see the house, tall and plain, pink and green, linking arms with all the other tall, plain, pink and green houses. It was a comforting sight, like coming home and opening the door to a kind, reliable companion. The sort of person you'd be grateful to end up with

* Lyric from the Slits' song 'Ping Pong Affair', *Cut*, 1979

after trying to date interesting, attractive people for years. I called the estate agent and made an offer.

A few weeks after moving in I had a huge party in the court-yard. Magnus, my neighbour and old boyfriend from school, built a bonfire two storeys high and placed a giant wooden effigy of a woman on top. As soon as it was dark, on a signal from me the DJ played Arthur Brown's song 'Fire', and Magnus, standing on a high balcony a couple of hundred feet away, released a contraption which shot like a flaming arrow over everyone's heads and straight into the heart of the bonfire, which erupted in flames.

I've lived in every compass point of London but moving east felt like coming home. I love that there's no tube station in Hackney so I have to get the bus everywhere. The 55 is my favourite, it's one of those new curvy ones designed by Thomas Heatherwick. I hail it at the request stop on Mare Street. There's a group of modern houses opposite the bus stop called Sojourner Truth Way. The first time I passed them I thought, *That's an unusual name for a housing estate*, and looked it up. That was when I found out about Sojourner Truth, the African American women's rights activist, born around 1797 in New York. She lived forty years a slave and forty years a free woman. I read her speech 'Ain't I a Woman?' and was glad I knew about her now. We should have been taught about her at school.

Look at me! Look at my arm! I have ploughed and planted, and gathered into barns, and no man could head me! And ain't I a woman? I have borne thirteen children, and seen most all sold off to slavery, and when I cried out with my mother's grief, none but Jesus heard me! And ain't I a woman?

From Sojourner Truth's speech given in 1851 at the Women's Convention, Akron, Ohio

People hardly lift their arms up to hail buses nowadays, not like in the seventies. There were so few buses back then that you couldn't take the risk of not being seen and the bus sailing past, so you thrust out your arm and made meaningful eye contact with the driver. Another old-fashioned custom was to call out, 'Thank you, driver!' every time you alighted from the bus. Mum used to do that, much to my embarrassment. No one counts their change in shops any more either, not cool. Shopping with my mother seemed to go on forever when I was young. She counted every penny of her change, twice, before she left a shop counter. Everyone did.

When the bus heaves into view we all play a game of chicken to see who can last the longest before someone capitulates and raises their arm about two centimetres while looking down at their phone. I've noticed that bus drivers often pull up closest to the person who hailed so they can get on first.

It's a forty-five-minute journey into town. I try and be early for meetings and appointments so I can ride the 55 all the way from Hackney to Oxford Street. I run upstairs hoping one of the front seats will be free but they're usually occupied by someone engrossed in their phone. (Bus etiquette dictates that you do not sit next to someone unless there are no double seats empty.) I'm tempted to say, 'What's the point of hogging the front seat if you don't want to look out of the window?' But I haven't reached that level of outspokenness yet.

I was sitting upstairs on the 55 one cold January evening when I tuned in to a slurred conversation between a man and a woman sitting behind me.

'You know that little bit between Hackney Wick and Hackney Downs?' said the man. 'There's a place there that's a tattoo parlour, except it isn't a tattoo parlour any more, it closed down and they sell drugs there.'

I leaned back in my seat so I could hear better.

'What? You mean over the counter?' the woman replied.

'Yeah, you go in the door and there's like a double mirror and they push the drugs through a little gap and you put the money through. Except I didn't, I grabbed the drugs and ran away. They're looking for me now. I can't go down that road.'

'You ran away without paying?'

'Yeah, done it twice. My mate stood outside and watched to see if anyone came after me. They all came out the second time. They're Turks in there. Said they'll cut my fingers off.' His voice was flat and monotonous like a robot's.

'Can anyone go in there?'

'I'll have to move away from the area. I'm frightened, I'm not safe. Yeah, anyone can go in there.'

'You really ran away with the drugs?'

'Yeah. I'll show you it when we go past.'

I glanced over my shoulder on my way downstairs to see what the man looked like. I knew what he smelled like – unwashed clothes, stale piss and rotting trainers. He was plump and puffy, with watery, unfocused eyes, glassy red marbles poked into a white doughy face like an uncooked pie. He didn't look as if he could run very fast, he looked like a drug addict. The woman looked like a drug addict too. The same grey skin, red nose and wet eyes.

I didn't think I was better than them. I thought I could have been them. I've known lots of people like those two, they weren't alien to me. There were a couple of moments in my youth when I could have been a junkie, if I'd said yes a few more times, if I hadn't stuck with the loneliness and the not-fitting-in, if I'd given in to peer pressure, been a tiny bit weaker. If I hadn't had such a strong mother. I wasn't judging the couple upstairs on the bus but I was glad to have escaped that life and not to be them. They were my Ghosts of Christmas Past, especially the woman, in her leopard-print coat and motorbike boots, peroxide-yellow hair with grey roots, dying for a cigarette, spending all day with a person she didn't like, trying to score. Always on the lookout for a scam, believing that this might be her lucky day, the day she got drugs for free. Every decision you make in life sends you off down a path that could turn out to be a wrong one. A couple of careless decisions somewhere along the line, that's all it takes to waste years – but then you can't creep along being so cautious that you don't have adventures. It's difficult to get the balance right.

I didn't look up at them when I reached the street. It's not good to stare at people in London. I was tempted to jump back on the bus so I could hear the rest of the conversation and find out if the tattoo parlour that sold drugs really existed, but instead I stood outside the Brazilian supermarket and tapped out their words on my phone. Then I darted into the road and waited on the dotted white line in the middle for the next lane of traffic to clear so I could cross. I was perfectly comfortable standing between two lanes of heavy traffic going in opposite directions. That's when it occurred to me that there are two types of people: those who wait for the whole two lanes of a road to be completely clear before they venture across and those who risk it and charge into the middle, not knowing when they'll get the chance to make a run for it to the other side. Neither is better than the other. The first one will have fewer problems and fewer adventures, and the second one will have more adventures and make more mistakes.

7 Lying next to Vida, vaguely aware of a football thudding repeatedly against next door's fence, I let last night's events drip into my head. A motorbike started up. Birds tweeted. First, Mum was dead. I wondered how come I was still breathing, still functioning, with my mother no longer on the planet? It wasn't how I expected to feel. *It'll hit me soon*, I thought, *and then I'll be lost.* Another hour disappeared into the ceiling and I felt nothing. But I was cheating because I wasn't letting myself think about the other thing that happened that night. I knew if I thought about that, the feelings would come. I listened

to a squirrel scrabble its way across the fire escape. It made a
clanging noise as its claws scraped on the metal. Still no tears
came for Mum. The whole time I lay there I didn't think about
the other thing either. Which was unlike me. I'm usually good at
facing things, no matter how unpleasant.

Millie Tant*

Thy valiantness was mine; thou suck'dst it from me.
  Volumnia to her son Coriolanus. William Shakespeare,
  Coriolanus, 1608

My mother made me into the type of person who is at ease
standing in the middle of moving traffic, the type of person who
ends up having more adventures and making more mistakes.
Mum never stopped encouraging me to try, fail and take risks.
I kept pushing myself to do unconventional things because I
liked the reaction I got from her when I told her what I'd done.
Mum's response to all my exploits was to applaud them. *Great,
you're living your life, and not the usual life prescribed for a
woman either. Well done!* Thanks to her, unlike most girls at the
time, I grew up regarding recklessness, risk-taking and failure as
laudable pursuits.

   Mum did the same for Vida by giving her a pound every time
she put herself forward. If Vida raised her hand at school and
volunteered to go to an old people's home to sing, or recited a

---

* Fictional character in *Viz* comic, a parody of a militant feminist

poem in assembly, or joined a club, Mum wrote it down in a little notebook. Vida also kept a tally of everything she'd tried to do since she last saw her grandmother and would burst out with it all when they met up again. She didn't get a pound if she won a prize or did something well or achieved good marks in an exam, and there was no big fuss or attention if she failed at anything. She was only rewarded for trying. That was the goal. This was when Vida was between the ages of seven and fifteen, the years a girl is most self-conscious about her voice, her looks and fitting in, when she doesn't want to stand out from the crowd or draw attention to herself. Vida was a passive child – she isn't passive now.

I was very self-conscious when I was young, wouldn't raise my voice above a whisper or look an adult in the eye until I was thirteen, but without me realising it Mum taught me to grab life, wrestle it to the ground and make it work for me. She never squashed any thoughts or ideas I had, no matter how unorthodox or out of reach they were. She didn't care what I looked like either. I started experimenting with my clothes aged eleven, wearing top hats, curtains as cloaks, jeans torn to pieces, bare feet in the streets, 1930s gowns, bells around my neck, and all she ever said was, 'I wish I had a camera.'

One of the only times Mum was disappointed with me during my teenage years was when I messed up my education. I was nineteen and studying fashion and textiles at Chelsea School of Art when my grandmother Frieda died and left my sister and me £200 each. I bought an electric guitar with the money and left my degree course to form a band – the Flowers of Romance, with Sid Vicious. I'd already dropped out of Hornsey Art School to work in a music venue two years before this, and Mum was desperate for me to get a qualification. Now I'm a mother myself I can imagine how galling it was for her to hear me say something like, *I'm leaving this art school halfway through the course too, Mum. I know that you loved learning and were made to leave school at sixteen and go out to work because your parents didn't understand the value of education, and I know you've spent the last twenty years being overlooked for jobs you're too smart to do because you don't have any qualifications, but I'm not going to get a degree, I'm forming a band with this spotty, monosyllabic boy called Sid Vicious . . . great name, eh?!*

It was her own fault. Mum's attitude to child-rearing made me into the kind of girl who'd do something reckless like form a band with a boy called Sid Vicious when I couldn't play guitar or sing and girls didn't do that sort of thing. She raised me to be a punk. By the time I joined my next band, the Slits, she'd rallied to the idea and came to every show we played in London, often bringing a friend from work. Most mothers would have been embarrassed to be seen with me in those days, and certainly wouldn't have shown me off proudly to their colleagues at Camden Council, where she was a housing estate manager. Mum was very good at being an estate manager. She was good at everything she did. I had complete faith in her, whatever she tried to do. Any job she went for, I took for granted she'd get. She was smart and determined, and I was ashamed that for a very long time I was unfocused and unmotivated, easily bored and only interested in music, art and romance. None of these pursuits were thought acceptable by schools or society in the early 1970s. At my North London comprehensive I was considered a dropout and a time-waster.

Mum cried when I left full-time education to form a band. That was only the second time I'd ever seen her cry (the other time was during the first few months I turned vegetarian, when we sat down to yet another plate of lentils). She didn't reprimand me though. All she said was, 'Do you *have* to get a guitar? It's the one thing Pascale has to herself.' My sister was learning to play flamenco guitar, but as I didn't want to play guitar, I wanted to be in a band – a totally different thing – I ignored Mum's objection. Pascale was fine about it, as she was when I copied her Maria Schneider *Last Tango in Paris* perm. She was very generous about things like that.

I set myself up for life with that reckless decision, that £200 and that electric guitar.

Frieda the Fierce

I've always been absolutely terrified every moment of my life – and I've never let it stop me from doing a single thing I wanted to do.
Georgia O'Keeffe, quoted in Olivia Laing, 'The wild beauty of Georgia O'Keeffe', *Guardian*, 1 July 2016

Mum didn't do it on her own, it took three generations to make me a punk. Before me there was Mum, and before Mum there was her mother, my grandmother, Frieda Basler. For six years, when I was between the ages of four and ten, we lived downstairs in Frieda's house in North London, but I don't remember much about her except seeing her false teeth in a glass by her bed, the smell of mothballs, and noticing that after she'd washed up her plate, fork and cup there was still food stuck on them (that happens to me now – eyesight).

Mum talked a lot about Frieda over the years, which is how I formed an impression of her personality. She was born in

Switzerland in 1891, when the Swiss industrial revolution was in full flow – until 1848 Switzerland was one of the poorest countries in Europe – and her parents were farmers. Before anyone was hired to work at their farm, Frieda's mother cooked them lunch and watched how they ate. If they ate fast, they got the job. 'A fast eater is a fast worker,' she used to say. I'd like to propose that a quick shitter is also a quick worker, although neither a quick shitter nor a quick eater will complete a task as neatly and thoroughly as a slow and methodical shitter or eater.

After my cancer treatment ended I kept going back to the hospital for tests because I had constant diarrhoea and thought I might have bowel cancer – you can become a hypochondriac after surviving cancer. During the investigations a nurse said she was going to teach me how to evacuate my bowels correctly. First she tricked me by asking me to show her how I would push out a poo. I felt embarrassed but reminded myself I'd been a punk, screwed my face up, bore down and pushed my arse into the blue plastic chair with as much effort as possible, hoping I wouldn't fart. 'Aha!' said the nurse. 'That's how everyone thinks they should do it but it's completely wrong and is very bad for your insides.' She told me that to shit properly you have to take a deep breath and gently expand your ribcage and your waist, making sure your breath goes to the sides of your body, not to the front – using the same muscles opera and *bel canto* singers use when they sing – and then the poo slides out without straining your insides. This is difficult for me to do because I'm in and out of the bathroom as fast as possible, not patient with the process at all. I can't understand why anyone would want to sit on the bog reading. I feel claustrophobic in small rooms, and anyway it's not good for your sphincter muscles to hang them over a bowl all opened up for ages. I use the method the nurse taught me whenever I remember, and it works every time. Forcing something, whether it's a shit, a song or a relationship, never gets the best results. Force is aggressive, whereas bravery and determination, traits my grandmother had in abundance, are much more positive attributes.

When she was sixteen, Frieda and her best friend planned to leave Switzerland and travel to England to start a new life – Switzerland had a very advanced train network compared to the rest of Europe – but the night before they were due to leave her friend got scared and dropped out. Instead of abandoning the idea, Frieda went to England alone. This was around 1908, Edwardian times. She would have been wearing a high-necked, long-sleeved blouse, a floor-length skirt over petticoats, a wide-brimmed hat and boots with lots of fiddly little buttons up the side, and carrying a bag containing all her possessions (probably not many). She was unable to speak English and, according to Mum, had two francs in her pocket. *Frieda was a risk-taker.*

Frieda made a good life for herself in England and married Charles van Baush, a Dutch South African who had fled his home country as a young man because he hated the politics. They saved up, bought a house and had five children – my mother, Kathleen, was the fourth. When her younger brother, Edward, was born, Kathleen stamped her foot and cried out, 'You've all dropped me like a hot cake!' Frieda sewed for extra money, knitting clothes for shops in the West End. She didn't use all the allotted wool though. She kept some back to make clothes for her children, stretching out and ironing the garments she sold to her clients to hide that they were undersized. *Frieda was a hustler.*

Charles voted Labour and Frieda voted Conservative – women were supposed to vote the same as their husbands in those days so she was going against the norm. Whenever a local or general election came round Frieda would say to Charles, 'If we both vote, we'll only cancel each other's votes out, so let's not bother.' Charles agreed and didn't vote, but Frieda nipped down to the polling station and voted when he was at work. She used to laugh about this trick with Mum. *Frieda was a con merchant.*

Frieda wasn't a bad person though. She lived through two world wars and joined the British Red Cross during the Second World War to drive ambulances. It couldn't have been easy for her, living in England during the war with her Swiss German accent. Her eldest son, Charlie, was a flying officer on Lancaster bombers. He was killed six months before the end of the war on his twenty-sixth mission. Mum used to think to herself, *At least he had a good life* – he was thirty, it seemed old then. Mum told me that because Charlie was the highest-ranking airman on the plane, Frieda thought someone from his family should hand-write a letter of condolence to the family of each member of the crew who'd gone down with him. The job fell to Mum but she couldn't think what to say – she was twenty-one at the time. She fretted all her life that she didn't do it right. I've got the calico pouch that Uncle Charlie's personal effects were sent home in. It's the size of an A4 envelope, with Frieda's name and address written haphazardly on the front in black ink using capital letters. It looks like a child wrote it. He was Frieda's favourite, but Mum didn't mind – she loved him too, he was playful and handsome. When she was six Mum asked Charlie if it would hurt if he drove over her finger with his go-cart. 'Let's find out,' he said, and told her to put her finger on the ground, which she did. He ran over it, bruised her finger badly and her nail turned black and fell off. Frieda bought Mum a pink sugar mouse as compensation, an unheard-of luxury back then. She made it last for a month by only allowing herself two licks a day.

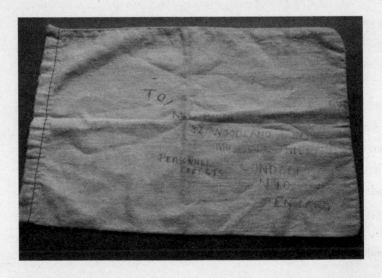

8 It was the night of my book launch. We'd hired the venue, the Lexington in King's Cross, months ahead. There was a lighting rig, a small stage and a bar, and people called all day for spare tickets or to get on the guest list. It was more of a gig than a launch as Anat Ben-David and Bryony Kimmings were performing. As soon as I got there I went over the lighting with the stage manager, then sat at a table and wrote out the guest list. Tessa, bass player from the Slits, was DJing. She'd already set up her records and was checking sound levels with her headphones on. I'd thought about what to wear non-stop for the past three weeks and decided on black jeans, my new Haider Ackermann Cuban-heeled black boots and a Dries van Noten shirt with different-coloured panels and a see-through back, a bit like Vivienne Westwood's old anarchy shirts. I felt as if I was throwing a party, not nervous, but I hoped everyone would have a good time.

We Are the Granddaughters of the Witches that You Could Not Burn*

Mum had a bitter streak, but I thought all mothers were like that. Most of my friends' mothers were disgruntled and used to say things like, 'I could have been a ballet dancer if I hadn't had children,' or 'I was going to be an artist before I met your father.' They were full of tales of what they dreamed of doing as children, or were on a path towards before having a family

* Ghada Amer, *Sindy in Pink-RFGA*, artwork, 2015

stopped all that. After I'd been through a couple of art schools and bands I realised that most of us fail at what we try to do, especially in the arts, but our mothers didn't know that. You don't know how hard it is or how unexceptional you are until you've been at it for ten or so years. They assumed they would have succeeded. I'm glad I just about managed to be born into a time that allowed me the advantage of looking back at my failures (and successes) instead of fantasising about what I could have been.

One of the reasons feminism took such a strong hold in my mind, and in the minds of many girls of my generation, is that we were brought up by repressed and dissatisfied women who had grown into adulthood during the war, learned new skills, tasted independence, and then had to dissolve back into the shadows of their dark-brown homes and watch from behind their ironing boards as the swinging sixties unfolded. In the words of Jacqueline Rose, they were 'part of a generation whose identity was above all to become mothers and who found themselves, after a devastating war, under the harshest obligation to be happy and fulfilled in that role'.*

To compensate for the freedom and the opportunities she missed out on, Mum did her best, with very little means, to make sure that my sister and I didn't suffer the same fate of domestic drudgery and dependence on a man that befell her. Sometimes it's easier to push someone else to do what you can't or don't have the nerve to do yourself. Mum was highly attuned to the subjugation of women and pointed it out to me at every opportunity, on TV, in the streets, in shops, politics

* Jacqueline Rose, 'Mothers', *London Review of Books*, 2014

and education. Her injustices lodged firmly in my brain and added to my own grievances, made me doubly angry with the world. I burned with both her anger and my anger whenever I confronted prejudice. Perhaps that's how it is for every woman. The repression your female ancestors suffered accumulates over the generations, resentment building in daughter, granddaughter and great-granddaughter like hair clogging a washing-machine filter, until along comes a child who is so pumped full of fury that she kicks all obstructions out of the way.

I became the receptacle for her pain, her fury, her bitterness . . .
I dragged it behind me as an ox drags its plough.
   Violette Leduc, *La bâtarde*, 1964

In the 1980s I quit making music and living in squats, tried to stop being an angry young woman and went to film school. I was fed up with feeling cold and hungry all the time. Eventually I became a television director but I couldn't understand how, at thirty-five and armed with a profession, I still felt like a furious outsider. I tried to rationalise it:

Must be because I'm thick.

Or because I don't have British blood, so I have the wrong temperament.

Or because I'm burnt-out and battle-worn.

Because I have a moustache.

Because I'm the oldest intern . . . the first female director at the company . . . in my thirties, don't have a child, the least educated the most outspoken unprofessional hysterical mad bossy scary manipulative ambitious . . .

But even though I look normal nowadays, with conventional

clothing and natural-coloured hair, and even though I own a home, have given birth to a child and clocked up a seventeen-year marriage, I still feel like an alien.

The sensation of being under attack has intensified as I've grown older. Even walking down the street is difficult. It always was, but I was younger then, I had energy and enthusiasm and hope. It's harder for me to put on my psychic armour and sally forth now. There are times when I can't face walking through the city. The advertisements, all the pictures of thin bodies, painted faces, men looking, judging – not so much me any more, I'm becoming invisible, still attackable though, but my daughter, other young women. The dark. Footsteps. Not making eye contact. Clocking distances, assessing his fitness, his age, his clothes, what shoes am I wearing? Can I run? Means of escape, street lighting, any other pedestrians? Everything registered, recorded, exhausting. I see male dominance everywhere. Some nights I can't bear one more male face on the TV. I don't want them in the corner of my living room. Or one more of their books. One more clever painting, one more lazy song.

For sixty years I've been shaped by men's point of view on every aspect of my life, from history, politics, music and art to my mind and my body – and centuries more male-centric history before that. I'm saturated with their opinions. I can think and see like a straight white man. I can look at a woman and objectify her, see her how a man sees her. I can think like a male criminal. To stay safe, you have to anticipate their thoughts and actions. I can think like a rapist for fuck's sake.

You are a woman with a man inside watching a woman. You are your own voyeur.

Margaret Atwood, *The Robber Bride*, 1993*

Some women can block patriarchy out and get on with life, the same way our brains filter out most visual input to our eyes, because if we could see every molecule that's out there, we'd go insane. I can't block patriarchy out. I was trained by my mother to notice it, to seek it out and to fight it.

I can see it, I can hear it, I can feel it, and I'm burning up because of it. Same as all the other 'witches'. Same as the ones in the Middle Ages.

Fatherless Girls

Never trust anyone who says 'Trust me'.
Mum

Of all the domineering, repressive men in the world, in my mother's eyes my father was the worst. I agreed with her. He was controlling and violent, and for a long time I was angry with her for choosing such a dud, even though I wouldn't be here if she hadn't. The upside to having no respect for my father, and no contact with him after the age of thirteen, was that I had the freedom to range way beyond the boundaries society set for young women at the time. If he'd been around, I wouldn't have had the confidence or been allowed to pick up an electric guitar for a start.

* I was led to this quote by the film producer Nadin Hadi

It wasn't just me; none of the Slits had a father. Both Palmolive and Ari's fathers lived abroad and weren't part of their lives, and Tessa's father died during the early days of the Slits.* We dressed outrageously, behaved aggressively, and fought every obstacle that came our way with a zeal that would have been impossible at that time in history if we'd had fathers. Fathers we hated or fathers we loved. Especially fathers we loved, we would have wanted to please them. In those days fathers were admired and obeyed. They ruled the home. The man of the house was given the best of everything – food, mother's attention, choice of TV programme and the comfortable chair (now it's the children). The Slits were able to run around the streets of London like Dickensian orphans, shouting, stealing, cursing, demanding equality with men and control from the music industry and society because no one we loved or respected was angry, looking embarrassed or telling us not to.

Now I come to think of it, our mothers weren't around much either. Ari and I had liberal, hands-off mothers, Tessa's mother lived outside London and they weren't close at the time, and Palmolive's mother lived in Spain.

My mother's attitude towards men freed me. 'Never rely on a man. Make sure you're financially independent. Never let a man own you,' she'd intone. And, 'Don't ever give the biggest slice of cake to a man, you take it for yourself!' was the sermon she dished out every Sunday as she passed around the plate of pink, yellow and brown Mr Kipling French Fancies.

---

* The Slits: Paloma Romero/McLardy, aka Palmolive; Ari Forster, aka Ari Up; Tessa Pollitt; and me

9 I can't recall everything I did before the doors opened, but I do remember running upstairs to the DJ booth and giving Tessa a signed book for her friend, then running back down to say hello to the people selling books and records. At some point I huddled in a corner with John Robb to work out what we were going to say on stage. The audience started arriving at about seven thirty. I was talking to my old schoolfriend Maura, when Dan, Faber's publicist, came over and said, 'Your sister's trying to call you.'

I was a bit irritated. 'What does she want? Is she stuck outside?'

He shifted his weight, looked me in the eye for a second and then looked away.

'No,' he answered. 'I think it's about your mother.'

Not Pretty

My daughter isn't as resentful and rage-filled about the inequities of her life as my mother was from her thirties onwards, and as I was from thirteen onwards. Vida is growing up in a time and culture that gives (white) women more choices in both their work and identity than Mum and I ever had.

I grew up in a society that expected girls to smile and be acquiescent. The message I received was that loud, opinionated girls were 'not pretty'. I learned to want to be pretty. When I was seven years old – before I wanted to be pretty – I won a prize at school. My teacher asked what gift she should buy me with the money (two shillings and sixpence). 'A cowboy gun and holster, please,' I said. I'd seen a shiny silver gun with a brown plastic handle embossed with a sheriff's star tucked into a black leather holster in the toyshop window. The teacher said I couldn't have a gun, not because a weapon was an unacceptable gift from a school – no one cared about that in the 1960s – but because I was a girl. My mother went up to the school and persuaded them to present me with the gun in assembly but wrapped in pink paper. The boys were given their guns unwrapped.

British society didn't offer working-class women many choices in the 1950s and 60s. The way I saw it, I had three: become a secretary, a primary-school teacher or a policewoman. My mother used to be a secretary, I saw female teachers at school, and once a week I watched a police drama on TV called *Z Cars* that had policewomen in it (even now most of the decent parts for women are in police dramas). TV and school were the only two places, apart from the shops, where I saw women doing something other than being a mother and a housewife. I didn't want to work in a shop, and after witnessing my mother's life, to be a mother or a housewife seemed like a death sentence.

British culture was simple and binary back then. There were two choices in most spheres of my life:

The Beatles or the Stones
BBC or ITV
Cadbury or Rowntree's
Wall's or Lyons Maid
Peanut butter or Marmite
John Peel or Tony Blackburn
Labour or Conservative
Arsenal or Tottenham
Levi's or Wrangler.

Everything was black or white, or black and white. I had two friends, two pairs of Levi's, two T-shirts and two pairs of shoes (Clarks for school, Woolworth's plimsolls for weekends).

I noticed that as Mum got older she stopped wearing dresses and skirts, and wore trousers instead. Her voice got lower and she didn't talk to men in a cajoling sing-song tone any more. She also smiled less and a frown appeared between her eyebrows. She became more solitary, less 'pretty'. I interpreted these signs as her becoming less happy.

In the whole of my childhood, my mother never once suggested that I should aim to be happy. No one discussed happiness at home or at school in those days. We were taught and brought up by people who'd lived through the Second World War, and they were brought up by parents who'd survived two world wars. You don't go around asking each other 'Are you happy?' after a war. 'Are you surviving?' is more like it. Because I wasn't burdened with trying to look and be happy (awful hearing parents ask their children 'Happy, darling?' and seeing the child's attempt to nod convincingly and arrange its little face into a bright expression), there was plenty of space in my mind for me to respond to my mother's encouragement to lead an interesting life instead.

My neighbour, Magnus, told me recently that his mother eventually became happy when she got dementia and forgot everything that had happened to her. When he asked her if she remembered his name, she said, 'Sainsbury's?' Another friend's mother found contentment when she started taking anti-depressants. She'd been quite bad-tempered up until then. He said it was a bit weird though, to see her floating around the house smiling all the time, especially after his father died. She just didn't give a shit.

Euphoria

Although Mum insisted that she was never lonely after her divorce, I didn't believe her. I was sure I detected an undertow of sadness.

'Don't you ever get lonely on your own, Mum?' I'd ask whenever I visited.

'No, I love it,' she'd reply, hunkering down in her armchair with a satisfied smile, blinking in slow motion like an overfed cat. She never forgot what it was like to be in a marriage throughout the 1940s, 50s and 60s: trapped, unable to get a mortgage if you were a woman, having to leave your job when you became a wife – most companies had a marriage bar after the war. Lots of women lied and removed their wedding rings so they could work. To be free of servicing a man, his washing and his cooking, not to be shushed whilst the news was on, leaving the washing up in the sink overnight if you were tired, these small privileges felt like luxuries to my mother, luxuries she never thought she'd be able to afford, and she cherished every one of them.

For eighteen months after the end of my own marriage I had the same sense of euphoria. My elation didn't last fifty years like Mum's did, but then she grew up in a more restricted time than me so appreciated her freedom more. Two years after my divorce I gave away our Burmese cat (he went to a good home). He was always complaining and demanding food and attention, even moaned when the heating wasn't on. After my husband and the moany old cat were gone I felt exactly the same delirious relief mingled with the adrenalin rush of a narrow escape as my mother did when my father left home. But after eighteen months my excitement evaporated and real life, bills and loneliness crept in, although I still feel a surge of relief every time I inadvertently wander down the pet food and cat litter aisle in a supermarket. I've never regretted the loss of any man – or cat – I've known. I have regretted losing women though. Every woman, good or bad, who's gone from my life has left a hole. I was on tenterhooks for years anticipating my mother leaving the biggest hole of all. I expected her to leave a crater. A crater can be beautiful, I kept telling myself. People go to Iceland and America especially to see craters.

10 I patted my back pockets and was annoyed with myself when I realised I'd left my phone in the basement. I should've kept it on me. I never went anywhere without it in case Mum needed me, but that night I was scared it would slip out when I used the loo because I was so busy and distracted – it had happened before. I ran downstairs and searched through my bag, telling myself to stay calm, not to panic until I'd called Pascale and heard the facts. I didn't think it was anything serious. This was the one night I was certain I could relax. Mum knew what writing the book had cost me: three years of trying to find a bit more time, a bit more money, supporting my daughter, negotiating a divorce, moving home four times.

Why aren't there more female artists?

Fuck off.

(And read *Women Artists* by Linda Nochlin.*)

* *Women Artists: The Linda Nochlin Reader*, edited by Maura Reilly, 2015

Tender Buttons*

I met Eryk-the-builder when he came to price up the renovation work on the Hackney house. He was tall and thin, with a shaved head and eyes so pale they looked like acid drops that had been sucked into flat, transparent slivers. His voice was low, not so low as to be threatening but droney and mesmerising like bees buzzing around a lavender bush. I drifted into a daydream as he talked about partition walls, clerestories and intumescent paint, wondering if he'd arrived in my life because I'd been sensible for once and chosen to move to a plain, normal house and employ an ordinary, easy-going architect who knew nice builders instead of hiring someone fashionable and expensive. A week after the refurbishment started Eryk saw my full name on an email and realised I was 'Viv from the Slits'. He told me that in 1978, when he and his then girlfriend were seventeen, they followed the Slits all around Europe. I was so flustered and flattered I tripped over a piece of copper piping as he spoke and stumbled into a hole in the concrete floor.

For a long time after moving to Hackney I was frightened to do anything adventurous or get involved with anyone in case I created bad associations. I wanted the house and the area – the only compass point of London I hadn't yet lived in, and the only streets I could walk down without feeling nauseous and overloaded with memories – to remain pure and unsullied. Don't ever try to do that. It's impossible.

I got to know Eryk slowly. I didn't want to rush into a

* Gertrude Stein, *Tender Buttons*, 1914

relationship and make another mistake. He seemed gentle and intelligent, with occasional flashes of spite. We were both interested in music, art and architecture, a bit cynical, and repulsed by the theme tune to *The Archers*. I liked his physical presence. His movements were languid, unimposing. A man's physical presence is very important to me. I'm sensitive about personal space and put off by too overbearing a manner.

I liked Eryk so much that I did that thing where you look at yourself through fresh eyes. What I saw made me want to shrivel up and dissolve into a smouldering pile of black clothes and pointy boots like the Wicked Witch of the East – which is exactly what I would dissolve into because that's what I wear most of the time. I was ashamed of some of my character traits and failings, like my lack of tact and short temper. I knew I was loyal and good fun but I wasn't sure if that made up for the bad stuff. *Every day, in every way, I'm getting better and better*, I chanted to myself – a self-hypnosis mantra from the French psychologist Émile Coué that I first heard in the 1980s.

Eryk was a strange one. Of course he was, I'm only attracted to strange ones. I wouldn't be able to see a nice normal man if I tripped over him in London Fields. Normal isn't familiar to me. Eryk was very passionate on our first date, felt me up in the corner of a dark bar, grabbed my arse, slid his hand inside my jeans and snogged me for ages at the bus stop. We were like teenagers. But the first time we went to bed together he kept all his clothes on, including his socks. I'm used to inexperienced and sexually shy men so I asked him if I could undo the top button of his soft brown shirt. 'Just one,' he replied without smiling. I negotiated with him that every time we saw each other (about every ten days) he'd allow me to undo another button. I liked his reticence, it made me feel bold. I felt sexually experienced compared to him and more confident about taking my own clothes off. After six months, Eryk agreed that next time we met he'd take his socks off, but I had to promise not to look at his feet. I did have a quick peek. They were no different from or worse than anyone else's feet, just soft and very white, like the fish that live at the bottom of the ocean and never see daylight. Whenever he was coming over to my place Eryk would text to ask what I'd like to do. If I said, 'Bed,' he knew that didn't mean sex. It meant we'd lie down, kiss and touch and read a book out loud to each other. We were reading Wilkie Collins's *The Woman in White*. I don't know if Eryk knew I wasn't bothered about us not having sex because we never talked about it. I thought if I probed him on the subject he'd close down. Something I've learned from the past and all the dates I've been on is to just let a person be who they are. If they do something that makes you uncomfortable or doesn't work for you, tell them. If they don't or can't adjust and it doesn't bother you too much, ignore it. If it does bother you, leave. That's what I always do. Leave. I thought that's what everyone did. When a relationship hits an obstacle you say mean things and then you leave. That's the way my parents did it.

11 I turned away from the smokers huddled around outside the entrance, leaned against the wall, pulled the collar of my jacket up to shield the phone and called my sister. She managed to say, 'Mum's turning blue, the ambulance crew are here,' before bursting into tears. I was relieved Mum wasn't dead, even though I wasn't expecting her to be. I told Pascale to

put me on to a medic. 'We've only got one more tank of oxygen,' he explained. 'Your mother has about twenty minutes left.' I wandered back into the club. I wasn't upset, I didn't feel scared, I didn't feel anything. Even though I'd just been told that Mum had only twenty minutes left I didn't feel there was any need to rush. *I'll leave later, in a couple of hours, after my talk,* I thought. *My first duty is not to let all these people down.* I pushed through the crowded room. I was talking to myself in my head: *Mum'll be all right, she's not going anywhere. No way she'll slide off the planet tonight. She's strong and wilful, she'll wait for me.*

Deckchairs

Anger is about status injury.
Martha Nussbaum*

By the time she reached her sixties, Mum had developed into such a confrontational person that I felt compelled to have a word with her about it. I said it wasn't necessary to be so aggressive all the time nowadays and she needed to keep up with the changing times. (Vida said a similar thing to me when I was fifty-six.)

It was back in the 1980s when Mum was sixty-something that we had the 'unnecessary aggression' conversation. British people seemed to suddenly sprout a whole new attitude to life. Margaret Thatcher was prime minister and even creative people started

* I was led to this quote by the anthropologist Martha Nussbaum by Maria Popova, www.brainpickings.org. See also Alison Bechdel's book *Are You My Mother?*

conforming and becoming acquisitive. Men and women began physically grooming themselves from top to toe like Americans. It was all a bit of a shock to the system. I wasn't aware of British men wearing deodorant before the eighties. The smell of body odour on the tube at rush hour made your eyes water. I miss normal body smells. Now that we're all masking our sweat I feel we've had a signal removed that helped us deduce attractiveness and character.

Mum and I had booked a bed and breakfast by the sea for the weekend, but the landlady was so offhand and rude to us we decided to check out and find somewhere else to stay. I was polite as we left but I could feel Mum bristling behind me when I paid. She managed to wait until we were trotting down the path with our bags before bursting out with, 'You should have told her why we were leaving and had a go at her!' Whenever I was conciliatory Mum thought I was being traitorous. I explained that things didn't work like that any more, that these days it was considered much cleverer – and nastier in my opinion – to smile to people's faces whilst you stab them in the back. The pain lasts longer for them and you walk away feeling smug and looking refined because you haven't lost your temper. I observed people conducting themselves this way whilst working as a freelance director at television companies in London, mixing with people who'd been privately educated and gone to Oxbridge. I was exposed to much more ruthless behaviour when I associated with these professionals than when I hung out with street kids in my punk days.

Mum and I kept on discussing the merits of suppressing anger as opposed to expressing it, huddled together in our deckchairs behind an orange-green-and-white-striped canvas windbreak.

It was the same sort of place she used to take us for childhood holidays. We couldn't afford to go on proper holidays so every year Mum took us to the seaside for just one day – Walton-on-the-Naze or Canvey Island in Essex. 'You can have anything you want – fish and chips, rock, sweets, candy floss and balloons, souvenirs, go on all the rides. We'll have our whole holiday in one day,' she'd say, as she took all her savings out of the tea caddy. We'd fall asleep on the train home, bags full of sandy swimming costumes and towels, sweets, toys and postcards, with Mum telling us, 'That day was as good as a two-week holiday!' She said it so many times that I believed her. Still do.

I had to give Mum lots of context and references to convince her that it was necessary to contain her anger, but she got it eventually and was grateful to me for bringing her up to date. She realised she'd developed the habit of always defaulting to a defensive position. Reverting to anger when cornered was Mum's automatic response to threat because she felt and had always been treated as if she were a nonentity, in all walks of life, from her home to her work to her society. It was when I was in my twenties that I tried to reject her way of thinking and not be furious all the time like her. No one wanted to be perceived as an underdog in the 1980s – or since the 1980s, come to that. Some of us embraced it in the 1970s and made a virtue of it. My mother had pumped me so full of her anger I couldn't throw it off. She must have thought I needed some kind of fuel to fill me with the courage to kick down doors and gain entry to an interesting life. So anger it was.

Fishwife

Bad girls aren't villains; they're transgressive forces within patriarchal cultures. Made to choose between wreaking destruction and accepting their own powerlessness, they pick destruction.

Judy Berman, 'The cool girls, good girls and bad girls of modern books', *Guardian*, 28 May 2016

Often, when I've acted in anger, I've been perceived as, been called and have felt mad. Not the quietly-weeping-in-my-room-can't-get-out-of-bed madness of depression, although I have had that. Or the erase-myself-from-the-planet-can't-bear-it-any-more-kill-myself-I-am-a-burden-to-those-I-love mental illness. I've been close to and feel compassion for that. But boiling-over-furious-red-faced-eyes-popping-burn-her-at-the-stake-clap-her-in-irons-tie-her-to-a-stool-duck-her-in-the-pond-teeth-grinding-howling-in-the-attic-lock-the-door-and-throw-away-the-key-raving-hollering-in-your-face-ugly mad.

One October evening in 2010 I set off with my guitar, pedals and a couple of changes of clothes to play a solo gig in York. It was a small, intimate venue and everyone there had paid to see me, except four men sitting at a front table. I later discovered they were a boss and his three male employees, who'd been given tickets as part of a work bonus. They shouted and caroused through my first four songs, which is fine in a big venue but not a tiny one. They were louder than me as I only had my guitar with its tinny, trebly sound for accompaniment. After the fourth song I asked them to keep it down because other people were finding it difficult to hear, but they ignored me. I felt like I was their mother asking if they had any washing they wanted doing. After they continued to shout through the next song I suggested they go to the bar if they wanted to make a noise, but they didn't move or stop yelling. Instead of the audience witnessing Viv-Albertine-the-ex-punk come back to shake them up, they saw a middle-aged woman being disrespected and ignored. I had two choices: give up and let people see a woman try and fail to be respected, or fight. I decided to fight.

I unplugged my guitar, jumped off the podium and walked over to the men's table. It comes back to you, your punk attitude, when you need it. They were sitting in a semicircle with their pints lined up in front of them and looked up in unison with *What you doing over in our corner, Ma? We didn't ask for extra peanuts!* expressions. 'Do you know how the way you're behaving makes me feel?' I asked. They shook their heads. I was surprised they responded. A mistake on their part. 'Like this.' I picked up the fullest pint glass on the table and, starting at the bloke on my right, swept the beer in an amber arc across the four blank faces, ending up with the bloke on the far left. None of them moved. They just sat there with their eyes and mouths wide open, dripping. The room fell silent. The four of them were quiet for so long it felt as if time had stretched and was suspended between us, like chewing gum pulled out of your mouth to see how long you can get it. Triumph surged up through my body and went right to my head. I lifted another glass from the table and drenched them again, this time in Guinness. Out of the corner of my eye I saw some members of the audience step backwards into the shadows.

The scariest-looking man stood up (he wasn't big but he had a feral glint in his eye), reddening with rage and clenching his fists.

I remembered what Sid Vicious taught me about fighting: *Do the worst thing you can think of first.* Except I threatened the worst thing first. 'If you want to take it outside, let's take it outside,' I said, putting the hardest, coldest look I could muster into my eyes. 'And I'll put this bottle in your face.' I picked up an empty bottle of Heineken with such fluidity of movement you'd think I did this sort of thing every day. The feral man sat down. The four of them muttered between themselves, then gathered up what was left of their drinks and headed towards the bar. The DJ put a jolly record on to signal that that was the end of the night, but I hopped back on stage, said 'I haven't finished yet' into the microphone and played the rest of my set. Quite a lot of the audience had left by then, but those who remained saw that the spirit of punk was alive and well, and completely out of place, in a middle-aged woman with an electric guitar, in an underground bar in York.

> I am never proud to participate in violence, yet I know that each of us must care enough for ourselves, that we can be ready and able to come to our own defence when and wherever needed.
>
> Maya Angelou, *Letter to My Daughter*, 2008

I'm sure that my choice of when and where to resort to – or threaten to resort to – violence must seem peculiar and unnecessary to most people, but the times I choose to be violent are the times that seem necessary to me.

Later that night I came across the boss of the group at the bar. He was talking to the barman, all excited that he'd been part of the night's 'entertainment'. We smiled at each other and I said I hoped his top wasn't expensive. 'It was actually,' he replied. 'It's Ralph Lauren.'

12 I stumbled through the crowd towards the bar, not knowing who I was looking for or what to do, when I bumped into my schoolfriend Maura again. I recounted the phone call from my sister, ending with, 'I might regret it if I don't go now though.' As I waited for Maura's response, a wave of cold prickles crept from under my shoulder blades, across my back, up to my neck, around my ears and settled on the top of my head. I searched Maura's face for some sort of clue.

'Yes,' she said. 'You might.'

Not the answer I was expecting, but that was it, the moment I knew it was all over – the book launch, the panel discussion, the night of celebration. The moment it dawned on me that quite a different night lay ahead.

Mrs FB

Mum's health declined rapidly during the last three years of her life. I didn't realise it at the time, but she was having lots of little heart attacks. I just thought she kept falling over. Whenever she didn't answer her phone for a few hours, I'd drive over to her flat, pick her up off the floor, check she had no broken bones, prop her in an armchair, make a cup of tea and a sandwich and then drive back home to Vida. It didn't occur to me to call a doctor until her fifth or sixth fall. I found her lying in her hallway trying to reach the phone, and that's when I realised it was serious. I was so absorbed with my own life – the divorce, moving house, finding Vida a new school and recording my album – that I just thought of Mum's falls as annoying obstacles. I was irritated that just as everything else was crumbling in my life, she was breaking down too. Not a charitable thought, but I thought it. I decided that the only way I could manage everything and everyone, and keep working, was to be three people at once. It seemed a logical solution at the time. I became more and more exhausted as I hurtled between all my commitments and the strain soon started to show. As always, my tolerance towards domineering men was the first thing to go.

One summer's day I left Vida with Mum for a few hours while I recorded some vocals for my album. At four o'clock I rang the doorbell to collect her and, excited to see me, Vida raced down the three flights of stairs to let me in. As we climbed back up, the door of the second-floor flat (the one below Mum's) opened and a tall man in his thirties poked his head out into the hallway. 'Keep the noise down,' he said. All that had happened was seven-year-old Vida running downstairs in the middle of the afternoon.

'Mind your own business,' I answered.

'Excuse me?' he responded, in that highfalutin tone that meant he'd heard exactly what I said and thought he'd humiliate me by making me repeat it. That doesn't work on me.

'Mind your own business,' I said again, loud and clear. We ended up on the doorstep, with him towering over me.

'What's your name?' he demanded. Maybe he thought he'd try and frighten me by being authoritarian. I'm not scared of authority. Shook that off fifty years ago.

'My name is . . .' He leaned in to catch the words. 'Mrs . . .' I paused. I wasn't sure what to say. I certainly wasn't going to give him any personal information. 'Mrs . . . Bollocks,' I said.

He froze mid-lean. Vida looked up at me. Out of the corner of my eye I could see Mum, who was hauling herself down the stairs to come to my defence, stop in her tracks and lean on the bannister, panting and smiling triumphantly, *That's my girl*.

The man recovered his composure and tried again. 'What's your *real* name?' he said. 'I'd like to know.'

'My real name is Mrs Bollocks,' I replied, with confidence this time. 'But you can call me Mrs *Fuck* Bollocks if you like.'

(The initials of my grandmother, I later realised.)

Mr Shilling

Before 'Keep-the-Noise-Down' moved in, a man called Mr Shilling lived in the flat below Mum for thirty years. He was a gentle person, nursed his mother night and day until she died, and then lived there on his own without any friends or visitors for another ten years. As he got older, Mr Shilling became more and more hunched over, scruffy and smelly. He liked to collect bits of scrap and poke around skips in the surrounding streets after dark for entertainment. One night he was searching through a skip in Belsize Park when two boys spotted him and decided to beat him up. They stamped on his head several times and stole his trainers – cheap old trainers, not a name brand. Mr Shilling ended up in hospital without any shoes.

Mum went to visit him, but he looked horrified when she walked into the ward and drew the sheet up to his chin to hide his bare bony chest. They'd only ever said hello to each other as they passed on the stairs. Mum was sorry she'd visited him and sorry she'd embarrassed him. He died three weeks later. Killed for looking weak, past his sell-by date. That's how it happened in Neanderthal times: you got weaker and slower until some fit young bastard put you out of your misery. They shoot horses, don't they?* Except Mr Shilling was happy enough shuffling backwards and forwards to the shops, looking in skips, cooking his meal at night and watching television. He wasn't doing any harm and he didn't want to be culled.

He reminded me of my father, who also turned into a strange-looking, crooked old hermit as he aged. Every time my father went out – he was French and went back to live in France when he was older – people stared at him. Mind you, he did have a Beatles haircut (so he thought, but it looked more like a Friar Tuck as he was bald on top), wore clothes from the 1970s and talked to himself out loud as he scuttled around the streets. Eventually he became so wary of the outside world that he wouldn't venture any further than the shop on the corner. After a while even that was too much and he stayed in all the time. One day a neighbour heard him crying out and found him dying on the sofa.

I'm attracted to loners. Both my parents became recluses in later life, and I'm becoming one myself. There's a lovely word from the thirteenth century describing women like the writer and mystic Julian of Norwich (she wrote *Revelations of Divine Love* around 1395, thought to be the first book to be published in the English language by a woman). At that time, a woman who completely withdrew from the world was called an anchoress. That term suggests to me that recluses are not mad, but anchored.

* *They Shoot Horses, Don't They?* (1969), directed by Sydney Pollack, starring Jane Fonda, based on the 1935 novel by Horace McCoy. The phrase refers to the practice of killing old and injured horses to put them out of their misery

13 By the time Vida arrived I knew what I had to do. I saw her smiling at me from the entrance of the club, hair freshly washed and shining, in her best dress and new shoes with little heels for the first time. I took her hand and led her into a corner. God knows what the expression on my face was like. My mind was working overtime as we took those two or three steps. How to say this? How to say, *You know this night that you've been planning your outfit for and looking forward to for months? Well, it's not happening. I'm lifting the needle off the record mid-song. And you know the person you love most? The one who never tells you off and loves you unconditionally? She's going to die tonight. That's what's happening instead, the thing you've been dreading.* How to say it? And not scar her for life? And get to the care home in under twenty minutes?

Do Not Resuscitate

I never asked Mum what she was thinking during her last few months in hospital. I didn't want to stir up thoughts of death in her, not when it was so imminent, in case she was frightened. We'd talked about her dying in the past, but when the looks between us (gaze not held very long, or too long) and gestures (more tactile than usual) signalled that death was getting close, I didn't want to appear too interested in the actual process and treat her like a specimen to be analysed. But what *was* she thinking? I was surprised that she kept ordering books from the hospital's mobile library. Why did she still want to read and increase her knowledge? She only had a few days left as far as she knew, what did she care about the Second World War or the history of slavery in the southern USA? (Although I've got thirty years left, if I'm lucky, and the thing I most look forward to is all the books I can read in that time.) Or was immersing herself in books a way to distract herself from thinking about dying? She couldn't bear to listen to her beloved radio any more or have the TV on, but often when I rounded the blue pleated-paper curtain – always pulled right around her bed for privacy – she was engrossed in a book propped up on the bedside table.

Reading, and fighting for her rights were the two passions Mum kept alive for the longest. 'You have to fight for yourself, Vivvy, right up to the end,' she advised me in her last few weeks. 'Does it really never stop, Mum?' I asked. She shook her head. Recently she'd insisted on being moved to another ward when a troubled female patient kept swearing at her. And she was so tired of being poked and prodded and operated on that she refused to endure any more invasive tests from her doctor. He was astounded that Mum wouldn't do as he said. He thought she must be insane. Why else would she disobey him, *a consultant surgeon*? He sent a psychiatrist over to her bed every single day to hassle her into changing her mind. She wouldn't budge.

What was Mum thinking? *Peace at bloody last*, I reckon. She was OK with dying. Do Not Resuscitate.

Luckily – or unluckily, because it's exhausting, but then for some of us to keep trying to play the game and fit in is also exhausting – my mother instilled that same combative spirit in me. It doesn't make getting work, going out for a meal and having friends or a relationship easy, but there's a certain inner peace to be derived from holding on to your principles. 'You look so young, you must have a clear conscience,' Mum said to me once. I don't have a clear conscience. I've done plenty of things I regret. If I do look young – and if there's a reason for it other than being single, sleeping too much, hair dye, bio-identical HRT, genes, not smoking or drinking, avoiding too much sun, and a squirt of Botox between the eyes once a year (stopped in 2016) – it's because I try to be truthful. I'm cleaned out, like I've had regular emotional irrigation treatments. Although with all the diarrhoea I suffer from, the reason may be much simpler than all that. Maybe I just look young because of all the *actual* colonic irrigation.

With only a month of breath still left in her, Mum and I sat together one afternoon and listened to the broadcast of a show I'd recorded for BBC Radio 6 Music. I arrived at the hospital to find her propped upright, a nurse at her side, the radio on her bedside table tuned to BBC 6 Music, and annoyed I was late. We wore one earpiece each of my headphones and listened to the whole two-hour show. Mum commented on every record I chose and every word I uttered between songs. 'Hmmm, not really my taste, that one,' or, 'I didn't like that one at all, I liked the last one better.' I found myself getting upset, as if it mattered whether my mother liked Sun Ra or not. Now I realise she just wanted to be taken seriously, to still be thought of as an intelligent person who had opinions. Mum fought to the last to be seen, even by her daughter.

Film Noir

I am become a hard, thankless, graceless girl, and it was the only
way I could do it.

Agnes Smedley, *Daughter of Earth,* 1929*

During the last year of my mother's life I was so sleep-deprived
that my senses became heightened. I blundered through the days
feeling like a character who'd been edited into three different
films by mistake: a Gothic ghost story, a 1950s family melodrama
and a dystopian fantasy.

Visiting Mum in the care home was the ghost story. Weaving
my way around the residents drifting down corridors, robes
trailing, swollen slippered feet barely touching the cabbage-
coloured carpet, wisps of frosty hair candy-flossing around
wobbly heads, I'd arrive at Mum's open door to see her lying
on her bed motionless, mouth wide open. *Oh no, it's happened.*
I'd hold my breath, waiting for her tiny frame to lift slightly.
I'd never seen her look so corpse-like before. *That's what she'll
look like when she's dead,* I thought (and she did). Before doing
anything I'd wash my hands – explicit diagrams and instructions
were in every bathroom of every hospital Mum passed through.
I'll never forget how to wash my hands properly now. Don't
forget the backs, the fingertips and that bit that looks like a
chicken leg. *If you're out and need a clean finger to extract
something from your eye,* Mum always used to say, *the little
finger on your left hand is the cleanest.* Then I'd sit next to the

* I was led to this quote, and to Agnes Smedley, by Vivian Gornick, *The Situation and
the Story,* 2002

58

bed, take Mum's hand into mine and ask, 'How am I ever going to cope without you?' She'd tut and say, 'Oh for goodness' sake, you'll be all right.' But even as I said it I knew I'd be OK. A tiny part of me was even looking forward to seeing how I'd navigate life without her. Like when I was a child back in Muswell Hill, learning to ride my bike, thinking I couldn't do it without Mum holding on to the back, but when I glanced over my shoulder as I teetered along, she was a tiny figure in the distance. She'd let go ages ago and I was fine.

After leaving the care home I rush to the station, sit on a train for a couple of hours, arrive in the vacant countryside, find a taxi and am driven down deserted winding lanes while staring out of the window looking for the flashes of primary colours strobing between brown trunks and green leaves that signal 'festival tents'.

Now the dystopian fantasy. Tumbling out of the cab into the rain I pull up my hood and look around for the production office (usually a grey Portakabin). Standing on tiptoe, I peer through a hatch at a *Wizard of Oz*-type Munchkin with a necklace of lanyards, perched on a stool. The Munchkin, examining me suspiciously – I imagine them thinking, *Ooh, she's old* – directs me to the stage I'm performing on by pointing to a muddy hill half a mile away and saying something like, 'See the ribbons flying from the top of the Helter Skelter? Head for that.' I nod and quash the rising sense of panic, tell myself I'm an adult, I'm not going to get lost, I haven't got Alzheimer's, and start listening again: '. . . past the pretend-slum-tenements outdoor disco, turn right at the psychedelic-bubble-machine cupcake factory, keep going until you reach the floating-giant-lily-pads-of-the-glen, opposite the chill-out palace filled with luminous fairy-balloons, then straight ahead you'll see the pointy-Gormenghast-enchanted-castle next to the strawberry-and-elderflower beers-of-the-forest tabernacle. That's your tent. You can't miss it.'

Joining the river of youth I'm swept along in a slipstream of denim shorts, flip-flops and Hunters. Everyone looks the same – same size, same shape, same nose, same colour. I look down at the ground. *Must concentrate on walking, don't want to fall over and arrive with mud all down one side of my body.* We march, slip and slide past stage after stage, until we pass the spoken-word tent and I peel off. Needing the loo, I head to a blue plastic cubicle smelling of shit, piss and bleach. Someone with long hair and a long scarf arrives at the same time and, to my despair, gestures for me to go first. I have diarrhoea. Always have diarrhoea. Leave the cubicle embarrassed, give Scarf Person a weak smile and wince inwardly at the thought of them entering the cubicle and . . . *never mind.* Pick my way through churned-up sludge to the backstage area, skid, stay on my feet, peep through the back of the tent. Confronted by a sea of blinking eyeballs trained on the lonely microphone, have a nervous twinge and navigate my way back through the mud to the blue cubicle.

After the reading and book signing – pre-released copies, available before the book launch – I make my way past the stages and through the fields and wait for a cab on a wooden walkway by a hedge in the gloom. Fall asleep on the train, jump into a taxi at King's Cross and arrive home – entering the family melodrama – around 1 a.m.

Pay the babysitter, check all the doors and windows are locked, tiptoe into Vida's room, give her a kiss, whisper, 'Mummy's home,' hoping my voice will register subliminally and she'll know she's safe, but she scowls, mutters something and rolls away from me. I watch her sleep. A crowd of sensations – tenderness, gratitude, guilt, love and anxiety – have a punch-up in my chest. Anxiety wins.

At 7 a.m. I contemplate calling through the partition wall to ask Vida if she minds making her own breakfast. (We lie head to head either side of the wall. Sometimes we drum rhythms to each other to communicate, as if we're captives in adjoining cells.) I manage to haul myself up at the last minute, make breakfast and have a conversation about Vida's school and friends. I want her to have no doubt she's loved; her GCSE exams are looming, her grandmother's dying, she needs support and reassurance. Fifteen is a vulnerable age.

My time with Vida anchors me, but the other two worlds don't feel real. Not the garish colours, music and camaraderie of the festivals or the sped-up, double-time ageing of my once sparky, opinionated mother, who seems to be crumpling into a smaller papery pile every time I see her.

14 We ran out of the Lexington, hair, coats and bags flapping, dodged around the cars and lorries on Pentonville Road and jumped into a cab. We were thrown backwards as it accelerated off, but we didn't put our seat belts on. I can't remember if we said anything. I think there were little bursts of conversation. Lamp posts and brightly lit shop fronts flashed through the window, washing Vida's face in orange, green, red and blue, all the neon colours of a city at night. Familiar streets whizzed past but I felt separate from

them, like a ghost peering back at the real world while I was being spirited away from it. I tried to convince myself that this was it, the moment I'd been scared of since I was a child, but a voice in my head kept cutting in. *No, it hasn't happened yet, there's still a chance she'll pull through, that she won't die tonight.* But which part of 'Your mother is turning blue, we have one more tank of oxygen left, it will last twenty minutes and then she'll be gone' sounds like she won't die tonight?

What Do You Want a Man for?

It was a blessing and a curse that my mother was so smart. *The blessing lies next to the wound,* as the old African saying goes. She was the only person I laughed until I cried with (until Vida). We laughed about words and expressions and human-interest stories in the newspaper, not at scripted comedy on the television. She was so sharp that her advice was unerring until she was ninety. She was good at maths and spelling – I love that in a person, don't know why, it's not a deal-breaker but I feel safe with a good speller – and I tried to keep her up to date with current thinking so her advice stayed relevant. After she turned ninety she couldn't keep up any more. Not that it stopped her. I can still picture her propped on a stack of pillows in the hospital, correcting my adding up (numbers don't change, they're reassuringly reliable) and commenting on my appearance. 'Not enough on the eyes and too much on the lips,' she said when I arrived with a new look – lots of mascara, no eye shadow and a slash of red lipstick. The one thing she could never understand about me was why I wanted another relationship after my divorce. 'What on earth do you want a man for?' she'd ask with an appalled expression, as if I'd said I wanted to kneel down in the dirt and eat mouthfuls of shit. In Mum's opinion there was no way a man was going to make my life any better. She thought I'd got off lightly, being divorced, buying my own home, doing interesting work and bringing up my daughter. But as I looked around at other people in couples it occurred to me that they weren't together for all the right reasons like Mum wanted me to be. They weren't with the perfect person or someone who loved them unconditionally and treated them kindly all the time, they were just with . . . someone. Someone good enough.

They may be your rock, but someone who's taught you, who knows you and loves you so well, can also be oppressive.

Soothsayer

If I didn't immediately drop a boyfriend who was careless with my feelings, Mum would say, 'He'll do it again.' And she was always right. I'd come back to her a couple of months later and say, 'You were right about him, Mum.'

Not long after my divorce we were in Waitrose together. 'I've met someone,' I grinned. I was happy that my emotional life wasn't over. I came out of my marriage with so little confidence that I didn't think I'd ever have a partner again. I was pleased I could still attract someone. 'Be careful. He'll end up hurting you.' First thing she said, straight out of her mouth. Sucked the pleasure right out of me.

'How do you know I'm not going to hurt *him*?' My voice wavered.

She pulled a tattered tissue from her sleeve and started sniffling into it. People stopped and stared, probably thinking I was a horrible daughter for making this sweet little old white-haired lady cry. I think Mum cried to cover up her mistake. She could see she'd upset me. I must admit I've sniffled a few times myself after I've said something clumsy and hurtful to my daughter. It's not straight-out manipulation when mothers do this; you're genuinely sorry for your mistake and annoyed with yourself.

The man I'd met who Mum said would hurt me – I'll call him Pig, not as an insult but because it resonates with the name he's adopted and makes me laugh – was in the music industry. After we'd been on a few dates Pig invited Vida and me to stay at his holiday villa in Spain for a week. I knew it was too soon to introduce Vida to a new relationship but we needed a holiday, I was broke, and the children from his first marriage would be there so I thought she might enjoy it. Vida and I arrived at the villa late at night and Pig introduced us to two women, quite a bit younger than me, draped in sarongs and skinny vests, who were also staying with him. We had a quick chat and a mint tea and then everyone went to bed. Vida shared with the children, I had a room on my own. Next morning, after rifling through my suitcase trying to find clothes that matched the rich-hippy type of thing the other two women were wearing, I wandered through the whitewashed villa looking for the others. I glimpsed a bright blue swimming pool with bashed-up sofas dotted around it shimmering through the window of the open-plan living room. Hearing voices coming from a side room, I popped my head round the half-open door. Sitting on the bed was one of the young women, naked, playing with my daughter and two other children. My mouth dropped open. I stuttered hello, ducked out before I gave myself away, and stumbled into the kitchen. Sitting at the kitchen table was the other woman, naked except for a thong, chatting to Pig, who was puffing on a spliff. Vida was nine. I hadn't told her anything about spliffs or naked women sitting at kitchen tables.

That evening, after the children had gone to sleep, Pig ran a bath for me in his en suite bathroom and I hopped in while he lounged on the bed and rolled himself a spliff. Lying in the hot water, the warm breeze from the open window rolling over my face and shoulders, I looked out at the Spanish sunset and thought, *He's not so bad.* I was drying myself with a thick white towel when he rushed into the bathroom naked, penis jiggling, hands flapping, spliff dangling from his mouth, hissing, 'Jack [his son] can't sleep! He's here! I've put him on the balcony. Quick! Go to your room, he mustn't see you!' Pig hustled me out of the bathroom, through the bedroom, onto the landing and pushed the door shut behind me as if we were in a West End farce. I stood on the terracotta flagstones, wrapped in the damp towel, trying to make sense of what had just happened. Why didn't he just tell Jack (who was ten) to go back to his room? Or go to Jack's room with him and read a story? Or all three of us could have hung out in Pig's room for a while. Jack knew I was his father's girlfriend. Why was it OK for him to see naked women and spliff-smoking but not to see his father's girlfriend in his room? It was too weird and illogical. I stormed through the villa – not easy to do with wet bare feet – pulling all the oriental rugs, draped artfully over the wrought-iron bannisters, onto the floor as I went.

Pig went on to exhibit even more peculiar behaviour during the week's holiday and I thought Mum must be clairvoyant predicting so early that he was a wrong 'un. But it's more likely that she'd lived long enough to know a woman is vulnerable so soon after a divorce and will potentially make inappropriate choices. Telling her his name was Pig and that he was in the music business probably helped her gain insight into his character too. Same with any fortune teller or gambler, it's all about the 'tells'.

She did it again with my album, *The Vermilion Border*. As soon as it was finished I rushed round to her flat and played it to her, but she looked up halfway through the first song, went all misty-eyed as if looking into the future and said, 'I feel like there's something else you're going to do. Something more is in you that you haven't done yet.' I was crushed. It had taken every ounce of my energy over the last three years to make the record and here she was saying I wasn't there yet. I still hadn't done enough. Another challenge was around the corner, another impending goal for me to aspire to. If Mum hadn't had a solid grasp on my life and the world in general, I could've dismissed her comments, pecked her on the cheek and scuttled off home, but she was so often right. Sometimes you just want to find things out as you go along, not have this bloody soothsayer in your face all the time.

Six months later I started writing a book.

15 Vida and I sat close to each other and held hands the whole time we were in the cab. After a few minutes it occurred to me to ask the driver how long it would take for us to get to Hendon. I knew Vida was watching me but I couldn't stop my face from collapsing when he said forty minutes.

'My mother's dying, we've only got twenty,' I said.

For Vida to hear the word 'dying' spoken aloud was not ideal but it was more important we got to Mum in time. The driver put his foot down – taxi drivers know about life-and-death situations. I called ahead to the care home, told the receptionist we were on our way and asked her to unlock the entrance doors. I've stood outside those doors ringing the bell for fifteen minutes sometimes, waiting for someone to come downstairs and open them. My mind was working like a machine. We needed every second we could get. I took off my shoes and told Vida to take hers off too, her little heels and my expensive boots. We scrunched everything we were holding – coats, scarves, bits of paper – into our bags and tied back our hair. It was like we were preparing for a race. Or a fight.

Sarah Connor vs Terminator

Since I was thirteen I've only dated boys, and later men, who I wanted to learn something from. Knowledge was the only currency I was interested in. I couldn't think what else a boyfriend was for. I didn't have a sex drive exactly, more of a conquest drive. For me sex was bound up with control. I was more excited by the thought of having power over the annoyingly privileged oppressor, or possessing the handsome boy, than any kind of tender communion, although I didn't realise that's how I was behaving at the time.

I didn't have orgasms when I was younger. I couldn't relax and let go enough for them to happen – not helped by the fact that this was a time when girls didn't know their own bodies and were told that 'nice girls' don't make noise during sex. I only felt near orgasm once in my early twenties. A sound came out of my mouth that I wasn't in control of, not one of those fake sighs you do that you've picked up from films to make the other person think you're enjoying yourself, but a deep moan. The boy on top of me clapped his hand over my mouth to shut me up – a guitarist in a radical band he was. I didn't get close to having an orgasm again for another twelve years.

The 1960s and 70s were such restricted times for women that I didn't want to do what I saw girls doing, that's why I copied and learned from boys. (It's the opposite for me now, women interest me more and I learn from them.) There was no feeling of wanting to *be* a boy, and I didn't want a penis, was very glad I didn't have one. I just wanted to have the freedom and opportunities boys had: to hitch-hike without fear, to rough and tumble and play-fight when we all went to the park, to be looked in the eye when I spoke, ordinary stuff like that. I thought if I assimilated male thoughts and emotions, I would be respected and have an interesting life too. As soon as I found out about art school, rolling spliffs, jazz, forming a band, how to polish my DMs, immerse myself in work and be an emotionless cunt, I moved on. The boys I couldn't conquer or understand exasperated me. I would persevere with them for a while but eventually give up on them and force the 'relationship' to end by being unpleasant.

When I was in my thirties I met a man I wanted to live with. I thought he was mysterious because he was so emotionless. He was such a cold fish my nickname for him was 'Termie', short for Terminator – I wanted to be like that. I was frustrated that Termie took too long thinking about whether he wanted us to live together or not, and I discussed with friends how to get him to commit. From the day he said 'Yes' I never had an orgasm with him again – which was annoying as he was the first person since the 'radical' guitarist that I'd experienced a proper orgasm with, including myself.

I tried, but I don't think I ever truly loved anyone – not even my mother – until I gave birth to Vida. She taught me how to love. *That's my daughter in the water, everything she knows I taught her,** I used to sing to her. Now I humbly acknowledge it's the other way round.

Hairy Knob

... the amount of maintenance involving hair is genuinely overwhelming. Sometimes I think that not having to worry about your hair any more is the secret upside of death.

Nora Ephron, *I Feel Bad About My Neck: And Other Thoughts on Being a Woman*, 2006

As a child, I often wondered what kind of woman I'd grow into. Squinting into the steel knob on the radiator in the bathroom every time I sat on the loo, I'd look for answers in my face. Examining my distorted reflection, bug-eyed, pug-

* Peter Blegvad, 'Daughter', sung by Loudon Wainwright III on *Strange Weirdos*, 2007

nosed, cavernous nostrils, mouth dragged down at the corners, I imagined this was what I'd look like when I was old. I couldn't envisage being older when I was twelve. It didn't occur to me to look at my mother in her shirt and slacks, lace-up shoes and short, functional haircut and guess I'd look something like her. That was too great a leap of the imagination. We weren't that similar physically and I never took much notice of her appearance. She was just Mum. Apart from my teachers and my mother, I didn't have a picture in my head of a woman I could aspire to be.

Now I'm older than I thought I'd ever be, and look better – on the outside, I'm a mess on the inside due to the cancer treatment and other illnesses and operations – than I thought a sixty-year-old could look when I peered into that chrome bobble. It takes a concerted effort for me to look good dressed, but it's nothing like the amount of work it takes for me to look good undressed. And that's mostly because of The Hair.

I have lots of hair on my head and people often comment enviously on it, but what they don't realise is that it's also all over my body, like Mr Tumnus, the faun with the legs of a goat from C. S. Lewis's *Chronicles of Narnia*. Except I'm more like a goat with the legs of a faun. The older I get the more unmanageable The Hair becomes. I dream about hair every night. Eyebrow hair, face hair, underarm hair, arse hair, pubic hair. I dream the hair on my legs is as long, straight, black and shiny as liquorice bootlaces, and the bootlaces trail out of the bottom of my jeans, dragging along the ground as I walk down the street. The strands are so long that people can't help stepping on them. In another dream I have one long, thick, dark brown hair sprouting from under my nose which reaches down to my boots, and try as I might, I can't pull it out. Or the hair on the backs of my fingers is so long and brown that I plait it and the plaits swish about as I wave my hands around when I talk. Last night I dreamt I didn't have time to go home before I went out, and by the end of the evening the hair on my upper lip and chin had grown into a thick tussock of pale-brown sea-grass and I had to hack it off with secateurs. I am seriously unhinged about hair. I've instructed my friend Trace to pluck my chin hairs, wax my moustache and stick a bobble hat over my grey roots as soon as I'm dead. (Now she has nightmares too.)

> Body hair, for many of us, is a constant micro-aggression, attacking us from within, no matter how many times we rip it out from the root, no matter how much we convince ourselves that it's really not that deep. It exists as a mental burden . . .
> Aisha Mirza, 'On Being Mad, Brown, and Hairy', 2016

I was even too embarrassed to say my father was from Corsica when I was young, right up to my thirties, because the name had the sound 'coarse' in it and I thought it would draw people's attention to the thick brown hair on my face and my legs.

It's not just The Hair that stops me being enthusiastic about undressing in front of someone else or having sex. The thought of sleeping with someone new conjures up a whole gallery of unappetising pictures: harsh morning light showing my cellulite; the retainers I wear every night (I spent a fortune on having my teeth straightened, I'm not going to let them drift back to their previous snaggled state). At least I don't snore or cough in the mornings (only because I use an inhaler). An older person coughing isn't the same as a young person coughing. In an older person it sounds like impending death. If you don't want the older-coughing-person to die, it's even more irritating. I hated it when Mum coughed deeply. It frightened me and made me irritable with her, even though she was healthy most of the time. All she did to keep fit was cut a page out of an old *Woman's Own* magazine illustrated with Canadian Air Force exercises, paste it onto the back of a cornflakes packet and prop it on top of the fridge. She touched her toes and windmilled her arms around in the kitchen occasionally, and in her eighties she joined a local indoor bowls club – she said the women who were still on HRT looked twenty years younger than everyone else. No spinning bicycles, Zumba, yoga, jogging, cross-training or weights for her. She also smoked roll-ups and ate hardly any vegetables, didn't eat sugar and never used soap on her face. She was smooth-skinned and slim and lived to ninety-five with all her marbles intact.

When I was at art school I used to go to keep-fit classes at the local church hall on Tuesday evenings. After the Slits, I went to a beginner's ballet class. That's all there was back then. Girls didn't jog past you in the street wearing track pants and trainers, not until the mid-1980s. Apart from the fact that it just wasn't done, women didn't exercise in public then, you couldn't walk past a group of builders without being verbally assaulted. Women weren't allowed to run marathons until 1967. It was thought to be physically impossible for a woman to run that far. Bobbi Gibb and Kathrine Switzer were the first women I heard of who ran long distances. I was thirteen by then. I never saw a woman play sports, miss a goal, fall over, fail, get dirty, look stupid, then jump up and get on with the game when I was young, not on television or anywhere else once I'd left school and stopped doing PE. Girls' and women's role in sport was to watch the men or make the sandwiches. The occasional sportswoman who did make it onto TV (during the Olympics) was derided for looking 'like a man'. There was no British culture or industry to support women being physically fit when I started attending aerobics classes in the early eighties. I couldn't believe the sense of power and release that I and the other women in the classes experienced from strengthening our bodies. Before long I was teaching aerobics myself. Exercise teaching for women was unregulated in the 1980s, it was so new. Everyone laughs when they hear that – *Haha, a punk teaching aerobics* – but it was liberating, getting sweaty and red in the face, building muscles and feeling them working when I walked home at night. Maybe now I had a chance if I was attacked. Maybe now I was strong enough to fight back. I felt empowered. Building muscle and getting fit felt like a radical act.

16

The cab belted along, jumping red lights, careering round corners, and for a couple of seconds I felt as if I wasn't in it. I was up in the sky looking down at the wet road, the tops of glistening umbrellas and the streetlights streaking across the shiny black taxi roof. Then I was back, holding Vida's hand and watching her face. Her pupils were deep pools of black liquid pouring over me. Here we were, the two of us facing death together, again. Fifteen years old and she's always with me when I go through these things. These adult things. Never taken aside and looked after. Never shielded from the shock or the pain. Single mother, single child, that's how it is. I want to protect her more than anything in the world, but life crashes on around us and all I can do is hold her until it's passed.

Sex

Before I was married I wanted to kiss every boy or man I thought was attractive (part of the conquering thing). Sometimes the kissing turned into sex because I didn't know how to stop it, or I felt I'd led them on, or because we ran out of conversation. I didn't think feeling pressurised into sex was a big deal in my teens and twenties. I wasn't informed about consent, and the general opinion in those days was that if you'd aroused a man, even accidentally – or he told you that you'd aroused him, or you were badgered for long enough – it was your fault and you owed it to him to give in.

Recently I asked a sixty-year-old schoolfriend who was thinking of leaving her marriage of twenty-five years, 'Will you mind if you don't meet someone else and never have sex again?' She closed her eyes and winced as if she were remembering something bad. 'I've had enough sex to last me the rest of my life,' she said. I knew what she meant. Starting at fifteen, we had both been having sex with men for forty-five years. Society can't sell it to us in any shape or form any more.

After my marriage was over I had a fling with an odd man the same age as me, which for some reason made me think it was fine not to use any protection. *He's so weird he can't have slept with anyone for years. I'm sure it'll be fine*, I thought. Stupid to risk it. I got myself tested for everything at a clinic afterwards. On my way out I asked a doctor if it was OK to have a cock in your mouth after it's been up your backside – asking for a friend. He gulped and said, 'Yes, it's fine.' This friend had done it with no obvious ill effects, but still I can't believe it's fine to have a poo-flecked cock in your mouth. Perhaps the doctor said it was OK because he was startled by such a direct question from a middle-aged woman, or my friend wasn't unwell because she had a very clean arse, or maybe he wasn't a doctor at all, maybe he was a porter or some random guy in the corridor. I don't know, I wasn't wearing my glasses.

I had to retrain my eyes and brain to find older men attractive when I started dating again in my fifties. The last time I was single the men I was looking at were in their thirties and I still had that youthful image fixed in my head. It was depressing at first, choosing from a pool that's not regarded as desirable or vital in your society. I was paddling around in that same pool myself. I'd walk down Oxford Street looking at bald men and men with grey hair and paunches and say to myself, *He's about my age, that's the demographic I should be looking at.* I realised I had a very small group to choose from: men over fifty who'd kept themselves vaguely together physically, were single, mentally stable, solvent and not gay were rare creatures. I managed to re-educate myself eventually. Now I'm only attracted to people my age. A young face looks like a blank page to me.

Most middle-aged men want a younger woman as a partner. (In my teens I was upset that I was too young to even dream of going out with any of the boys in my favourite bands, like the Stones or the Beatles. Now they're all with women who weren't even born when I had that thought.) Men could train their eyes to appreciate the beauty in older faces and bodies like I did – it would help if we saw more older women in the media, your sense of beauty adjusts with constant exposure – but I don't think men are willing to put in that kind of effort. You have to make a conscious choice, like deciding to eat healthily or give up alcohol, and stick with it.

I could have dated younger men during the last five years, but lovely as some of them were, I didn't want to keep wincing inwardly whenever I referred to something that called attention to my age. Or not be able to share the difficulties of growing older, or have to keep explaining references. I'd like to be with someone kind who can hold a conversation and is in my age group. If that's too much to ask, I'll do without.

A large part of wanting someone to love and look after you is to do with the instinct for survival. I'm sure every person over fifty has thought about getting ill, becoming incapacitated and dying alone. I've weighed up men with that thought in the back of my mind. If a guy coughs his lungs up every time he laughs, I can't help but think, *I ain't going to be stuck looking after this one, wheeling him about and clearing up his poo whilst he grumbles at me until one of us dies.* Caring for someone you've been with for thirty years is understandable, but when it comes to someone you've only known for one, it's not an appealing prospect. When you're young, death and a long, serene old age together is a romantic haze on the horizon. When you're older, it's right up in your grill. Getting on and off buses slowly, borrowing each other's glasses to read the small print, hospital visits, indigestion, insomnia, hearing loss, whistling noses (sounds quite sweet actually), irascibility and impatience is the reality of a twilight romance.

Worse than being stuck with someone ill or being alone forever is the thought that I'll grow to love a person very much and won't have them for very long. Finding another person to love is finding another person to lose.

17 I asked the cabbie if I could pay in advance. 'Just give us twenty, love,' he said. I felt a surge of gratitude but it didn't occur to me to thank him. Vida and I lunged out of the cab onto the driveway and ran across the gravel clutching our belongings. The glass doors were open and a nurse was stationed on either side of the entrance. They had understood my request and taken it seriously. Gravel turned to carpet underfoot and we were in the entrance hall, passing the signing-in book, a bowl of plastic flowers, a portrait of the Queen. I pushed open the Georgian-wired inner doors and we rounded the corner – like a scene in a Scorsese gangster film, all shot in one take – raced up the mottled brown linoleum stairs with black rubber non-slip edgings and onto Mum's floor. As I ran I chanted to myself, *Please hang on, please hang on.*

Dead Flower Water

My second attempt at dating after Pig (but before Eryk) was with a wiry, vulpine-faced man I met at an open-mic session in Hastings. I'll call him Fox. I went along to the pub to play a couple of songs and saw him leaping around the room, drumming on the optics, the top of the bar and the brass foot rail. He smacked a bloke on his arse, scraped a chair on the floor, clapped his hands and it all added up to an exciting rhythm. Fox was the compère for the evening and just before I went on stage he whispered in my ear, 'You'd better be good.' I wasn't worried. I strapped on my guitar, started up with the intro to 'Confessions of a MILF' and thrashed my way through to the end of the song as if nobody was in the room.

Fox had a tense energy about him. Some people, whatever their age, look like they've given up. Their body language is soft, crumpled; that's not my kind of energy, not that I like the nervous foot-twitchers either. A certain tautness and alertness, even in your eighties and nineties, is good. My mother had that kind of energy.

I met a new crowd at the Hastings pub, very different to the parents at my daughter's school. My best friends there were two trans women: a tall, elegant, harmonica-playing blonde and a sharp-witted guitarist with a chic Louise Brooks bob. Sometimes we played together as a trio. It was a wonderful, liberating new world, a lot like my old world of the 1970s. One night a group of us danced until three in the morning to 1960s soul, the scent of sadness clinging to us like the whiff of dirty water from a vase of dead flowers. As I danced, I pictured my husband and young daughter tucked up in their beds. I knew how wrong I looked, jerking my body around with strangers in an attic room on the edge of a blowy seaside town.

Crap Date

Six months after our first meeting, I asked Fox if I could go back to his flat with him after we'd all played our songs at the open mic. He'd been flirting with me for months but had never taken it any further and asked me out. The old-timers in the pub glanced at me with dubious expressions as we left together. Fox lived in a large square room in a Regency house by the sea. We sat side by side on his mattress, no bed, while he smoked weed and played the bongos. Then he invited his father, who owned the house and lived downstairs, to come up and drink beer with us. After an hour I signalled to Fox with my eyes that it was time for Dad to go. After Dad left, Fox opened a cardboard box, placed it on his lap and spent an hour showing me photographs of his childhood. I got the feeling he was putting off a physical encounter. When we were at the pub and there were lots of people around us he couldn't keep his hands off me, always touching me and trying to push my face into his sweaty armpit, growling and making sexual comments, full-on stuff like that. Now we were alone the tension in his body, all that wild-man flirtiness and pent-up sexuality, had evaporated. He was a completely different person without an audience. This was disconcerting, but not as disconcerting as when he hugged me and exclaimed, 'Oh! You're soft. Like a woman.' (Here we go. I'd forgotten about this part of dating, the part where a man makes thoughtless comments about your body which you never forget. It started at thirteen and has never stopped: classic English pear shape, big hips, flat chest; huge jugs; little tits; high arse; low arse; big arse; did you know the end of your nose dips when you smile; you've got a moustache; you're quite plump down there, I thought you'd be more bony; you've got a double chin; hairy legs; long toes; thin mouth; a back like a boy; a grey hair; when you smile you look like Jack Nicholson as the Joker (this classic from Pig). They won't remember saying those things, and even if they did the comeback would be 'I was only joking.' If I had a quid for every time a man said that to me . . .)

I have no idea what Fox meant when he said I felt 'like a woman'. He could have been bi and my body felt different to a man's, or maybe he usually only went with very young girls, but most likely he was trying to undermine me in some way.

After a couple of hours I commented on his changed persona. 'What? You want me to take you to bits? Is that it?' he said, as if I was a nymphomaniac or something. *Well, yes. That's what your behaviour has been promising. That's what everyone back at the pub thinks you're like. That's what you've projected for the last three months.*

He kissed me a few times, touched me here and there in a lacklustre way, couldn't get an erection, then fell asleep and snored. Lying next to him on the bare mattress under a moth-holed, rancid-smelling old coat, I thought back to how he'd hyped me up, hiding his impotence behind bluster and showmanship. He was forty-five, drank a lot of beer and smoked a lot of spliff, but it hadn't occurred to me that this would affect him physically. The last time I dated men who drank and took drugs they were young enough for it not to affect their virility. Not one man I've dated since my divorce who's had erectile dysfunction (ED) – and there have been quite a few, it happens when men get older, especially if they drink a lot – has admitted they have a problem, no matter how carefully I've approached the subject. Even when I confess my own shortfalls – insecure about my body, damage from chemotherapy, no good in bed, The Hair – they say nothing. Every time this happens I end up questioning my sanity and attractiveness, my confidence spirals downwards and I find myself pondering buying new underwear. I was such a confident woman when I first spoke to them.

These guys would prefer you went out and hanged yourself on the nearest lamp post than admit to having ED. They intend to carry it with them to their graves. They'd rather not have a girlfriend for the rest of their lives, let you be emotionally scarred and insecure, kill yourself even, but whatever happens, *they ain't tellin'.* And they think you haven't noticed, that they've got away with the deception, like children who think you can't see them when they put their hands over their eyes. The tragic thing about all this is that if men spoke about their shortcomings, they'd discover that loads of women don't mind. I don't mind if I have sex or not, or how proficient a person is in bed. Other things are more important to me than sex, like having a laugh together, affection, shared interests and kindness.

Anyway, there I was, wide awake, lying next to a stoned, snoring man, new to all this dating malarkey, feeling stupid, guilty, disappointed and ugly – time to leave. I slid out from under Fox's arm, put my boots on and let myself out.

Driving home along the deserted coast, light-grey sky, dark grey sea, I locked my elbows to keep the wind from buffeting the car onto the wrong side of the road.

18 We pelted down the corridor. A nurse looked up from her station and I had to stifle my automatic response to smile. I glanced into the rooms as we ran. There was the woman with the budgies, and the man with a nice wife who popped into Mum's room once and gave her an ice lolly. At the end of the corridor I saw a cluster of nurses in white coats and ambulance staff in green overalls. I tried to gauge from their faces if Mum was dead or not, but I couldn't tell. Then we were inside her room. Nurse Mia was in the corner and Pascale was sitting on the mattress next to Mum's head. Vida and I rushed towards the bed with so much force that we almost fell over each other like Laurel and Hardy. I was aware of how frivolous we looked,

arriving all red-faced and overdressed. I wanted to explain,
We're not the sort of people who go to parties and get emergency
phone calls that someone's dying and turn up at the deathbed all
breathless and in our finery like characters in **The Great Gatsby**
or a Katharine Hepburn and Cary Grant film. Please don't think
we're those kinds of people.

Drive

I was sitting on a chair in the phone shop waiting to be served
when I heard a man talking to a sales assistant, and something
about his voice made me look up. Motorbike boots, jeans, leather
jacket, holding a crash helmet, slightly greying hair tucked
behind his ears. *Not bad*, I thought, and looked back down at
my pamphlet. 'Viv!' he shouted across the shop floor. 'I was just
thinking, *that's* a beautiful woman! And it's *you*.' (Because I'd
driven I was dressed in an old jumper and jeans, no make-up,
hair all over the place.) Richard-from-the-past, he turned out to
be. Dangerous, these creatures. The fact that you have a shared
history makes them seem trustworthy, but shared history doesn't
necessarily equate with 'good person'. I often forget this when
I haven't seen someone for years. Richard pursued me when I
worked with him about twenty years ago – I can't believe there's
such a thing as twenty years ago – but I rebuffed him because
he was married and had two young children. He was extremely
handsome back then, with longish light-brown hair and bright
blue eyes. After we talked in the phone shop, Richard asked if he
could take me out and gave me his number. I couldn't believe it,

asked on a date by a guy I met in the phone shop – who needs dating apps? I took a while to contact him and he came straight back with where and when. Very good, no games.

Dating attempt number three.

Richard suggested we go to a gig at the Victoria and Albert Museum in Kensington on Thursday evening. He had ideas for a date, had done his homework and chosen an interesting venue – he might be an adult. On the day we were to meet I had my roots retouched and my hair blow-dried – this makes my hair look normal as opposed to a ball of dried-out seaweed. Nora Ephron, so good on hair, noted this stage in women's lives: 'After a certain age, the only time you have a good hair day is when you've paid for it.' Rain poured down all day. At five o'clock Richard called. *Here we go, he's cancelling, can't be bothered because of the rain.* I answered the phone with a light, not-expecting-bad-news kind of voice. 'Can you come and pick me up?' he asked. 'I don't fancy getting soaked.' He didn't know I had a car. He did know I lived in East London and he lived on the other side of town in North London, near Tufnell Park (Tough Nell Park is one of my pseudonyms, as is Simone Snorkelle – after the Simon Snorkel fire engines from the 1970s – thought up by my friend Trace, who was obsessed with them and the lovely 70s font).

I was so relieved Richard wasn't cancelling that I said yes, I'd pick him up. He told me the name of the street but not the house number, and I set off towards Kentish Town. The rain was so heavy it was as if someone kept throwing a thick grey horse blanket across the windscreen.

I parked and texted Richard. *Be down in a sec, where are you parked?* he texted back (still not telling me the house number). He jumped into the car with a woolly hat pulled down over his

head, a cravat at his throat, kissed me on the cheek and off we went.

'Last time I saw you I turned down having sex with you. I've regretted that for years,' was the first thing he said.

'Really? I don't remember that at all, so you can stop torturing yourself about it. I do remember you pestering me for sex every time I saw you, even though you were married with young children.'

'I want to apologise for that.'

'Go on then.'

'I'm very sorry.'

Not a great start. We aquaplaned through the potholed streets as he reminisced about the old days. 'Oh yes, I slept with her, and her,' he chirped as we discussed mutual friends. 'Slept with my ex-wife when I was babysitting our kids one night and she got pregnant again! Ho ho.' I decided to enjoy the date, knowing I wouldn't see him again. I tried to convince myself that it was good to get to know different people, hear about different lives.

We pulled up outside the V & A. There was a queue around the block, hundreds of people standing in the pouring rain. Richard peered out of the window. 'I didn't think it would be this busy so I didn't book.' We talked to the ushers at the door but there was no way we were going to get in.

'Shall we just go and get a coffee down there then?' asked Richard, pointing at a brightly lit touristy cafe a couple of streets away.

'Let's go to this drinking club I can get into instead, something with a bit more atmosphere,' I suggested. I felt embarrassed signing in a guy in a cravat. As we crossed the room Richard deliberately lagged behind me so I'd get to the bar first. He was avoiding paying. I called to him and asked what he wanted. 'A pint of lager.' He ducked past me and sat down.

'My new place is just around the corner. I've just done it up. Do you want to see it?' I asked.

'Are we going to have sex?'

'No.'

He took a swig of his pint. 'Oh. No, then.'

After a while I said I was tired and was going to head home. Richard asked me to drive him home first. I agreed. I know it sounds perverse, but I wanted to see the date through to the bitter end. I wanted Richard to think it had been a success.

'Can we go via Brick Lane on the way back? There's a place there that does great kebabs,' he called out to me as we ran through the rain to the car. The date was becoming so ridiculous that I was laughing inside. At the kebab shop Richard jumped out, bobbed his head down to the window and enquired – sounding very much as if it was an afterthought and hoping I didn't – if I wanted a kebab too. I declined. 'You won't drive off, will you?' he called over his shoulder. I should have driven off but I didn't want him to know how disappointed I was, so I stayed. Ten minutes later he emerged from the shop and ran up to the car swinging a blue plastic bag sagging under the weight of sawn-off meat. The windows steamed up, the meat smelt like human sweat. Off we went again. This was my fourth hour of driving. It would take another hour to get across London to Richard's road and another hour to drive back home. A date consisting of six hours' driving. We parked at the same junction I'd picked him up from a lifetime ago and he scampered off, clutching his bulging plastic bag.

Richard texted the next morning to say what a wonderful night it had been and asking could we meet again? I thanked him and wished him well but said I'd rather not. He threatened to stalk me if I didn't answer his texts or see him again. I ignored all further communications and eventually he stopped. I *think* I won that one.

19 **Mum was alive, twisting and turning on the bed. The first thing I noticed was her eyes. Although she was looking around the room, they were vacant and clouded over with a milky blue film, like the blind clairvoyant in *Don't Look Now* – I always thought the clairvoyant was scarier than the murderer in the red coat. I tried to get inside Mum's mind. *Is she having hallucinations? Who's she looking for? Or looking at? Does she remember it was my book launch tonight? If she does remember, she'll be annoyed we all missed it because of her.* I started gabbling. I had so much to say before she went and**

I didn't know how long she had left. 'The launch went well, Mum. Loads of people were there ... Thank you for everything, you made me what I am ...' On and on, pretending I wasn't frightened and that I was riding in on a wave of triumph and success.

Bonkers

'Do you think I'll ever meet another guy, Mum?'
'There'll be plenty of guys, Vivvy. What worries me is the one you're going to pick.'

Why is every man I go out with so bonkers? Do I choose these men because I have low self-esteem and am scared of rejection? Because I think they're so broken they'll never leave me? Or is bonkers familiar because my family were all a bit bonkers? Or are we all bonkers by the time we're in our fifties? I know I'm attracted to Asperger's types, but is this as good as it gets?

When I first described Eryk, the man I met after Richard-from-the-past, to Mum she raised her eyes to the ceiling and said, 'He sounds like a dead loss.' I was determined to prove her wrong this time, especially as she was leaving me. *I'm not going to have you dictate who's good and who's bad for me any more. I'll make up my own mind, thank you very much.* I worked extra hard at the relationship with Eryk just to go against Mum, like I did with friends she disapproved of when I was at school.

But it wasn't just Mum. Everyone I knew was dubious about Eryk. 'You can do so much better,' they said when they heard about his unreliability and indifference towards me. I didn't think I could do better. I thought he was the best I could do, what with my own foibles, my age, physical problems, work that sometimes engulfs me, a child and tiredness. I was lonely and my mother was dying. I needed to feel connected to someone, however odd he was, just like I needed a home, however close to a rat.

Perhaps 'defective' is a middle-aged person's default setting. Like the life cycle of a pear we go *unripe, unripe, ripe, off.* Except the men I meet seem to go *adolescent, adolescent, adolescent, old,* with no ripe bit, no wise bit, no emotional maturity before they wither.

The listless Eryk filled my thoughts all through my mother's decline. I thought about him more often than her dying. Once he left a message on my voicemail after not calling for ages and I played it to Mum as she lay croaking in her hospital bed. Trying her best to appear interested in my pathetic love life, she asked to hear his message again, but as she passed the phone back to me she accidentally pressed a button on the screen with her arthritic finger and called him back. I punched the cancel button in a panic and rounded on her, 'Don't ever touch my phone again!' Her face collapsed.

I shouted at my dying mother because I was attempting to play it cool with a weak, apathetic man I'd only known for a few months. Shameful.

I put up with more and more careless behaviour from Eryk as Mum neared death. I 'recruited him to serve my loss', as Helen Macdonald wrote in *H Is for Hawk*, about a man she met not long after her father's death. Macdonald's words struck a chord, but no matter how badly he behaved, I kept clinging to the unseaworthy vessel that was Eryk with the desperation of a drowning woman.

The Third (Button) Man

Eryk and I went on quite a few dates, but as he avoided intimate encounters I still hadn't undone all the buttons on his shirt or seen his penis after knowing him for six months. At last the day came when I was allowed to undo the third button. We were lying in my bed. He had his shirt (two buttons undone), underwear, trousers and socks on, and I was in my bra and pants. I slid my hand over his chest and fiddled about trying to undo the third button, wondering if he'd forgotten our pact. He was as still and timorous as a virgin. *Surely he's not a virgin? Not at fifty-three. Maybe he's gay. That would be awful, if I'm forcing myself on him. More likely he's a psychopath. I've read that psychopaths pretend to be sexually innocent with the woman they're seeing and do the bad stuff in secret.*

Eryk let me undo the third button and ran his fingers down my arm, applying just the right amount of pressure. I liked that he didn't do very much. None of his actions were irritating or intimidating. He was also a good kisser. Something happened to his lips, he made them go soft and pillowy until they fitted mine perfectly, and the kisses lasted for ages, we got lost in them. I touched his shaved head and looked into his pale, Putinesque, *puttanesca* eyes. Then he rolled over, grabbed *The Woman in White* from my bedside table, opened it up and started reading out loud. I was disappointed that he couldn't wait to get on with the story (good as it was). At the end of the chapter he snapped the book shut, sat up, rebuttoned his shirt, laced up his pointy brown brogues and said sternly, 'That's enough for today.' There was no point asking him to stay. I'd tried a couple of times in the past but he just shook his head. He wasn't a communicator. I'm very much a communicator, but there I was, trying to have a relationship with a cold, pale-eyed man with a van.

20 Mum looked so uncomfortable on the bed. She'd rolled into a furrow created by my sister sitting on the mattress. It was one of those air-filled pressure mattresses, so it wasn't very stable. It was painful to watch Mum crossing one leg over the other and rolling her shoulders as if she was trying to climb out of the trough. I didn't understand why Pascale couldn't see what was happening and get off the bed so Mum could lie flat. I was scared she'd get angry and ruin the atmosphere if I said something, so I kept quiet. I tried to hold Mum's hand and Vida's hand at the same time, but it was awkward because of Mum's position in the trough. I was highly attuned to Vida, aware that she was witnessing the death of her beloved grandma, so as I talked to Mum I was also secretly talking to her, reassuring her. I modulated my voice, making it quiet and deep. As Pascale's older sister and Vida's mother, I thought I should set the tone.

Liquid Assets

One lie, one broken promise, or a single neglected responsibility
may be a misunderstanding instead. Two may involve a serious
mistake. But three lies says you're dealing with a liar, and deceit is
the linchpin of conscienceless behaviour.

Martha Stout, *The Sociopath Next Door*, 2005

A year went by and no bond formed between Eryk and me.
I tried hard to build our attraction into a relationship – and
when I try at something, I really try – but it was hopeless. He
was so pathologically secretive that I began to suspect he was a
compulsive liar. Often I'd find out after a date (from a mutual
friend or a bit of Facebook stalking) that he was going on holiday
or to a grand wedding the next day, but he hadn't mentioned
it. He did this many times, not just about small things, about
everything. I never saw his flat. He wouldn't discuss his home
life or share his thoughts and feelings about the past, present or
future. He only wanted to talk about places and things. Either he
was hiding some terrible secret or he was incapable of intimacy.
He was cold and hard, a shiny frozen shell with a hint of
darkness inside (sounds like a chocolate Magnum).

We broke up one evening in 2014, after meeting for a drink
at the Pub on the Park on the edge of London Fields. I glanced
through the window on my way in and saw him leaning against
the bar, wearing a brown vintage shirt and dark jeans. He looked
so good – long slim body, no bum and the top button of his shirt
undone showing his flat clavicles. Eryk asked what I wanted to
drink. I ordered a vodka and cranberry juice and a glass of water.

He pulled a bunch of fifties from his jeans pocket (I love it when a man carries cash in his pockets, no wallet). 'Builder's money,' he laughed. We sat on a chocolate-brown pleather sofa in the corner. He'd disappeared off the radar for the weekend so I asked him where he'd been. 'Can't tell you, you'll get upset,' he said with a half-smile. I got it out of him eventually. He'd been to Berlin with his ex-girlfriend. He smirked a bit when he said it. I detected a splinter of pleasure in his eyes, as if he enjoyed the pain he was inflicting.

I'd seen that look once before, at the beginning of our relationship, when we were on my bed kissing and I took my top and bra off for the first time. He broke off from the kissing to tell me he'd recently met a man I used to go out with who'd dumped me. Said it while I was sitting there with no bra on. I've relived that scene in my imagination so many times. In it I get off the bed, put my T-shirt back on, tell him to leave and never see him again. Why didn't I do it that afternoon? Because I was desperate for affection and distraction. Why did he say it? I mulled over this question during the following months (waste of brain energy) and came to the conclusion that it was a diversion tactic. He was protecting himself by belittling me – the best form of defence is attack – and what was he protecting himself from? Performing in bed.

After hearing the Berlin story and clocking the sly expression in Eryk's eyes, my body took over from my conscious mind. I snatched up the vodka and cranberry juice, tipped it over his head, then wrestled his pint off him and sloshed it over his crotch. ('Too much throwing liquid!' said Sally, my first reader, about this and the York gig chapter. I know, but both incidents happened and it was better than hitting them, which was what

I wanted to do. I think the reason I throw liquid when I'm angry, and possibly why other women throw liquid, is that it humiliates a man while minimising the risk of reciprocal violence.) Eryk leaned away from me, beer pooling around his arse on the seat, vintage shirt straining across his chest. A mental picture of buttons flying off in all directions with satisfying pops and pings flashed through my head. I grabbed the two halves of the shirt and pulled them away from each other, but the material was so old, instead of opening up it shredded in my hands. The feeling of the delicate fabric rending was intoxicating. 'No, Viv! This is my favourite shirt!' Too late. It was in ribbons.

I ran out of the pub, across the road and under the railway arch towards home. As I emerged from the gloom of the tunnel into a pool of yellow streetlight I felt all my anger evaporate. The lamp post seemed to suck it out of me, like a genie returning to its bottle. The night was so still I could hear rainwater trickling down the mossy wall behind me and landing, toc, toc, toc, on an empty plastic bag.

Wheatfield with Crows

The railway arch at the end of my street doesn't have a name, it has a number, NE22485, and is constructed from soot-stained, reddish-brown bricks stacked in a curve, like a Roman arch, and iron girders. It's a real Jack the Ripper, foggy old London, prostitutes, pickpockets and murderers kind of bridge. The walls are dank with green slime, and grey pockmarked mortar bulges from between the wet bricks. Every spring a buddleia takes root behind the drainpipe. The branches drift out over the pavement and scrape your cheek if you don't judge the distance right as you pass. There's a moment in the buddleia's lifecycle, purple flowers blooming, cabbage white butterflies flitting, when it's beautiful and triumphant, sprouting out of the broken wall without an ounce of earth to flourish in. *That's what we humans have to do*, I think whenever I see it, *keep blooming despite the barren circumstances we sometimes find ourselves in.* After a few weeks the buddleia becomes a weed again, with grime-splattered leaves and crispy brown flowers that never fall off. You can only fight so hard, and for so long, before your environment engulfs you.

I never use the next arch along, even though it's higher and brighter than NE22485. It is metal, with little ledges for the pigeons to perch on, which increases the odds of being shat on by at least 70 per cent. You only need to look at the road splattered with white blobs to work that one out. I know 'my' arch so well that I stride through the shadows with confidence, even at night. The plastic light fitting, set high up near the top, as high as a double-decker bus, is encrusted with layers of pale-grey pigeon droppings and cobwebs. It looks like Miss Havisham's wedding cake. There's usually a pile of black plastic rubbish bags torn open by foxes on the corner, with a trail of ketchup leading to an abandoned fried-chicken carcass. Lame pigeons hobble around pecking at the tiny latticed bones. A yard with walls constructed from blue metal shipping containers occupies one corner and men I can't describe (because I never look at them, don't want to appear interested in any way) load giant transparent plastic water bottles into scruffy vans. Something doesn't look right about that place. Nothing's

clean – the bottles, the van, the yard. I don't drink from those
water coolers now when I go into somebody's office. On the
other corner is a Victorian semi-detached house which used
to be a squat. The side wall is painted with a mural of Van
Gogh's *Wheatfield with Crows*. The body of a man was found
buried in the basement in 1997. He'd been battered to death
with a hammer – which was also buried – by his flatmate, the
mural painter. Apparently the painter had had enough of his
companion playing music and banging around all through the
night. The body wasn't discovered for ten years. The painter
would have got away with it too, if it hadn't been for that
meddling religious sect he joined in Australia. They told him he
had to go back to England and confess, which he did, and seven
years after the crime he went to prison for it.

21 Mum's nose and the tips of her fingers were turning blue and the paramedic asked me if he should take her to hospital. Mum had a Living Will saying she didn't want to be resuscitated, but I asked her again if she wanted to go. You never know. Faced with the real thing, Death, you might not feel the same as you did when you made that calm, rational decision six months ago. Mum clamped her lips together, frowned and shook her head once. She couldn't speak – she hadn't been able to speak for three weeks – but she could still think. The paramedic was satisfied and left the room. Pascale and I started blabbing at Mum, talking over each other: 'I love you,' 'You've been a great mother,' 'You've lived a good life.' Mum tried to lift her head off the pillow. She gulped in a big breath, puffed out her cheeks and let out a throaty roar. It erupted from the very depths of her being. Not a happy sound, more the sort of noise you make when you're trying to shout for help in a dream, an unintelligible bark dredged up from the bottom of your lungs. I reached into the back of my mind. *I must get this right for her, must interpret her needs at this crucial moment. What is she trying to say?*

'Be quiet?' I ventured.

She nodded.

Madeleine Moment

... sometimes the key arrives long before the lock.
Rebecca Solnit, *The Faraway Nearby*, 2013

I wasn't sitting by my father's side as he lay dying. I received a phone call from France saying he didn't have long left, so I went to visit him in hospital but could only stay a week. When I got back to London I rushed round to Mum's flat to tell her he was nearly dead and tried not to sound too delighted about it, even though she had just as gleeful a glint in her eye as I did.

My father, Lucien (I can't call him 'Dad' easily), had been hassling, crying, demanding and emotionally blackmailing me on the phone and whenever I visited him for years. He threatened not to leave me anything in his will unless I persuaded Pascale to visit him too. French Napoleonic law states that you have to leave your money equally to all your children when you die, whatever your feelings about them. I didn't know this but I still refused to coerce Pascale, and told him it was up to her. I visited my father because I felt sorry for him, and also I wanted to try and work through the fear of maleness that had built up in me during my childhood. He was an ignorant man and violent towards my sister and me when we were children. I didn't like him, no one did, and he didn't like anyone back. *Why doesn't he just die?* I thought for years. He obliged three weeks after my visit to France, at the same time as my marriage fell apart, and he left me enough money to pay for a solicitor and get out. I couldn't have done it without him dying. It wasn't just the money, I'm not sure I would have had the emotional strength to contemplate a divorce if he wasn't out of my life. My father's absence created enough space for me to reassess the other man in my life and see him in a clearer light.

I was Lucien's only living relative (apart from Pascale, who lived in Canada), so after his death I went to France to organise his affairs. It was the height of summer, and sorting through the rubbish he'd hoarded in his flat over forty years was boiling hot and dirty work. One afternoon I came across a handmade trunk wedged into the bottom of a large mahogany wardrobe. It was painted blue with aluminium edges. He'd made it himself. He was always making crates and boxes and filling them with things. I dragged the chest out of the wardrobe and onto the floor. It landed on the tiles with a crack.

A tattered plastic carrier bag full of wooden-handled Opinel paring knives of assorted sizes was the first thing I pulled out. French men love these knives. They have one wide blade indented with a tiny curved groove for your thumbnail that folds out from a tawny wooden handle. My father used his Opinels all the time, to slice apples, cheese, sharpen a pencil, clean his

fingernails, cut an almond from a tree. He'd hold the knife in one hand and a nub of cheese in the other, curl the blade towards his thumb, stopping just as the metal touched skin, then gobble the cheese off the blade.

Underneath the bag of knives was a bundle of papers. I lifted out a fistful and sat cross-legged on the cool floor – *Don't sit on cold floors, you'll get piles*, said Mum's voice in my head – to check if there was something important hidden among all the bills and newspaper cuttings. I'd already found his Last Will and Testament wedged between layers of smoothed-out madeleine cake cases. Coming across my father's will under the pile of frilly glassines heartened me. *Albertines and madeleines, together again, just like in Proust.* Even though our surname was only linked to greatness via a character in a novel and some eggy little cakes, it somehow seemed significant. The first time I ever liked my surname was when I read about Albertine in Proust's *In Search of Lost Time*. Until then I hated the foreignness of it and the taunts of 'Albert', 'Albatross' and 'Albuquerque' at school. The second time I liked my name was when the footballer Demetrio Albertini played for AC Milan and Italy. Over time I came across more namesakes, such as the artist Bill Albertini and Princess Elisabeth Albertine, of African descent, whose daughter married King George III. The best finds were the Algerian author Albertine Sarrazin and her book *L'Astragale*, and 'The Albertine Workout', a poetic dissection of Proust's fictional character by Anne Carson. Each discovery was another little ledge to hold on to, giving me faith that I wasn't from such terrible stock after all and could make something of myself.

Other documents I found among Lucien's papers were:
a typewritten copy of Rudyard Kipling's poem 'If';

a *carte du combattant*, proof he was in the Free French Navy during the Second World War;

a little book with a sage-green linen cover titled 'Aliens Order 1920 – Certificate of Registration. You must produce this certificate if required to do so by any Police Officer, Immigration Officer or member of His Majesty's forces.' Lucien was trying to become a British citizen. The black-and-white photograph inside the green book was dated 1945. He gazed out of the picture and up to the left, eyebrows raised, large brown eyes drooping at the outer edges, making him look sad and sensitive. Thick fair hair brushed back from a young forehead, high cheekbones, neat ears, mouth pursed as if he was about to kiss someone or say something French. A dimple in his chin. Overcoat collar turned up, a sliver of white shirt, thin black tie. The image could have been a frame from a 1940s French film. I peeled the photograph off the page and turned it over. On the back was written 'November 1st – 1944 – I could say what I feel about you for this is the first time I do' in Lucien's hand, followed by 'The word to say "I love you" is not enough to mean it' in my mother's writing.

Lucien (Albert) Albertine was twenty-three and my mother, Kathleen Ruth van Baush, twenty-five when they met at Queens Ice Skating Rink in West London. There weren't many young men left after the war and Mum thought she'd hit the jackpot when she clapped eyes on the handsome French sailor in

a white hat with a little red pom-pom on top. He was two years younger than her, but what the hell. 'You can either be a young man's fool or an old man's darling,' her mother, Frieda, warned her. Mum told me that she and her friend Joy had never been ice skating before. They only went along that night for one reason – to see if a girl in their office was lying about being a good skater. Mum and Lucien fell in love at first sight. All three girls met their future husbands that night.

There were two cardboard folders in the trunk. One was a faded buff colour, labelled *Letters – Kathleen & children*. Adrenalin shot through my body when I saw these words. No warning, no time to control the anxiety. A series of images flipped through my mind: spirit level, carpenter's pencil with flat lead, measurements in feet and inches scribbled onto pieces of plywood, stubbly chin grinding as he ate. (Mediterranean men's jaws seem to move from side to side when they eat. They look like they're enjoying their food, whether it's a piece of chicken or a square of chocolate. You can sense their pleasure, see them savouring the flavours. British men's jaws go up and down with little chopping movements, like they want to get the process over with.) I heard my father's laugh, a childish giggle which didn't go with his big body, the way boxers often have high voices that don't go with their bulk. I saw the red marks on my legs left by the leather belt he hit me and my sister with when we misbehaved.

I lifted the bundle of letters out of the folder and discovered my parents' marriage and divorce certificates tucked between them. They married in 1947 and their divorce was granted in 1970 on the grounds that each party was guilty of cruelty to the other. I only looked at two of the letters: a note detailing

101

Lucien's maintenance arrears from the Petty Sessional Division of Highgate Magistrates' Court – seven pounds a week he was supposed to pay, I knew that figure well, it was a risible sum even then, and Mum often spoke angrily about it – and a ruling from the European Commission of Human Rights dated 1970, responding to my father's complaint that he'd 'lost all contact with his children of whose present whereabouts he does not know'. The reply stated that a court welfare officer saw the children and 'they did not wish to meet their father under influence of mother'.

The second folder was blue, faded at the corners to a pinky yellow, and contained a document titled *The Diary of L A Albertine (Esq) 1965–1967*. These were the last two years we all lived together as a family. I didn't read any more letters or the diary, just shoved everything back into the trunk, but the next day I went to Galeries Lafayette, bought a large canvas bag the colour of wet brown earth, half the size of a sack, and emptied all the papers, diaries and knives into it. The following week, when the funeral was over and all the cleaning and tidying was finished, I boarded the train to London carrying two suitcases,

my father's rattan chair and the big brown bag. I was stopped at the border because of all the Opinel knives, but when I told the French customs officer in broken French that my father had just died, he nodded and waved me through.

Something Nasty in the Wardrobe*

The first time I visited Mum after Lucien died her grey eyes swept over my face like a prison searchlight looking for an escapee. She knew it was likely I'd come across something damning – Mum knew enough about life and death to know that when going through a person's lifelong accumulation of papers and possessions it's inevitable you'll unearth some secrets, and she had so many secrets. I didn't mention the papers, which felt like a betrayal as I usually told her everything, and stowed the brown bag at the bottom of a cupboard in my flat. But whenever I passed the cupboard I felt uneasy, like I'd locked a living thing in there. I was aware that if I threw the bag away, my anxiety would probably disappear with it, but I left it in there. Even when I moved to Hackney I took the bag with me; this time I stashed it in a shed. I wondered if I was being a masochist by hanging onto my father's diary. I questioned myself, *Which action is bravest, throwing away the diary or reading it? Why do I think I always have to be brave?*

* See Stella Gibbons, *Cold Comfort Farm*, 1932

22 I detected a bitter glance from Pascale after Mum agreed to my suggestion that we be quiet. It occurred to me she was jealous that I'd guessed right, like I'd shown I knew Mum best. Mum was in a bad state. She could hardly breathe, her throat was blocked and she was making curdled, death-rattly sounds as if she was choking and gurgling on phlegm. Mia, who'd been standing quietly in the corner, stepped forward with two tubes attached to what looked like a washing machine on wheels. 'I need to clear your mother's airways,' she explained to Pascale, who was still sitting on the mattress next to Mum's head. 'No,' Pascale replied. 'I'm not moving.'

Encased

Pascale was born when I was eighteen months old. My reaction to her arrival was to climb into her playpen and not get out again, unless I really had to, for a year. I felt robbed. I wasn't ready to not be the baby any more, I wasn't done with it. I wasn't done with Mum. Pascale didn't want to be in the playpen. As soon as she could crawl, she was off round the garden, eager to explore the world – we were living in Australia at the time, where there were lots of dangerous bugs and spiders. I felt safe huddled behind the wooden bars of the cage. I'd gather the blanket and soft toys in close and suck my thumb. When I was sent to school a year early because Mum couldn't cope with two of us at home I felt even more wronged. I hated being deposited at the school gates and watching Mum wheel the pushchair round in a circle and stride off with Pascale, leaving me behind.

I cried and shat myself every day. That childhood desire to be in the playpen has never gone away (shitting still a bit of a problem too). I still like to feel safe and contained. You try all your life to be an adult, but something deep down inside you will always be that child.

It wasn't just daytime, I liked to feel confined at night too and begged Mum to heft layer after layer of grey army blankets, winter coats and, if they still didn't feel heavy enough, old curtains on top of me when I went to bed. Once I was suitably weighed down I'd push the top of my skull, where a newborn's fontanelle is, up against the headboard. I still have to remind myself not to do that. I equated being crushed or squeezed with feeling safe. Every night after she tucked me in Mum would go to the bottom of the bed, tunnel under the sheets, blankets and coats, grab hold of my ankles and pull me back down the bed so my head was in the middle of the pillow, but as soon as she left the room I'd wriggle back up again. (Other rituals Mum performed on me at night were exercising my legs by gripping my knee and ankle and circling one leg at a time so I wouldn't be bow-legged, weaving plaster in and out of my toes so they wouldn't be crooked, and taping a penny onto my stomach so I'd have a flat navel, all of which worked.)

My need for boundaries and pressure is never far below the surface. I was even reluctant to have my braces removed after wearing them for two years in my forties because I liked how they hugged and gripped my teeth. And when Eryk said, 'I've encased you,' after he finished constructing the walls and partitions in my Hackney home, I thought that was hot. I've since discovered there are other people in the world who find it comforting to be held or pressed tight. Temple Grandin, one of the first adults to publicly identify as autistic, suffered from chronic anxiety and found she became less distressed when she shut herself in the holding device that calmed the calves at her aunt's ranch.* She later invented the 'hug box', a piece of equipment designed to calm people who are on the autistic spectrum.† After reading about Grandin and how the need to be held tight or weighed down can be an autistic trait, it occurred to me that I may be on the autistic spectrum myself (or a calf).

Half a Sixpence

Imagine you were asked in a maths paper at junior school, 'Which would you prefer, a shilling or two sixpences?' and you answered, 'Two sixpences,' because thinking of the two tiny silver coins jingling together in your pocket made you feel good and you loved those cute little sixpences. But when the test paper was returned you saw a big red cross through your answer, and that night your mother explained to you that it was a trick question, two sixpences and a shilling were worth the same amount – which you knew, but you'd still prefer two sixpences. It wasn't that you were stupid, you just saw things from a different angle. Sixpences had character, shillings didn't. And you felt richer with two sixpences because there were two coins, not just one. But despite all these explanations, you were still wrong and you kept getting tripped up by these trick questions over and over

* www.templegrandin.com
† You can now buy weighted blankets for children with ASD and ADHD

again, in exams, in relationships, friendships, jobs and interviews. In fact, these misreadings of situations happened so often that you started to view the world as a tricksy and untruthful place. Then you noticed that the people who saw the tricks behind the questions were popular and always at the top of the class. Baffled by life and its unseen rules, you began to doubt everything around you. You felt you had to approach *all* of life as a trick, just to get it right a few times.

The sixpences episode happened to Pascale, but it could just as easily have happened to me.

There were no allowances made for people who were a bit different in the 1960s, especially children. We didn't know or use terms like 'autistic spectrum', 'Asperger's' or 'Attention Deficit Disorder'. Even being 'artistic' was considered a defect. Teachers, parents, classmates and the medical profession thought children who didn't conform were just difficult, annoying misfits. Girls were considered even more of an aberration than boys.

> For women with autism our capacity and interest in conformity is diminished – we are no friend to the patriarchy.
> Nicola Clark, 'I Was Diagnosed with Autism in My 40s', *Guardian*, 30 August 2016

Even now girls are under-diagnosed in this area because they are more adept at adjusting their behaviour, able to observe and mimic social interactions. This means ASD symptoms in females may be masked and go undetected. As Sarah Hendrickx, a writer who received a late diagnosis of ASD, remarked in the *Guardian* in 2015, 'Research is now catching up and revealing that girls and women can present a different autistic profile and this is why they continue to be missed.'*

I think my whole family was on the ASD spectrum. My mother and father both had extreme and unusual personalities (plus my father was an engineer, a classic ASD profession – along with mathematician – before computer programmers). ASD types are often attracted to each other; this is called 'assortative mating', and it has been suggested that the recent increase in numbers of autistic children in Silicon Valley is due to this phenomenon.† Assortative mating probably drew my parents to each other, and also explains why I'm interested in unconventional women and men.

I had some peculiar traits when I was young. I couldn't leave the house if there was a wrinkle in my sock and wouldn't finish eating if a fly buzzed past. I was so easily distracted that Mum had to lock down a room and remove all stimuli to get me to finish my food. I also had a tendency towards obsessiveness (clothes, music, boys, smells, colours) and an exaggerated response to stress. I'd panic if I lost a hairbrush. If I misplaced something I felt my world was out of balance. I had diarrhoea every day on the way to school due to nervousness, right up to the age of seventeen. I was also extremely aware of the emotional undercurrents between members of my family, and later on, between everyone I encountered. (I can also be the complete opposite – clumsy and missing the point by miles.) I experienced my life as if I was on drugs, paranoid, watchful, every emotion exaggerated and magnified. That's how I've felt every day from as far back as I can remember.

* Sarah Hendrickx provides training on ASD: www.asperger-training.com
† Steve Silberman, *Neurotribes – the Legacy of Autism*, 2015

23

Mia was shocked that Pascale wouldn't move away from the bed. I wasn't. 'You can come round this side and do it,' I said, trying to sound normal. I desperately wanted Mum's death to be normal. I was embarrassed about Pascale's behaviour. *Here's my mad, bad family rearing its ugly head again.* I tried to keep the mood light because it was more important to me than anything that, if Mum did go that night, Vida's memory of the whole thing would be bearable. Mum and I had worked hard over the past five years to make her impending death acceptable to Vida, not something to fear or be hidden away and not spoken about. We'd done our best to prepare her and I didn't want Pascale ruining it. Mia tried again. 'It's much easier for me to reach your Mum from this side, where the plug is.' Pascale ignored her. Mia's shoulders hunched up to her ears as she trundled the machine around to the other side of the bed and used a plug by the door. Vida and I shuffled out of her way. The wires were stretched so tight the equipment only just reached Mum's mouth.

Grey Garden*

In the early years, when we lived at Frieda's house, Pascale and I were allies. We'd spend hours together drawing or making pop-up books. We'd build dens in Nanny's garden until it got dark, then Mum would notice we were missing and call us in.

* *Grey Gardens,* a documentary about mother and daughter Edith and Edie Bouvier Beale, 1976

We giggled about nothing for hours under our father's outdoor workbench while it rained, again until Mum noticed, told us off and dragged us inside. We lived in our imaginations as we had very little stimulus at home: no books, no visitors, hardly any friends. Once we dared ourselves to kiss each other on the lips to see what all the fuss was about, but sprang apart in horror as soon as our mouths touched. I can still remember that feeling of soft smooth skin on soft smooth skin. It was horrible, like kissing myself.

Pascale was nine and I was eleven when we moved out of Frieda's and into our own house in Muswell Hill. That's when our arguments became more frequent and more physical (punching and general hitting). I found her more irritating and annoying than before, but we still protected each other's secrets and covered for each other when we were in trouble.

Four years after moving to Muswell Hill my parents separated and Mum, Pascale and I moved into the council house next to Hornsey Gas Holder No. 1. That's when Pascale did something I thought was strange: she stopped confiding in Mum and me. She'd met this new group of friends, boys and girls from outside school. The main boy was older than me and had long dark-brown hair and a moustache like Mickey Finn, the drummer from Tyrannosaurus Rex. I was jealous when he gave her a big brown toy rabbit with a purple velvet jacket for her birthday. I understood that she didn't want to share her new friends with me – I'd nicked some off her once before – but I was upset for Mum because up until then she and Pascale had been so close. Mum worked hard: five days and two evenings a week as a librarian and a third evening as a cleaner to make sure we had new clothes and didn't look poor. She had no life. I felt we at least owed her our confidences. She also stayed up late every night studying to pass her library exams so she could move up a grade and earn more money. The head of her library in Crouch End said she was too old to go in for the exams at forty-nine. When she passed with credit he sent her paper back to the examining board and told them to double-check it.

Mum did everything she could to make sure our lives and our appearance were not too affected by our lack of money. Her holey, greying knickers with fraying waistbands pegged to the washing line in the garden every Saturday morning were testament to that. I was ashamed of myself every time I looked at those knickers. We always had new ones, and new socks and shoes. Pascale and I looked immaculate. Our petticoats and shirt-waisted dresses were starched by hand so the skirts stood out from our knees, not too stiff, not too lank, with just the right amount of 'bell', skinny legs protruding from the crisp hem like spindly pink stamens dangling from a fuchsia bud.

Despite all Mum's hard work, and my attempts to coax her out by regaling her with my own experiences, Pascale never shared anything personal with me, and as far as I know with Mum, again. In her early twenties she emigrated to Canada and didn't contact Mum for years. There'd been no argument between them, they didn't fall out. Mum couldn't understand it and nor could I. I'd never have done anything as extreme as leave Mum and then ignore her, even though I was supposed to be the rebellious one. Pascale sent me her address eventually and I wrote begging her to at least send Mum a postcard occasionally saying she was OK, but although she kept in contact with me, she still wouldn't reply to Mum. I saw her leaving as a betrayal. I've never forgiven her.

Scheherezade

After the divorce, losing our home and Pascale leaving, I thought that if I didn't work hard at distracting Mum, she might give up on life out of grief and disappointment. To counteract what I saw as Pascale's desertion, and fearful of the effect it would have on Mum, I became as cunning and desperate as anyone fighting for survival in my attempts to keep my mother alive. I told her about all my adventures to fill up the holes in her life. I stepped into the breach. That's how my confessional nature developed, how I became the big mouth I am today. I think I did pretty well too. Mum lived to ninety-five and I'm not exaggerating when I say I feel partly responsible for her longevity.

I had nothing to offer her in return for everything she did for me, no money or success. My only currencies were my time and my wayward life. So every night I told her stories the way Queen Scheherazade told stories to the king, except Scheherazade did it to keep herself alive and I did it to keep my mother alive. I really believed that by entertaining her I was stopping her from killing herself. *I know what to do. Mum wants to know what's coming next.* I understood 'Scheherazade's terror: the terror that comes from the literal or metaphorical equating of telling stories with living, with life itself'.* I adhered to this strategy right up to Mum's death, sharing experiences that I probably should have kept to myself, telling tales of drug-taking and STDs over a cup of tea at the kitchen table, graduating to infertility and marriage breakdown as I got older. There was never any condemnation from Mum, although she did gasp and shake her head sometimes. Whenever my life collapsed – which was often – I'd move back in with her, and no matter my age or what I was up to, she always put a hot-water bottle in my bed at night. Finding that hot-water bottle after narrowly avoiding rape or a beating during my punk years made me feel loved.

Mum advised, supported and steered me through my many disasters. Whether I'd said something stupid to someone at a party, made a mistake at work, fallen out with a colleague, was lonely, applying for a job, in a difficult relationship or spiked with drugs at a nightclub, she helped me make sense of the situation and find a way forward. The world baffled me, people baffled me, I couldn't understand them most of the time. They baffled her too. Sometimes it took a four-hour phone call, or a series of phone calls spread out over days, for us to work out how to

* From David Bayles and Ted Orland, *Art and Fear, Observations on the Perils (and Rewards) of Artmaking*, 1993. I was led to this book by author Amanda Smyth

respond to a predicament I was in, but we got there in the end. It took two people for me to function in the world, Mum and me. 'Two heads are better than one, even if they're both wooden heads,' my grandmother Frieda used to say.

When I was growing up not many girls or women reached their potential because back then a woman's role was to become a wife and support her husband in his endeavours. I only managed to forge an interesting independent life because Mum was always by my side.

Fuck it. I married my mother.

I'll never hear her voice again. She used to call me Vivvy, or Vivvy-bonks.

24 After Pascale refused to move for Mum's throat to be cleared, I felt my body deflate and the I-am-normal-and-so-is-my-family facade became too difficult to maintain. All the ugly emotions that should have stayed locked up inside me for another fifty years came slithering out. I could sense all our past resentments and rivalries vying for space, feel them pushing up against me in the little yellow room. Grotesque, thuggish, unforgiving creatures throwing twisted shapes and threatening shadows as they swung from the curtains and flapped around Mum's head. 'Hell is empty, and all the devils are here.'* Now I knew what it meant.

* William Shakespeare, *The Tempest*, 1611

The Prodigal Daughter

Pascale finally wrote to Mum from Canada and started visiting once a year. By this time the pattern of me blabbing about my exploits and Mum dissecting and commenting on them was well established. Whenever Pascale came to England she joined Mum as listener and evaluator of my life. I was complicit in the arrangement and saw nothing wrong with the set-up. It never occurred to me that it might be unhealthy. I thought I was being funny and interesting and entertaining, filling the awkward gaps in the atmosphere.

Pascale became increasingly concerned with Mum and her health as the years passed and started hassling me (from 3,500 miles away – just saying) to sort out Mum's life. But Mum didn't want a new oven, fridge, mobile phone or computer. If she needed something like a copper bracelet for her arthritis, an electric blanket or a non-slip bath mat, she'd tell me. If it was something expensive, she kept quiet and went without. She was from the war generation, not from the *let's-throw-it-away-and-get-a-new-one* generation. She didn't take taxis, eat something sweet every day, shower every day, go on diets or analyse her feelings. She used to say, 'The worst four words in the English language are "We need to talk".' The idea of therapy or hashing over your emotions made her feel physically sick.

I didn't like being nagged and ordered around from afar and nor did Mum, but she refused to say anything to Pascale about it. Whenever I mentioned that Pascale's harassment was annoying, Mum responded with 'Pascale was so helpful to me when she was young. You understand if I make more of a fuss of her than I do of you, don't you?' Or, 'You're both so different. Pascale needs *love*, you need *things*.' I nodded, but seethed inside. (What's wrong with love *and* things?) Pascale waltzed back into Mum's affections after disappearing for years, garnering all the praise like the prodigal son. It was odd because Mum hated that parable and often said how unfair she thought it was.

When she wasn't in England, Pascale set me tasks and checked up on me until I'd done them. That was how it felt to me, although I'm sure that wasn't her intention. I developed a constant flutter of fear in my stomach which erupted into panic if I saw an email from her. *What errand has she set me now? What haven't I done?* I'd jump when the phone rang or my email pinged and felt nauseous when I saw her name on the screen, dreading what her next missive would demand of me. I already felt guilty. I knew I wasn't doing enough for Mum. I saw her almost every day, phoned her every night, bought her food and talked to the social services for her, but I didn't get round to things like taking her to the dentist. I hadn't been to the dentist myself for the last five years, Vida hadn't been for two.

The animosity I felt towards Pascale was confusing. She'd been a good sister to me. If ever I was in trouble – cancer, divorce, burglary – she was the first person, other than Mum, I longed for. Whenever I felt threatened I wanted Pascale. I thought of her as strong and loyal and capable. If you were in a fight, or needed to break into your own house or face down a bully, you'd want Pascale by your side. She gave me money to put towards a childminder for Vida and flew to London three times when I had cancer and needed the kind of help that only family can give. We didn't get on once she arrived, but she came, and that's what was needed. I, on the other hand, have never done the same for her, partly because I was ill for so many years, but mainly because I was never asked. I never knew when Pascale was in trouble. She never told me.

During the last five years of Mum's life, Pascale started visiting her twice a year. She organised Mum's flat, tidied up, threw things away and arranged the delivery of beds and special toilet seats from the NHS. It was a relief to have her take over those duties for a few weeks. Mum was becoming difficult, telling carers not to come back, refusing to see doctors and nurses and eschewing food unless I bought and cooked it. The only person she would let do anything for her was me, and I was exhausted.

Chair

For a moment we glared at each other . . . full of mutual resentment and something darker, the old sense between sisters that there is only really room in the world for one girl. The sense that every fight could be to the death.

Philippa Gregory, *The Other Boleyn Girl*, 2001

A few months before Mum died I called Pascale in Canada and said, 'I don't think she has long left, you'd better come now.' It was difficult to gauge how long Mum had to live, months, weeks or days, but I wouldn't have been able to live with myself if Pascale had missed her death. The onus was on me to get the timing of that phone call right. The tension between Pascale and me was just about bearable when there was all that sea and time difference between us, but after my call she flew to London and moved in with Mum and it became apparent that there wasn't room for two caring, attentive daughters in Mum's life.

Pascale would sit scowling at me from the corner of the kitchen when I visited them. She didn't move from the armchair beside Mum's rocking chair. She stayed rooted to that chair for two, three hours at a time. Didn't make a cup of tea, answer the phone or go to the bathroom, just squatted there like Cerberus guarding the gates of the underworld. *She can't possibly have plonked herself there to stop me sitting next to Mum, can she? She can't be that unhinged. I must be disturbed for thinking it.* I wanted to sit next to Mum, to hold her hand and smile at her. I often only had an hour or two in between work and going home to Vida, but I didn't dare ask Pascale to move. If I was right and she was deliberately hogging the space next to Mum, my request would cause a scene. I didn't want to ruin the illusion of a happy supportive family in front of Mum when she was so near to death.

I noticed Pascale doing the same at the hospital, not leaving the chair by Mum's bed. In fact, she wouldn't move from Mum's side wherever we were, no matter how short my visit. *Am I not going to be able to sit next to Mum ever again when Pascale is in the room?* And she was always in the room. I didn't know what to do, whether to accept the situation or mention it and risk an argument. Then one day during a phone call with Mum, when we were discussing what to do with all the stuff in her flat after she'd gone, I said, 'I bet Pascale will go back to Canada and leave me to sort everything out like she did with Lucien.' (Angling for a bit of sympathy.)

'Oh well,' Mum replied in a disinterested voice. 'Someone's got to do it.' The camaraderie was gone. She didn't care, she had Pascale to look after her now. Or she couldn't be bothered. Or she was too fed up with our squabbling and too near death to fake concern. I didn't say it aloud but a strange retort popped into my head: *You know what, Mum? I'm not playing the game any more either.*

25 Maleficence was in the air. Through narrowed eyes I watched my sister entrenched on Mum's bed and tried to summon some self-control. *Don't degrade Mum's death, don't give in to your anger,* I told myself, but Vida being robbed of her grandmother's death was too much to bear. I couldn't hold the fury in any longer, I just knew I was going to blow. There were so many things I'd dreaded would happen the night of Mum's death, but the one thing I didn't anticipate was that the decades of tension between Pascale and me would reach boiling point as we sat around Mum's deathbed. I'd imagined the two of us holding hands, sobbing, united in our grief.

The Entertainer

During yet another uncomfortable visit to Mum's flat, with Pascale crouched on the chair and me perched at the table, wittering away, filling the silences, I had an epiphany. *Hang on a minute, I'm just the joker here. Always have been.* I tried to quell the thought. But I couldn't shake the idea. I mulled it over on the drive home and became convinced I was right. *I've always been in the middle of this family, brokering the peace, distracting*

119

them with my antics. I felt like Ada Lovelace, I could see the mathematics of it all so clearly. I'd solved a puzzle that I was part of. That's a very difficult thing to do.

I decided to test my theory next time I saw Mum and Pascale. All I had to do was not perform the role of entertainer for five minutes and see what happened. It would be a simple enough experiment to execute. I was aware that this might not be the best time to cut out all sentimentality and make a cold, calculating decision to change my role in the family but I was in survival mode. I felt I had to protect my sanity, even if it meant letting Pascale take the last few weeks with Mum from me. Such an inconsequential habit to change, you'd think, not to be the talking, sharing buffoon any more.

Bad Seeds

Suppose
you saw your mother
torn between two daughters:
what could you do
to save her but be
willing to destroy
yourself – she would know
who was the rightful child,
the one who couldn't bear
to divide the mother.

Louise Glück, 'A Fable', *Ararat*, 1990

The next time I visited Mum I tested my Viv-the-jester, mother-and-sister-the-succubi hypothesis. I sat on a dining chair at the table as usual. Mum and Pascale were already in the armchairs, side by side. This time I waited for them to talk, to do the work, lighten the mood. I smiled but didn't offer up any mishaps, failed attempts at relationships, stresses at work or worries about Vida. I commented on the weather and then stopped speaking. Silence. The family dynamic collapsed like a Yorkshire pudding whisked from a hot oven into a cold kitchen.

No one spoke. There was nothing to do but look around the room with a fixed smile and pretend that everything around me had become fascinating. The second-hand wooden dining table draped in a pink plastic tablecloth (it's not that Mum had bad taste, she didn't have any money) marked with blue biro squiggles and brown coffee-cup rings. The Victorian occasional table in the corner, the dining chair opposite that I dunked in bleach about twenty years ago to get rid of the varnish, exposing all the different shades and types of wood that had been banged together to make it (Mum wasn't pleased). An old fridge right next to a new fridge with a television and two radios on top (in case one broke). Filing cabinet, pots, tins, piles of newspapers and a paper shredder. By the time I'd completed a circuit of the kitchen and my gaze alighted back on the two of them, Mum had a puzzled expression on her face and Pascale, still hunched in the chair, was glowering. This time I knew for certain she wasn't going to move. The tension in the room was excruciating. I wanted to break the spell, to make it all OK again. I had to fight the urge to gabble but managed to push the words back down my throat.

Neither Mum nor Pascale knew what wasn't right that afternoon. They hadn't time to work it out, and anyway it was such a tiny shift, me not sharing my troubles, that they wouldn't have been able to pinpoint what had happened. Before I did it part of me wondered if I'd imagined the whole thing, but sitting through those agonising minutes confirmed my suspicions and hardened my resolve to stop. When you change a pattern or a habit within a family you have to be brutal and slice it out. Families don't like change. If one of you changes, everyone has to change.

Half an hour was all I could bear before I jumped up, said, 'I've got to go now,' put my coat on, let myself out and ran down the three flights of stairs – past Mr Shilling's old flat – and into the street.

When I reached the front gate I looked up at Mum's third-storey window to see if she was waving goodbye like she usually did, but there was no twitch of the yellow satin curtains this time. I felt giddy, like a true rebel, much more rebellious than when I was in the Slits. To revolt against a lifetime of habit and family expectations was much harder to do – and possibly mean and foolish, when your mother is dying and you're supposed to be good and kind – than rebelling against society. I jumped into my car, pushed the key into the ignition, leaned back and stared through the windscreen. *The first time I haven't tried to entertain them*. A momentous day. The day I knew for certain that all this time I thought I was being the good one, the loved one, the favourite, I was the fool.

The lamp posts flickered on. A man with big black spectacles and two tiny white dogs emerged from the house next door. Windows lit up, curtains pulled shut and I sat in the car outside Mum's flat reflecting on what a cushy ride the so-called 'bad one' has. They don't have to call, write or attend family gatherings, all the boring stuff. They mooch around like nobody understands them, flounce off if anyone dares question their behaviour, disappear for as long as they like and turn up again when they want something or suddenly get scared somebody's going to die.

I turned the ignition key and revved up the engine. *So this is what it feels like to be the dreaded misfit. The one the rest of the family moans and complains about after you've left the room.*

An enormous relief.

26 The ambulance crew reappeared. A paramedic beckoned me over and said there was nothing more they could do for my mother and they were leaving. I nodded and tried to look calm. 'But before we go,' he added, 'I must warn you that when your mother is about to pass she'll claw at the air, gasping for breath as she runs out of oxygen. It'll be upsetting for you to see.' I nodded again, wishing Vida hadn't heard him, but she was glued to my side. We went back to the bed. Pascale was still sitting on it but now she had her arm wrapped around Mum's head and was flicking at her ear and talking to her in a sing-songy voice. Like she was petting an old cat.

The Yellow Wallpaper*

When the doctors and the council agreed that at ninety-five years old, nearly dead and having paid taxes since she was seventeen, Mum could go into a home, Pascale and I set about decorating her new bedroom. I found the care home through my friend Kate, whose own mother lived there. I knew from Kate that the carers were very kind to the residents. Pascale nearly mucked it up by losing her temper and slamming the phone down on the social worker who was helping. I had to apologise and coax her back on board. After all this, Mum announced, 'Isn't Pascale wonderful, finding the care home for me!' I started to protest, but stopped myself and replied, 'Oh well, it's not about me versus Pascale, is it?' Mum gave me a strange look, like she'd been rumbled. I didn't understand her reaction at the time, but her expression was when suspicions about her character first started to form in my mind.

Pascale and I brought photographs, a chest of drawers and a rocking chair from Mum's flat, and when she was wheeled into the little yellow room with daffodil-patterned curtains, she looked around and said, 'This is the nicest bedroom I've ever had!' I don't know if she meant it or not. If she was telling the truth, I think it's sad that the nicest bedroom Mum ever slept in was a yellow box in a purpose-built care home. Although it's also possible she was thinking of Pascale and me rather than herself and trying to soften the transition for us.

Every time I visited Mum at the care home I brought her a

---

* The title of a short story by Charlotte Perkins Gilman, 1892

fresh cream cake. What did it matter? She didn't have long to live, she could eat as many profiteroles as she liked. She must have said something about the cakes, or maybe Pascale saw the remains, because within a week she was bringing in her own cream cakes for Mum. I didn't know about this until Mum confessed she'd been forcing two cream cakes down every day so as not to upset either of us. I stopped bringing cakes after that. No point in mentioning it to Pascale, we'd only end up arguing about it. We could fight over any little thing. If we'd been born in earlier times, we'd have murdered each other. Or had someone else do it. At the very least I'd have locked her in a tower.

This was not the first time cake had been our battleground. We often fought over whose slice was the biggest as children. Sometimes we resorted to getting the ruler out. Five years ago we fought over how much Christmas cake Pascale had eaten, almost all of it right before the Christmas lunch I'd spent hours cooking, which she then couldn't eat because she was full. The row escalated and Pascale turned to Vida – then eight years old – and said she felt sorry for her for having such a shit mother. We didn't speak again for a year.

On one of her visits to London Pascale accused me of accepting little bits of money from Mum. True, but only little amounts, a tenner here and there, much needed and not that well appreciated, I'm ashamed to say. But this time I didn't let it go and argued back, *I'm the one who's here, and anyway, it's only to help me with Vida.* In response, Pascale told Mum that I said I found her exhausting and a bit of a pain to look after. I'd confided this to Pascale a few hours earlier. We didn't speak for a year and a half after that one. Then she wrote and apologised: 'Sorry if I upset you.' I can't stand that 'if' in people's apologies. You know perfectly well the other person is upset, there's no 'if' about it. Say 'I'm sorry I upset you,' admit what you did was wrong, or say nothing at all.

Our relationship followed this cyclical pattern for thirty years, similar to the 'cycle of abuse' theory developed by Lenore E. Walker in the 1970s. We'd try to get along, we *wanted* to get along (and I know Pascale let go of lots of things I did that hurt her too), but as soon as a conflict arose, over Mum or cake or something else, the argument would escalate, Pascale would say something unnecessarily hurtful and we'd withdraw from each other for a year or so. I don't know if she did the same but I often swore to myself I'd never see her again. She once told me that it took her at least a year to realise she'd gone too far. Towards the end of Mum's life this arguing and then ignoring sequence happened every single time Pascale and I met. Round and round we went, both feeling right, both feeling wronged.

27 I watched with horror as Pascale cradled Mum's head and flicked at her ear. We both knew Mum hated being touched and fussed over. She was always telling Pascale to stop touching her at the hospital, to stop fixing her hair and wiping her face. It wasn't personal, it's just that Mum wasn't brought up in a touchy-feely time. She wouldn't even let me hold her arm when we crossed the road and she stopped eating during her last month because she couldn't bear being spoon-fed. Pascale probably thought she was stroking Mum's ear, but to me it looked like flicking. I still think it was flicking. Mum couldn't say anything to stop it, she couldn't speak. I wondered again if I should speak for her. A scene from *Terminator* 2 popped into my mind, the one where Linda Hamilton is strapped to the bed and the male nurse licks her face but she can't do anything about it. Funny how I kept thinking of movie scenes. I must have been trying to conjure up a frame of reference. What were you supposed to do in this situation? I hadn't been taught what to do at a deathbed, how to behave, what's allowed, how to assert yourself. Who has more rights, the dying person or the bereaved? It's us who have to live on. No one discusses these things. Restraint is the British way, so that's what I did in the end, restrained myself. Pascale kept on flicking. Poor Mum.

Rug Rats

. . . her death had released us all to be the worst possible versions of ourselves.

Nora Ephron, *I Remember Nothing*, 2010

I gave Mum a handmade rug for her birthday about ten years ago, woven from thick deep-blue wool and patterned with random abstract twirls. I had it made especially for her. When Pascale visited from Canada she saw the rug, went out the next day and bought Mum a synthetic, yellowy-brown one. When Mum moved into the care home I brought the blue rug from her flat. It fitted neatly under the furniture along the back wall of her room – you couldn't see much of it but it added some cosiness. Pascale put 'her' yellow rug in the middle of the room, but it was in the way of the equipment that the carers wheeled in and out every day – they needed to use a hoist to get Mum to the bathroom – so they rolled it up and put it in the wardrobe. This was explained to Pascale, but she put the yellow rug back down in the middle of the room. The nurses were intimidated by her. She defaced one of their pictures of the Queen in the hallway (funny in a different context), which was quietly removed and thrown away. I was worried the nurses wouldn't look after Mum so well with all the effort it took to get their equipment in and out of her room and Pascale irritating them, but as far as I could tell they enjoyed spending time with her. They lifted their equipment over the rug multiple times a day without any more being said. I offered to take the blue rug out of the room and have no rugs at all, but Pascale said no. Mum couldn't see either rug from the bed but she didn't want to upset Pascale and leave the planet on a sour note. She desperately wanted us to be friends and not lose touch with each other. 'You've only got one sister, surely you can get along? You only have to see each other occasionally,' she said to me. But it was too late for that. You can't mend such a deep rift between two people in the last few weeks of your life. Better to let it go, let the fools do what they have to do.

28 It must have been about midnight. I remember thinking the room wasn't a happy yellow any more. It was 'repellent, almost revolting; a smouldering unclean yellow' with 'a sickly sulphur tint'.* The walls seemed to have turned grey, shifted from sunny egg-yolk to that blue-grey tinge you

* Charlotte Perkins Gilman, 'The Yellow Wallpaper'

get inside a hard-boiled egg if you don't run it under cold water after taking it out of the pan. I looked out of the window at the bare branches fringing the railway line and watched them shivering in the wind. I'd read somewhere that when a remarkable person dies nature throws up a wild storm to mark their passing. Where was Mum's storm? Didn't the universe know how special she was? I looked back into the room and for the first time it struck me as odd that Mia was still there. I thought people were supposed to be left alone when their relatives were dying, not have a nurse standing by the whole time. Could Mia feel the tension in the air? Was that why she hadn't left? Did she know Pascale and I weren't to be trusted? That we were immature and unstable? I noticed Vida was trying to hold her grandmother's hand, but it was difficult because Mum was still rolling down the slope created by Pascale's weight on the mattress. I decided to say something, even though I was risking a scene. I thought if it was for her niece, and I said it calmly, Pascale might let Vida sit next to her grandma for a bit. And Mum would get some respite from all the ear-flicking and be able to lie flat.

I spoke slowly, kept the anger out of my voice, and suggested to Pascale that she let Vida have a go sitting on the other side of the bed. 'Let her hold Grandma's hand for a while,' I said. 'You can take turns.'

'No,' she said. 'This is my spot.'

Two Dreams

Mum is bundled up in white bandages like an Egyptian mummy. She's huge, a giant chrysalis, or baby, wrapped in swaddling clothes, as heavy as a sack of stones. I keep putting her down to rest my arms, but as soon as I do, I feel guilty and pick her up again. I'm exhausted, distraught. 'Mum, I can't hold you any more,' I tell her. 'You're too heavy.'

I'm straddling a rock face, my arms and legs stretched apart in a star shape. Mum is clasped between me and the rock's surface. I press my body against hers as hard as I can, trying to stop her from slipping out from under me. But she's sliding away and I'm losing my grip. She'll fall a long way down if I can't hold her. I can't stop it happening. Mum drops away from me and crashes to the ground. Smashes onto her feet. I'm sitting in the shallow warm sea, my skirt billowing in the waves, wailing, 'Mum! Mum! Mum!'

29 I wasn't surprised Pascale said no to Vida, not after she wouldn't move for Mum's throat to be drained. But I was shocked that she was willing to throw away the only family she had left. *Surely she knows what's at stake here?* I thought, and said to her, 'You'll regret this behaviour for the rest of your life.'
   'Fuck off.'
   She spat the words at me with such hatred. Over Mum's body. It felt blasphemous. All the air smashed out of my lungs.

I couldn't have been more winded if she'd whacked me in the chest with a plank. More insults spewed out of her mouth. I can't remember what she said, I was transfixed by her lips twisting and curling. Now Mia knew for certain that we weren't a normal family, and I knew for certain that Mum's gentle death and Vida's tender goodbye weren't going to happen. I gave up on Pascale right there and then, on Mum's Last Night, in the last hours of her life. *This is where it ends*, I thought. *I want a sister very much, but I can no longer endure this one.*

Death Is Smaller than I Thought

Mum died at four o'clock in the morning on 4 June 2014. One last conversation would have been nice, one more laugh together, one more Liquorice Allsort. I'd have liked to congratulate her on having no debts and commiserate that she didn't have much money to leave behind after working all her life. I would have loved to tell her all about the funeral; that she chose well, a plain, pale-wood coffin, two cars. There were no twigs though. I didn't get twigs and leaves for the wreaths like she wanted. I chose yellow, purple and white spring flowers instead. It was easier and looked beautiful. Got away with that one. The coffin was carried into the chapel on the shoulders of four men – I didn't think they did that any more. She would have chuckled at that. She entered like a queen to 'Jerusalem', her favourite hymn, and I thought, *This is the first time Mum's been treated as she should have, and she's not here to see it.* The service, conducted by a female minister, was elegant and understated, and just the right length. There was hardly anyone there: four of my close friends who knew Mum, a carer she was close to, Vida and me. Mum had lived so long that the few friends and relatives she did have were dead. It's not a mark of anything important, how many people are at your funeral – especially if you're a behind-the-scenes sort of person as mothers so often are – just as how much money you've earned or how may Facebook friends you have aren't measures of your success. I saw some big fancy gravestones at Père Lachaise cemetery in Paris last summer, but everyone's in the same earth. (Although when we met at a funeral recently, I did ask my friend Mick to round up some people for me when I go. He will as well. He remembers things like that.)

We brought Vida's little electric piano to the funeral and she sang the Jeff Buckley song 'Lover, You Should Have Come Over' to Mum (it was the song she knew how to sing and play best). We both wept throughout the whole thing. I didn't know whether to stand up mid-song and tell her she could stop playing if she wanted to. *It's all right, darling, you don't have to do it.* I felt cruel sitting there not saying anything while she broke down, and I heard Mum in my ear telling me off for putting her through it. I let her finish though. I thought, *If she wants to stop, she's old enough to stop.* (When I asked Vida about it months later she said she wanted to finish, it was important to her.) I said a few words about Mum and placed a pouch of rolling tobacco and a packet of green Rizla rolling papers on her coffin. I'd found them hidden inside a cooking pot secreted at the back of the kitchen cupboard when I cleared out her flat.

Before she smoked roll-ups, Mum smoked Craven A cigarettes. The old Craven A factory is in Mornington Crescent, a large art

deco, Egyptian Revival building with two giant statues of black
cats flanking the entrance. The cats disappeared for years when
the building fell into disrepair, reappearing when it was restored
in the 1990s. There were rumours going around North London
that one of the cats was found in a back garden in Jamaica, which
sounded unlikely until years later I read that the owners of
Craven A, Carreras, had a factory in Jamaica. Craven A cigarettes
gave Mum an air of distinction: the square pack with strong red,
black and white graphics; the gold strip that you had to tear right
around the middle of the packet to rip the cellophane in half; the
cork filter. Craven A were hardcore. No one else I knew smoked
them, certainly no women. The only other woman I've heard
of who smoked Craven A was the pioneering French–Algerian
author Marie Cardinal's mother. 'They came in to serve the tea.
Its aroma, interspersed with that of the Craven A cigarette my
mother was smoking and the hot toast, forms a precise unit in
my memories, so that any one of them encountered anywhere
summons up the others . . .'* In between puffs, stray strands of
tobacco clung to Mum's lips and she'd push her tongue a little
way out into the air, which I thought a very delicate gesture,
collect up the tiny cluster of brown squiggles on the tip like
a gecko snaring an insect, and then pinch them off with her
forefinger and thumb. She told me that whenever Lucien shouted
at her, she'd stroke the cellophane of the Craven A packet in her
pinafore pocket and think, *When all this is over I'm going to
have a cigarette.*

When she became too unwell to go up the road to the shops
on her own Mum sat me down at the kitchen table, said, 'I've run

* Marie Cardinal, *The Words to Say It*, 1975

out of tobacco,' and asked if I'd buy her some more, even though
her lungs were weak and she'd been told not to smoke.

'Of course,' I said. 'How much do you want?'

She closed her eyes like her prayers had been answered. Her
relief was out of proportion to the request.

'What?' I asked.

'I told my friend Sylvia I had to ask you to buy me tobacco,'
she explained. 'And Sylvia said, "Now you'll find out how much
you're loved."'

I was pleased I'd passed that test. Some may think it would
have been more loving to refuse, but love is in the eye of the
beholder.

At the funeral – which Mum had arranged with the Co-op
and paid for in advance (what a blessing) – I read a poem by
Adrian Mitchell which I heard on *Poetry Please* on BBC Radio
4 about two years before she died. Lying in bed late at night
listening to the programme, I was moved to tears by the words

and called Mum immediately. You should always call a person when you think of them, I've learned that along the way. 'Funny you called,' she said, 'I was just going to call *you*. I just heard this poem on Radio 4 . . .' Mum never listened to Radio 4; she happened to have it on that one night. She was very affected by the poem too. She bought a copy of the book and left a little note in it for me, to be collected from her flat after she died. I adapted the poem slightly for the funeral; the following is the adapted version. The original is in Mitchell's 2012 collection *Come On Everybody*.

Death Is Smaller than I Thought

My mother died some years ago
I loved her very much.
When she died my love for her
Did not vanish or fade away.
It stayed just about the same,
Only a sadder colour.
And I can feel her love for me,
Same as it ever was.

Nowadays, in good times or bad,
I sometimes ask my mother
To walk beside me or to sit with me
So we can talk together
Or be silent.

She always comes to me.
I talk to her and listen to her
and I think I hear her talk to me.
It's very simple –
Nothing to do with spiritualism
Or religion or mumbo jumbo.
It is imaginary
It is real
It is love.

II

My mother composed me as I now compose her.
Alison Bechdel, *Are You My Mother?* 2012

30 I closed my eyes and tried to summon up some self-control. *You've had Mum all these years, had the best of her. If Pascale wants her death, let her have it.* I must have stood there for a full three seconds, or five, I don't know, trying to do the right thing, to be good and let it go. Next thing I knew my legs were moving – I didn't tell them to move – and I was leaning over the bed. Everything was slow, really slow – like half speed. I watched as these two long disembodied arms stretched out across Mum's body. They looked like spindly white branches, so far away. I felt as if I was perched high up on the top of a tree with a camera on my head peering down at them. At the end of the white branches were two knobbly red hands ribbed with blue veins and long twiglety fingers splayed out showing the webbing. Ordinary hands they were, middle-aged, female, no rings or jewellery, nothing of consequence. It's all a bit of a blur after that. Time sped up. Teeth crunched, body lunged, hands grabbed . . . and I found myself trying to tear every last strand of Pascale's hair out of her head.

How to Kill Your Mother

I think being a mother is the cruellest thing in the world.
Nella Larsen, *Passing*, 1929

You have no idea how grief will take you. The same with severe illness, motherhood, any profound experience. You don't know yourself. Others don't know you. Those events show you who you are. And you'll be surprised, shocked even. You'll feel the way you feel when you've done a particularly offensive-smelling shit – *That couldn't possibly have come out of me* – and start to rationalise it – *Must be that whole bag of pistachios I ate earlier, or perhaps I'm unwell.* You can't believe you could do something so foul and unrecognisable. Something so outside of yourself.

Instead of feeling sad after Mum's death I kept thinking about how mean she was, how manipulative she'd been and how I'd been tricked by her. I had no control over my thoughts, I didn't know why I thought them. They surged unchecked through my mind like sewage in a flood. I was cold and critical when speaking about her. Friends couldn't believe it, they thought I'd be distraught. 'But you were so close,' or 'Aren't you being a little harsh?' they'd remark as I sat across the kitchen table with a cup of matcha tea. This was when I cooked up The Favourite Theory with my friend Trace, whose own mother had also died recently. Trace and I think we've hit upon something quite interesting with The Favourite Theory, but the Greeks probably wrote about it centuries ago. I wouldn't know, I didn't study classics. Since I was a teenager I've picked my own way through literature, so my reading is specific to my interests. Now I understand the value of reading books that aren't of your choosing: once you can decide what to read your education narrows. This is The Favourite Theory:

A mother selects one of her children and grooms them to be her carer or companion in later life.

The favourite can be the socially awkward one, the misfit or the only option. Fathers don't tend to regard their children in the same way. Heterosexual marriage is still an institution that expects the woman to take care of the man, so men don't usually need a child to perform that function. And a single, solvent, middle-aged man can marry, or at least fantasise about marrying, a younger woman who will stay with him and remain fit and able while he deteriorates into old age. No woman, especially if she's middle-aged and has a couple of children, would ever be deluded enough to think, *Oh, I know, I'll get divorced in my fifties and find a nice young man who'll look after me in my dotage.* It doesn't happen. It's not what young men do. (I've noticed droves of left-wing 'intellectual' men in their fifties and sixties are now marrying women twenty, thirty years younger than themselves. This was considered politically incorrect and unintelligent amongst the radical set in the 1970s.) But we're all programmed to survive. Women are no different to men in that respect.

Sistahood ain't sainthood.
Joan Morgan, *When Chickenheads Come Home to Roost*, 2000

We all have our strategies. Lions kill their cubs so they don't become rivals, male otters hold their pups ransom for food, the black widow spider devours her mate after sex for vitamins (and because she was disappointed?). It's all perfectly natural.

In The Favourite Theory the mother starts scouting early for her prey. Consciously or subconsciously, she casts her eye over her children, mentally separating one off like a sheepdog teasing a weak lamb out of the flock. Her choice of favourite confuses the other children. They can't understand why she's so fond of the weak one, the hopeless one, the unsuccessful one, and she will profess that she's only indulging the lamb-child because they are not quite as able as the others and need her help. But this child will have been chosen because they can't run as fast or as far from her as the others can.

I've known mothers who have offered a child money or to reward a child in their will. My mother didn't have any money to bribe my sister and me with, or much of a choice in the training-a-child-to-be-a-carer stakes – we were both wild, undisciplined girls. Until my sister hit her teens, I'm sure Mum thought Pascale was her best bet. During our parents' marriage breakdown and separation, Pascale's fierce and unquestioning loyalty towards Mum made her indispensable. I was less malleable, although Mum interpreted my more impartial approach as disloyalty.

Is that the reason Pascale stopped communicating with us in her teens and left England in her early twenties? Did she realise that she was going to end up being Mum's carer or stooge if she stuck around? Did she sense that if she didn't get out and break the ties she'd be shackled forever? This is purely conjecture on my part, but it's possible, and very smart of her, if she did.

After Pascale moved to Canada and I was all she had left, Mum couldn't do enough for me. I was delighted that she was all mine at last. But was it love, I wondered after her death, or was she grooming me?

One morning, two weeks after Mum died, and still angry, I clattered down the fire escape to the shed in the back yard, wrestled open the dented metal doors and hauled my father's brown bag out onto the decking.

31 Pascale's hair was bunched up in my fists, twisted round my fingers and clamped between my knuckles. We were lashed together so tightly that the strands cut into my flesh like cheese wire. I braced my knees against the bed-frame to steady myself and ground my knuckles into her scalp to gain more purchase – if I lost my grip, I'd lose my advantage – and dragged her head towards me. I couldn't stop. Not even a flicker of a thought about stopping entered my mind. I'd made my move, the only direction now was forward. To finish her off once and for all.

The Brown Bag

Take, if you must, this little bag of dreams,
Unloose the cord, and they will wrap you round.
W. B. Yeats, 'Fergus and the Druid', 1892

Anxiety hammered inside my chest as I emptied the contents of the brown bag onto the kitchen table, found the buff folder and pulled out photocopies of the letters Lucien wrote to Pascale and me after he left home. They were sent through the county court and forwarded to us because Mum wouldn't give him our address. In every note he asked if he could meet us, and despite the disdain I'd harboured for him over the last fifty years, it was heart-rending reading the letters; to understand, now a parent myself, how devastated he must have been; to realise that he never gave up, repeatedly asking permission to see Pascale and me. His attitude was unusual in an era when it was generally accepted that men had little interest in or time for their offspring.

Lucien   10.11.74 – *To Viviane and Pascale:* I regret what has happened for all of us. I made several attempts to renew our relationship. Life has been unfortunate enough for the four of us in the last seven years. I was hopeful of a friendly reunion but instead I received a letter from Kath saying that it could not be possible. In spite of it all I still say that I like you all and wish to be friends, we are not the only divorced family in the land, we would be better off helping each other. Bless you both, I hope you will have a happy life, give my regards and best wishes to your mother.

23.08.76 – *To Kathleen:* Years now since we last met, please remember that we have all been through enough not to be afraid to meet and chat and that neither you nor I are any better or worse creatures than any other pair we may know.

01.09.79 – *To Kathleen:* I would be pleased to meet you anywhere you care to name – and naturally I would like to renew my relationship with Viviane and Pascale. Please give them my love, hoping to hear from you soon.

16.01.80 – *To Viviane and Pascale:* I hope you don't mind me writing to you from time to time and I hope you are well. I would like to see you again and for the past few years I have been saving for a good holiday, if you would like to come I would be very pleased and grateful of course. I'll pay for it all and I'm sure you will enjoy it.

Mum showed us the letters. She wasn't stupid, she didn't want us accusing her of deception if we came across them, or Lucien, in the future. 'Do what you like. Write to him, meet him if you really want to,' she'd say, but I knew she would see it as a betrayal if I showed any interest in my father. Sitting at the kitchen table reading his letters forty years after he wrote them, I realised that my mother had put me in the false position of thinking I was acting with a free will in choosing not to have a relationship with him. She absolved herself of responsibility by behaving as if she'd given us a choice in affairs that she was manipulating.

There was one more document I hadn't looked at in the bag: his diary, a bundle of pale-lemon-coloured, tissuey sheets of paper held together with a large brass paper clip. Pages and pages, translucent with age, covered with neatly regimented blocks of type, the print faded to a delicate dove grey, enough words to fill two books. I lifted the bundle of paper up to my face and breathed in. It smelled musty and male, and I was transported to the inside of my father's chest of drawers, each one lined with brown paper and containing a few ironed and neatly folded shirts. His clothes were always clean but they were impregnated with a stagnant smell. You could bottle the fragrance coming off my father during the last two years he lived with us, it was that strong: Resentment and Failure by Chanel – Pour Homme. Everyone would recognise it and no one would want to wear it.

Cherry Trees

I found out everything I ever wanted to know about my childhood by reading those flimsy, jaundiced pages chronicling the last two years of my parents' marriage. Lucien writes at the beginning of his diary that his solicitor told him to keep an account of the marriage as evidence in the divorce case. It wasn't possible to obtain a no-fault divorce in the 1960s. You had to prove adultery or maltreatment and wait three years until a divorce was granted. 'And,' he adds, 'I have no family in England and therefore have nobody to talk to.' He chronicled our home life from August 1965 to May 1967. Bearing in mind that he wanted to win custody of my sister and me, and was therefore skewing the contents of the diary to demonstrate that Mum was slack in her maternal and housewifely duties, nevertheless I could recall every incident he documented. He started by complaining about our grandmother, Frieda. (I've added occasional comments in italics.)

Lucien   In the six years we spent living at Kath's mother's house, her mother never once did any babysitting for us. I'm sure the children remember that when we lived with their grandmother she didn't want to know them. She never looked after them once, never gave them a penny, never bought them anything even for their birthday or Christmas and never allowed them upstairs to her flat.

It's true that, despite all the tales Mum told us about our wonderful, strong grandmother, Frieda was very cold towards Pascale and me. I never questioned her attitude, not even to wonder if all grandmothers were like her. She was just 'Nanny' and not very kind or friendly.

Pascale and I shared a bedroom on the ground floor of Frieda's Victorian house, and during the long summer nights I'd lie in bed listening to high heels snapping at the pavement as women clacked past. We always seemed to be in bed so early in those days. On every fourth or fifth step the heel would scrape along the ground. That sound, like a chicken clucking or a throat clearing, fascinated me. I'd count the footsteps until it happened again, trying to decipher a rhythm, but there was never any pattern to it. I thought that scrape was all part of wearing women's shoes and looked forward to making the same noise myself when I grew up. I had nothing much to worry about then except foxes under the bed. Outside the window a lamp post shone through two cherry trees, throwing dappled orange shadows that danced on the sage-green curtains. I told Pascale that the spindly, sparsely blossomed cherry tree was hers and the luxurious, blossom-laden one was mine. A hollow victory as she was too young (we were five and three) to know one was better than the other, or else she didn't mind. Pascale adored me when she was young. She thought I was clever. I also told her six was the highest number in the world, that she could have six as her special number for a treat, and I'd have ten.

The spring Vida turned five I took her to see grandmother Frieda's house in Woodland Gardens. The cherry trees were still there, their polished brown trunks with thin grey splits slightly taller and thicker, the canopies of branches heaving with pink clusters. I felt as if I'd travelled in time and was in two places at once: inside Nanny's house in 1959, listening to the high heels on the pavement; and outside in 2004 with my daughter, running around the cherry trees. I'm glad I didn't know how my life was going to turn out when I was that child lying in bed staring at the curtains. I'd have been terrified of the good things that happened just as much as the bad.

Vida and I played with the drifts of fallen blossom for an hour, tossing them in the air like confetti, piling them into heaps, constructing castles and pathways and tucking them into our hair. That afternoon is one of the happiest memories of my life.

Lucien   In those days it was the talk of the neighbours that Kath's mother wasn't taking a bit of notice or interest and in fact disliked her two little grandchildren. Kath couldn't wait to get out of there, she even had to go and ask her mother if it was alright to flush the toilet at night. Eventually her mother asked us to leave her house through a letter from her solicitor. As far as Kath was concerned Nanny was 'No longer her mother' and she was 'A disgusting woman trying to push us out into the street with two young children'.

Knowing Mum and Frieda, how smart they were and how conniving they could be, I suspect they cooked up the solicitor's-letter ruse between them to give Lucien a nudge towards buying a home.

It's odd that we weren't liked by our grandmother though. What was that about?

32 I was in the middle of snatching and wrenching
my sister's hair when I caught Vida's eye. She
looked straight at me, shook her head and mouthed, 'No,
Mummy,' with a pleading expression. I knew what she was
communicating: *Now is not the time or place for you to do this.*
I don't often disregard my daughter's advice – she's much wiser
than I am – but I was in too deep. I felt a twinge of guilt, but
not enough to stop. I was reminded of the time I caught our cat
in the corner of the shower cubicle with a baby rabbit twitching
in his mouth. I shouted at him, 'No, Kazzy!' He looked back
at me with such guilt and apology as he sank his teeth into its
flesh. He couldn't control himself. I knew from right back when
I leaned over Mum and grabbed hold of Pascale's hair – no,
I knew before that; I knew when the thought of being kind,
turning the other cheek and letting her commandeer Mum's
death slid down to my feet and fury rose up from the tips of my
toes – that, like the cat, some baser instinct had kicked in, and
there was no turning back.

Steve's Super Whip

Our father took the hint and we moved out of Frieda's place
and into our own 1930s mock-Tudor semi-detached house in
Woodberry Crescent. I was ten years old and that's when our
troubles really began.

Lucien   My fortnight holiday ends today. I have done all the
           shopping and cleaning and looked after the children. I

spent £7 on food, one picnic and a day at the pictures with them.

I handed the children back to Kath and left £4 on the mantelpiece. Kath got up at 10.45 and by 12 noon we'd had nothing to eat as per usual.

I have some understanding of Mum's late mornings and lack of housekeeping. I descended into the same apathy myself during the last year of my own marriage. I couldn't face the days, but as soon as my husband and I separated, I kept our home clean and tidy again and got up to make Vida breakfast every morning. But why did Mum fall apart just when she'd achieved the dream of owning her own home? Was it that, as the explorer Ranulph Fiennes once remarked, it's when your goal is in sight, with just a few miles to go, that all the will and stamina which has been motivating you dissolves and you're most likely to give up?

Lucien   04.09.65 – Saturday. Got up at 9.45 had two Shredded Wheat, shaved and went to the bank. Kath not up yet. Came home, changed sheets and pillows and made children's beds – swept top floor and dusted. Did my washing. Note: Done my own washing since 1st August 1965 [*only a month ago*], also ironing. Always done my own mending. [*That's true, all men who'd been in the forces could sew.*]

06.10.65 – We had practically no food for the weekend. The children had chips only and nothing else on Saturday.

Mealtimes were not a pleasant experience in our house and nor was the food. Mum said Lucien was mean as he only gave her £4 a week towards housekeeping for all of us. She said he was stashing money away to spend on fancy colognes and new underwear for himself and mocked him for preening in the mirror and wearing aftershave. French and Italian men were thought of as *perfumed ponces** by the English from the 1950s to the late 70s for caring about how they looked and smelled. Mum thought that if she bought hardly any food, Lucien would feel guilty seeing his children eat so little and buy some extra for us.

Lucien   10.11.65 – Tonight is the first day since last Friday that Kath brought some shopping home. Three bananas, one loaf of bread, two tins of evaporated milk, two tins of vegetables, a quarter of cheese and three pounds of potatoes. [*Food in the 1960s.*] I had bread and butter and Marmite and a cup of tea and went to bed.

12.11.65 – I went to Tesco. I spent £2.9.6d and kept the bill. In the afternoon I went shopping again and spent 15 shillings. Kath told the children to tell the teacher their father wouldn't give them any dinner money. Viviane said she wouldn't say this, but would say instead that she had forgotten it. Kath was angry with her and wrote all the details of the money she had to borrow on the back of Viviane's dinner-money envelope for school – I hope it doesn't embarrass the child.

* From *Withnail and I*, 1987, directed by Bruce Robinson, starring Richard E. Grant and Paul McGann

I'm sure I didn't show anyone the envelope. I never ate lunch at secondary school anyway. I used to spend the whole week's lunch money that Mum gave me on Monday morning in the sweet shop and starve for the rest of the week. I was used to living with the sensation of hunger. Instead of eating lunch, my friend Judi and I spent every break loitering outside Steve's Super Whip, the ice-cream van parked in one of the school playgrounds. There was a joke going round school that he was a travelling sadist who thrashed schoolchildren in the back of the van (*Super Whip*). Judi and I tried to make friends with Steve, hoping he'd take pity on us and give us a free ice cream. We especially coveted the wafer that was shaped like an open oyster shell, half dipped in chocolate, pumped full of whipped vanilla ice cream and sprinkled with a rainbow of hundreds and thousands – it was the most expensive ice cream on the menu. For a whole year Judi and I didn't talk to friends, play sports or read during lunch. Instead we fastened ourselves to Steve's van. Only once did he give us a free ice cream: a cheap blue ice lolly to share between us. I cringed with guilt for years every time Mum said, 'At least you never had free school meals.' She didn't want us to be stigmatised for being poor so she scraped together the money every week, even though we were entitled to free school meals. I never told her that I spent the cash on sweets and my lunchtimes pestering the ice-cream man.

Lucien   27.10.65 – I think Kath hides the butter. She leaves plenty of margarine around. Unfortunately I don't like margarine, in fact the four of us dislike margarine and since the margarine hasn't been touched by anyone for the past fortnight, I think I can say that Kath eats butter and hides it. [*The wording of this makes me laugh.*]

11.12.65 – I got up at 9.50 and prepared the children's and my breakfast. Kath came down at 10.30 and began creating that I had cooked 3 tomatoes. She said she had bought them herself, that they were special Canary's and yet she wasn't getting one. [*'Canary's' were big tomatoes from the Canary Islands. The first seeds were planted there in 1885 by an Englishman called Mr Blisse.*] Kath said, 'Why don't you eat your own food?' Then Viviane gave her one half of her tomato. I said, 'OK I'll try not to touch anything if I know it to be yours.' After breakfast I started clearing half a shelf to keep my food but Kath intervened saying, 'Why can't you keep it in your bedroom?'

From that day on, Lucien kept his food on a separate shelf in the kitchen cupboard and scratched or biroed a large capital 'A' onto the labels of all his tins. He also commandeered a corner of the fridge, where he stashed steak, butter and eggs. He ate all his meals at the end of the dining table crouched over his plate, munching in silence with his back turned to us. I didn't understand why. I thought he wanted to eat nicer food than us and was too mean to buy his children the same quality and quantity that he ate himself. That's what Mum told us anyway.

We didn't see much of Lucien after we moved to Woodberry Crescent. He spent hours in an upstairs room studying for his engineering exams. He had no friends, no other relatives and didn't fit in at Ford, the car company he worked for in Dagenham. He was a simple man and thought that if he made wooden boxes for the blankets to be stored in, eventually got round to mending the leaks and left £4 a week on the mantelpiece for housekeeping, he had the right to dominate his family. He couldn't grasp that it wasn't enough just to be born a man any more, that he had to be kind and make compromises to be loved.

Lucien   24.03.67 – I have been in my room all day studying. I've had one cup of tea and one apple. When I went down at 6.30 p.m. to have a drink of water I couldn't get in the kitchenette, Pascale and Kath obstructed the way. I was so distressed at their attitude (even Viviane must have thought they were carrying things too far because she shouted at Pascale, 'Move your blooming foot out of the way!') that I did not return downstairs for an hour or so.

I would never have said 'blooming' (pronounced 'bl'min'). Either I said 'bloody' and he didn't want to write that in the diary and make me sound like a delinquent, or he added 'blooming' to make his account sound more dramatic. But the other part was true, and I didn't quite understand why – apart from the fact that he was annoying – we all, especially Mum and Pascale, treated him so cruelly.

33 Mum programmed me to fight, not to be walked over, never to give in. But even with all her years of training I couldn't have been as savage and unrelenting as I was with Pascale that night if I hadn't practised being the bad one in Mum's kitchen during the past month. I didn't care how hideous Pascale and I, two women in their fifties scratching and clawing at each other, looked. I wasn't going to regret for the rest of my life that Vida and I didn't have any proper time with Mum at the

end. That Vida and I weren't allowed to sit next to her while she was dying, or say anything about Pascale moving from the bed or Mum's ear being flicked. To be left with the memory that I was too scared to make a fuss so I just sat back and let it happen.

Rude Girls

By the time I was eleven years old the atmosphere at home was so strained I spent as much time as possible outside, chatting with friends on street corners, playing on the swings at the park, walking up and down Muswell Hill Broadway staring in shop windows, and sitting in my friends' bedrooms while they were downstairs having tea. Pascale was out a lot too. Mum didn't seem to mind where we were, but Lucien thought we were too young to be roaming the streets.

Lucien 12.03.66 – Pascale said she was going for a walk and when I asked her to tell me whereabouts she replied, 'Just for a walk.' When I insisted, she stamped her foot saying it was her business. She is nine years old.

17.04.66 – When Viviane went out this afternoon with a friend, she dolled herself up with scent and lipstick – she is only eleven years old. I said she is much too young. She was shocked when I tried to advise her and adopted a rude attitude – I don't think I am old-fashioned.

25.02.67 – In Muswell Hill Broadway I met Mrs Kitchen, a neighbour, and she said, 'The group Viviane goes out with is no good. I know the boys and they're a bad lot. I saw her at the Wimpy Bar last week. The way your daughter dresses in mini skirts and fancy socks and the rest of it, she'll end up on drugs and in trouble.' She told me she attempted to talk to the children but they just looked back at her stupidly in defiance and contempt. [*Haha, yes we did.*]

20.10.67 – I came home starving but suddenly felt so dejected I only had a cup of tea and a slice of bread. I no longer feel hungry. When I went up to say goodnight to Viviane I found her crying. She told me she was worried about having spots on her face because she always went to bed too late. Kath is out. I must be given custody of the children. It is my belief if they are left in her care they'll grow up to some form of delinquency. She brings them up to look after Number One, don't trust anyone, especially your father.

Mrs Kitchen was right in a way and if, ten years later, she'd heard I was playing guitar in a band called the Slits, looking like a cross between a prostitute and a thug, she would have felt very smug. I did go to the Wimpy Bar occasionally, but only to sit with friends. I couldn't afford to eat there. I hung out with three boys called Dom, Adam and Paul. Dom had a motorbike, which he later had a crash on and died. The boys were very 'Leader of the Pack' in my eyes, but in reality they were only thirteen, fourteen and fifteen, still went to school and lived at home with their parents. I never wore scent or lipstick. Lucien must have been painting a dramatic picture to undermine Mum, but he wasn't all wrong. Pascale and I were fast becoming feral.

Mum told us to ignore our father's comments, said he was mad and an idiot. Pascale, being younger, followed Mum's lead and treated Lucien with scorn. I was ignorant of the dangers I could encounter on the streets. The worst things that happened to me at the time were seeing a couple of flashers and falling off a gate I was swinging on and splitting my head open. Neither event prompted any reaction from Mum. I agreed with her that Lucien overreacted when we got back late or disappeared for a while – he called the police a couple of times. I thought nine- and eleven-year-old girls hanging around the streets until late in the evening, their whereabouts unknown (we didn't have a telephone at home), was perfectly normal.

Bad Man

I thought less and less kindly of Lucien as each month passed. He and Mum argued frequently and if I was ever lucky enough to miss a quarrel, she recounted it to me when I got home. Her vivid accounts of Lucien's cruelty and unreasonableness combined with my own observations of this bullying, out-of-touch and embarrassingly weird-looking father I was lumbered with – his rumbling voice and thick brown hair combed forward into a wavy fringe – all added to my belief that there was an ogre in our midst.

Lucien   13.09.65 – Unless I say hello, the children are gradually being encouraged to ignore their father. I received more affection and respect before I bought the house Kath clamoured for so much. Her attitude has changed 100% since. She has got a house now and the devil may care how

I pay for it. She is bringing the children up to look upon their father as a bad man. She said twice in front of them, 'You want to be careful whom you marry, you don't want to end up with someone like him.' God knows what she tells them when I'm not around.

21.10.65 – When I come in, it is nothing and no one in sight. Our home and family life is now almost nil. In spite of my sweets, or pocket money, the children act towards me with such indifference that I have to repeat to myself that it isn't true, it hasn't happened, I am still their father. It isn't quite so bad with Viviane, she is eleven and beginning to judge for herself. Although she subscribes little to the few words I say, she also tends not to subscribe entirely to all her mother says either.

05.11.65 – How can I go on seeing two innocent children being indoctrinated with this kind of attitude towards their father, fellow human being and in particular, towards MEN in general? [*His capitals.*]

17.12.65 – When I returned this evening everybody else was in bed asleep. I looked at the children.

34 I hoisted Pascale up by her hair and dragged her across the bed. She was heavy, but I was so pumped up I had super-strength. Vida raised her pale young arms and tried to hold her aunt's body off her grandmother's face. I knew I was putting Vida in a terrible position but I wasn't thinking about

the present, I was thinking of the future. I didn't have time to explain all that to her. And it's not as if I didn't care whether Mum had a nice death, or was squashed by the weight of Pascale, or passed away to the sound of us fighting. It's more that I thought Mum wasn't the most important person in the room any more. It sounds terrible, but I decided we were, Vida and me – the people who were going to go on living. I glanced over at Vida and twisted my face into an expression that was supposed to mean, 'It's all right, I know what I'm doing,' but I probably looked like a mad ghoul. I must have lost concentration for a second when I looked at her because that's when Pascale manoeuvred my thumb into her mouth. I shouldn't have let that happen, I made a mistake there. I didn't let go of her though, not even when I felt her teeth sinking through the layers of my skin and into gristle.

Grimm

An unhappy alternative is before you, Elizabeth. From this day you must be a stranger to one of your parents.
Jane Austen, *Pride and Prejudice*, 1813

Although I didn't respect my father and was slightly revolted by his maleness, his hairiness (which I've inherited) and his obtuseness, I was still upset at the callous way we treated him. I was ashamed of my complicity in his persecution but I had to pick a side and he was not on the winning one. I felt uncomfortable that none of us greeted him when he came home from work. Listening to him trudge upstairs to his room without acknowledgement was distressing. Not a kind or polite word was spoken to Lucien in our house for weeks on end, except by me occasionally. Sometimes I risked going against Mum to show him some affection, but whenever I did she called me a collaborator, 'Like in the war.' She said I was weak and greedy. Weak because I felt uncomfortable ignoring Lucien and wanted to make the atmosphere at home pleasant, and greedy because I sometimes sat on his lap so he'd give me a sweet. I *was* a bit greedy. I liked sweets and the only sweets we were given when I was young were a Haliborange tablet after tea (a vitamin C and halibut oil pill which had a tangy orange flavour) or a teaspoonful of dark molasses. Whenever I asked if there was anything else sweet to eat Mum said, 'Have an apple.' I'm sugar-mad now.

The worst thing Mum used to say to me, and she said it often, was, 'You're just like your father.' Considering she so obviously loathed him, it was a terrible and crushing insult. I wish she'd realised back then that the sort of daughter who sat on her father's lap for a sweet, or left him a note because she felt sorry for him, was also the sort of daughter who'd feel responsible for her mother later in life.

Lucien   30.03.66 – Viviane bought me a pair of socks for my birthday. When I came in she was out. She returned about 5.30 and told me she had run away into the Broadway because her mother was cross with her for doing so.

               04.07.66 – Viviane has continued to say hello and goodnight to me and these last few days has made a point of telling me where they are going. If it wasn't for her I wouldn't know where they are most of the time. I don't say much to her because I don't want to see her unhappy but I think she realises what her mother has been putting me through.

03.01.67 – Whilst we were watching a hooligan's episode of *Z Cars* [police drama] on TV, Kath told the children never to let any man treat them like she had been treated, associating me with the bad characters on the screen in the eyes of the children. Pascale started calling the husband a 'stinking husband', a 'rotten man' and so on. I told her quietly she was very rude and she replied, 'It's nothing compared to what you are.' She said that I would have left the house by now if I was a gentleman and that she will be glad when the divorce comes. She is nine years old and twelve months ago I was her daddy.

Kath has thrown away all our happiness including her own. I can no longer find any love in me for her. There is no doubt we loved each other very much in days gone by. I shall never forget all we have gone through together and all the places we have been together. I am so sorry for both of us and the children. One day when they are grown up I intend to tell them my side of the story.

Well, here you are, Dad. Now I've heard your side of the story, I thought as I sat at the kitchen table reading his diary. He never got the chance to tell me his point of view before he died. By the time we were reunited I was in my late twenties, and he was so pleased to see me that he didn't want to scare me away by bringing up the past. He did try broaching the subject a few times, but I shouted him down and became tearful and accusing. I wish he knew I'd heard his side at last.

Go Now

> If I was bound for hell, let it be hell. No more false heavens. No more damned magic. You hate me and I hate you. We'll see who hates best.
>
> Jean Rhys, *Wide Sargasso Sea*, 1966

According to Lucien's diaries, Mum favoured Pascale, which I hadn't remembered until I read them. This hurt me most out of all the revelations. I was reminded of how Mum spoke and behaved towards me during those two years, like she didn't think I was very nice, and how that made me feel as if I wasn't a good person. I used to think of myself as someone who always wanted *things* and *clothes*, who sucked up to my father, didn't stand up for my mother or my sister enough, and was selfish and vain. I didn't realise until I read the diary that this image, which I still can't quite shake off, was constructed by my mother.

Lucien 05.05.66 – At 9.00 a.m. Pascale came into my room and asked if I wanted the Sunday paper and would I pay for her comic? I said yes. Viviane asked if I would pay for hers also, so I gave Pascale another shilling. Kath pounced on Viviane – accused her of being a spendthrift and took Viviane's shilling out of Pascale's hand saying she wasn't going short and see everyone else spending money on comics. Viviane was in tears so I told her I would go and buy her a comic. She said, 'Please don't, Daddy, because I owe Mummy 5 shillings and she won't let me have a comic unless I give it back to her.' She was saving for a new swimsuit.

Then Kath burst into Viviane's room and demanded her 5 shillings for the swimsuit back. With tears pouring, Viviane went to her money box and gave it back to her. I told Kath I had never seen anyone act so hard towards their children and they had done nothing naughty. She told me to shut up, that I was mental and that she hoped to be rid of me soon. She looked devilish, almost demented. She went to my bedroom, flung the door wide open, walked in, picked up the newspaper that Pascale – just back – had put on my bed and threw the pages all over the room then rushed out holding her nose telling the children, 'The stink in there is putrid.'

I remember that swimsuit. Mum felt guilty for shouting at me, and a few days later she gave me the money back and a bit extra and told me to buy something unusual, like a bikini (I'd only had a one-piece before). I went to Jane Norman in Wood Green on my own and bought a black bikini, but the two pieces were joined together with black net. It was quite grown-up. When I got in I said to Mum, 'I've bought another one-piece,' to tease her, and she said, 'What have you done that for?' Then I showed her the swimsuit, and she said it was lovely.

Lucien   11.05.66 – Kath repeatedly tells Viviane she had better make up her mind soon what side she is going to be on in the divorce. I said it's the judge who decides this and Kath retorted that she will have a say in it and 'If I say you can have her, then you will have her.' I replied that I would abide by the court decision and if, as I hoped, they gave me the children I would have them both gladly. She snorted and left the room saying, 'Some hope.'

I would have preferred to stay friends with both my parents, but that wasn't an option. I was scared I'd be left with my father if I didn't demonstrate to Mum that I was firmly in her camp. I didn't want to be too cruel to him (even though I did find him highly irritating and oppressive), but I didn't want to lose Mum. I was terrified of losing Mum.

35 Mum must have sensed us scuffling behind her head because her eyes popped open with surprise. It was the most alive she'd looked for months. *That's perked her up,* I thought. *There you go, Mum, still entertaining you, right to the end.* She couldn't see anything because Pascale and I were tussling behind her against the back wall, but she must have been able to feel it. I wondered if Mum thought all the shaking and shuddering of the bed was the three Furies come to exact their bloody revenge on her, prompting her to remember something she'd done in the past which she felt guilty about and making her think she deserved a horrible end. No wonder she snapped her eyes shut again. Pascale is bigger and stronger than me, has been since she was twelve or thirteen, so I knew it was going to be a tough fight. But in all our fifty years together,

even though we'd often been physically aggressive with each other, she'd never seen me behave like this. I knew there would be consequences for my actions: Mum's last moments ruined; my relationship with my sister irredeemable; Vida's memory of her grandmother's death traumatic; and possibly the loss of my thumb. All big losses but nothing compared to what I was fighting for. What was I fighting for though? Even now I'm not sure. Something so old and so deep, it has no words, no shape, no logic.

Normal

> They are sisters, savages –
> In the end they have
> No emotion but envy.
> Louise Glück, 'Confession', *Ararat*, 1990

With the tension in our childhood home escalating and everyone shouting at or ignoring each other – except Mum and Pascale, who were like a two-pronged pitchfork jabbing away – Pascale and I turned on each other. The natural sibling rivalry between us was exploited by our parents, who constantly characterised us in opposition to each other. To Mum, Pascale was loyal, I was a collaborator. Pascale was strong, I was weak. Pascale was a saver, I was a spender. In contrast, Lucien thought I was kind, Pascale was cruel. I was sensitive, Pascale was brutal. I was smart, Pascale was stupid (she was a darn sight smarter than him and better at most subjects than me). Two girls born eighteen months apart should have been able to get along – in fact, until we moved out of Frieda's house I don't remember there being any significant trouble between Pascale and me – but our parents cast us as adversaries and fought over us like we were the spoils of war.

Lucien   22.02.66 – The children have been picking on each other for some time, at around 9 p.m. they started fighting again. Kath will not say a word, especially if Pascale is the instigator. The result is that Viviane, being older, realises that Pascale is left to get away with a lot by her mother and feels frustrated. A little while later when Pascale made some nasty remark about her, Viviane kicked a stool under the table and Pascale's glasses fell on the floor. Kath became infuriated, smacked Viviane and told her she wouldn't be getting any pocket money for 12 months. Viviane said sorry, Pascale hardly ever does.

Mum was very sensitive about Pascale wearing glasses. She didn't want her to feel embarrassed or hindered by them. (Children were much crueller to each other in those days and schools did nothing to stop taunts of 'four eyes' and other unkind names.) Mum made pretty little pouches for Pascale's glasses that tied up with ribbons and matched her dresses, and told me – quite rightly – to stop doodling glasses on photographs of people in newspapers and magazines lying around the house.

Lucien   Later this evening Viviane and Pascale fought. Viviane slammed the kitchen door so violently that she broke a glass panel 3′ x 15″. Kath smacked Viviane and told her she's stopping her pocket money. [*As I remember this, Mum didn't smack me, I was sent upstairs.*] I told

Viviane off as well. As soon as I did that, Kath took the child's side.

Pascale and I were having an argument. She said something that enraged me and I went to hit her, but she was out of the kitchen in a flash, pulling the door shut behind her. I felt humiliated that she'd got away with the nasty remark and also proved herself a faster mover than me, so I hammered on the glass panel of the door with frustration and in protest, thinking it would make a good loud noise. My arm went straight through the glass, shattering the whole panel. Mum said later I must have done a kind of karate chop because there wasn't a scratch on me.

Lucien   24.04.66 – Viviane told me that her mother took her to the
              doctor because she was having fits of violence, and he gave
              her some pills.
                    Kath knows very well that she is sacrificing her
              children's happiness, her own and mine, but she would
              rather do that than come to her senses.

I don't remember the pills, but I checked my medical records and on 23 April 1966 Beplete tablets – a barbiturate – were prescribed to me for 'Screaming fits'. I was eleven and a half years old; it was just before my 11-plus exam. Even then it was an extreme medication to use on a child. According to medical journals, Beplete was a high-dependency class B drug, a sedative – creating a diminished level of consciousness – occasionally used for seizures. It can cause anxiety and withdrawal symptoms. I don't know why only I was prescribed the pills. I was no more violent than Pascale.

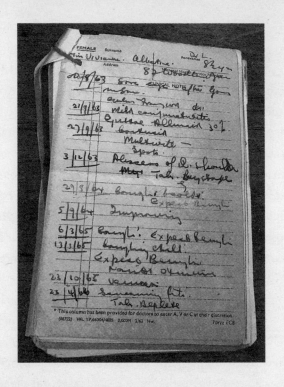

I ricocheted between my parents during those two years, trying to placate and be liked by both of them but afraid of committing the ultimate offence: being deemed disloyal by my mother. Pascale lived under a different tyranny, indoctrinated by Mum (who was trying to turn Pascale into her little attack dog) and constantly picked on by Lucien. The more aggressive Mum made Pascale, the more harshly Lucien behaved towards her. She didn't stand a chance. What nine-year-old child would, in the middle of an emotional war zone? Pascale and I argued and fought every day, with no idea how to resolve disagreements amicably – we had no role models. No arguments were settled peaceably between our mother and father. For a long time (about fifty years) I comforted myself with the thought that I was the only sane person in my family, like Marilyn, the normal niece in *The Munsters*, but after reading Lucien's diary, I realised I wasn't normal at all.

36 Mia was reduced to a shadow flickering on the edge of my field of vision. All I could see was the three family members I had left, Vida, Mum and Pascale, like I was looking at them through a long cardboard tube. My sister's jaw was still clamped around the thumb on my left hand, the hand that holds the neck of my guitar. She just kept on biting deeper into my flesh, severing our ties. I needed my thumb, I wanted to keep it, but I wanted my sister off the bed more. My blood sprayed out in a fan shape over Mum's sheets and fountained up the wall behind her head. It was a terrible scene, worthy of the Borgias. *At least there's no blood on Mum's face*, I thought. I was thankful for that.

Proxy

Lucien   19.10.66 – The children started throwing things at each other. A small toy hit me and spilled the cup of water in front of my plate. I showed them the belt I was wearing and told them if I had given them a good hiding from time to time perhaps they would not behave any more as they were behaving.

Kath has brainwashed them with a set of stories, telling them I gave them the belt a few years back when in fact it was her who asked for a belt saying that it hurt her hands more than the children to correct them. She distinctly asked me if she could keep my old belt for that if need be. I have not seen her use it but I think she has no right to tell them I hit them with it when I just reminded them of its existence a couple of times.

But I remember the belt hanging on a nail just inside the cellar door when we lived at Nanny's house and being told to go and get it and Lucien hitting us with it. Or do I? I looked up from the page and tried to picture Nanny's house, the cellar, our bedroom, us on the bed crying. Was Lucien telling the truth and he only threatened to use the belt but didn't actually hit us with it? I don't trust my memories now. Most of what he'd written in his diary was true, but I couldn't believe that Mum planted false memories in our brains. When we lived at Frieda's, Mum used to tell Lucien how naughty we'd been when he arrived home from work. Years later I thought, *If she hadn't told him we'd been naughty, he wouldn't have hit us.* Did she ask him to give her his belt like he said? Was she smacking us by proxy so that she looked like the good cop and he was duped into being the bad cop? Was she that scheming? Was he that gullible? I remember drawing around the red marks on my legs with a biro after I'd been hit by him, but they may have been impressions made by his hand, not the belt. I definitely remember red stripes on my skin surrounded by wiggly blue lines.

Gaslight

Lucien   05.03.67 – Midday yesterday Kath informed me she did not want me to enter the lounge any more, that it was her room from now on and I was to keep out of it. She repeated twice, 'You keep out of it you hear.' I replied I was entitled to sit in the lounge.

24.05.67 – The situation is too much and too tense for anyone to endure. Either Kath is right or very wrong or I am right or very wrong. If I am wrong then I can only conclude that I am sick. If so, then I am in need of care, advice or whatever else that may be necessary. I am prepared to submit to psychiatric investigation, provided my doctor advises it. Something must be done to avert some disastrous conclusion mainly where the children are concerned. I am not trying to dramatise, this is a serious situation.

   I am more convinced now than ever that Kath is trying to make the children despise me enough to secure their support in court and I have little doubt that she will ask them to testify in her favour. They – more so Pascale – act towards me with such indifference that I have to repeat to myself that it isn't true, it hasn't happened, that I am still their father.

Lucien broke in the end. I remember standing on the doorstep one day, peeping at him over the privet hedge as he walked away from our house, eyes down, shoulders hunched, head jutting forward like a tortoise. He looked like he'd been under a car crusher. Mum appeared and stood next to me. Even she was shocked. She said it wasn't until she saw him from a distance that she realised what a bad mental state he was in. Said he looked like a schizophrenic. He wasn't a schizophrenic, he was depressed. You can tell a depressed man from his walk. It's not necessarily a slow walk – they can beetle along, off to work or the pub – but the tension in the shoulders, the curve of the spine, feet not lifting far off the floor, even a deliberate, superhuman effort to stand up straight and swagger is a dead giveaway. Walks have always been important to men: the puffed-out chest and confident stride of a businessman, the bully's swagger, or the limp and dip of gangstas and dudes. They're all attempts to signal that this man is in charge, in control, not to be messed with, that he is fit and able to fight. A warning to other men that they'd better not risk attacking him. *This guy is not ready to be culled.* A man's walk is a primeval warning system, a survival mechanism. And when the walk has gone, the man has gone.

37

I was losing a lot of blood from my thumb. I couldn't let it go on any longer, I had to retreat. Flailing through my memory bank, trying to think of what to do, how to stop the pain, I was so desperate that I pleaded with my brain to help me and, in response, my mind just opened up. Everything I'd ever learned was revealed to me at the same time, as if a spiv had swung open his coat and exposed hundreds of rings and watches sewn into the lining. I swept across this jumbled landscape searching for a little gem of wisdom to get me out of my predicament. I was sure I possessed a useful piece of information somewhere. I sorted and groped, shifting my focus about inside my skull. Nothing. *Where is it? Go down further. Come on, come on.* I was panicking. All the blood, it felt like time was running out. Just when I was about to give up hope I hooked onto a scrappy little fact and began hauling it up to the surface, dredging what I hoped was a pearl from the deep. The information seemed to take forever to arrive in my conscious mind. I remember thinking, *Here it comes, here it comes*, before I even knew what it was. The answer busted into my head with such force I nearly blacked out.

'To get a pit bull to unclamp its jaws, insert two fingers into its nostrils and pull upwards.'

Conkers

After two years of unbearable tension, Mum, Pascale and I went to visit our Aunty Phyllis in the country for a week to have a break. The summer before this, Haringey council had paid for me and Pascale to go away for a week because we were in such a state of agitation. Pascale went to a children's convalescent home in Bournemouth. I was to be sent somewhere else but refused to go at the last minute and stayed at home.

Lucien   08.04.67 – Kath has taken the children away without asking me or telling me where she is going with them or when they will return. The only way I knew was a note from Viviane saying they will probably be back next Monday.

26.05.67 – In order to maintain my sanity and protect myself I have only one alternative and that is to leave my home, pushed out by Kath, Pascale and to a lesser extent, Viviane. I realise I count for nothing in the children's eyes, let alone Kath's. I have to face the fact I have no family left. I went to my room and started packing as if driven by some force and will other than my own. My last feeling being helplessness.

28.05.67 – Today I left. The removal was carried out by a young chap and his private van who I contacted Saturday evening. The time of leaving was around 11.25 p.m. at night and I felt incapable of describing how I felt.

This was the last entry in Lucien's diary. Well, I did it, I was brave and opened the bag. Good for me.

Mum didn't keep the house after the divorce as Lucien suspected she would. She couldn't possibly afford it. We moved to the council house by the gasworks and she got on with bringing us up. Lucien moved to Dagenham, bought a flat and a car, and grew his hair into a Beatle-do.

Pascale and I were interviewed during the court case, not in the main courtroom but in a little antechamber out the back. The judge took his wig off to 'look less frightening', he said. We stood before him dressed in our maroon school uniforms and new white socks. Mum had polished our shoes until they were as shiny as conkers. I did the speaking as I was the eldest. I said that we wanted to live with our mother; we hated and feared our father and refused to live with him.

And that was the end of it.

Lucien started his adult life in England as a handsome, arrogant young Frenchman, but he was a foreigner in a country that was wary of foreigners. He was also narrow-minded and a slow thinker; he wasn't able to adapt to the changing times. Eventually he was kicked out of the way and the world moved on. He wasn't culled as swiftly as Mr Shilling, but he was thoroughly crushed by the end of his life and only just managed to limp to the finish line. I didn't see my father again for seventeen years, and when I did, he still had that Beatle hairdo.

Drowning

You shall know the truth and the truth shall make you odd.
Attributed to Flannery O'Connor

I'm frightened. I feel like I'm falling. Falling and failing. I feel sick. My mother, whom I've idolised and respected and thought loved me unconditionally, was – is it overdoing it to say this? – cruel. How can I overcome my upbringing? How can I be a good person, or a good mother, after that upbringing? How can I love or be loved? Could Mum love? Maybe my 'mad, stupid, ugly' father was the only person who's ever loved me after all.

I wandered around Hackney for weeks in a sick fog, feeling as if I might vomit at any moment. I'd always wondered if Mum knew that Lucien was going to leave home while we were on that holiday with Aunty Phyllis; whether she and Lucien had cooked it up between them and that's why we were taken away. At last I knew the truth, if it's even worth knowing. Mum must have been as surprised as Pascale and I were when we arrived home to find the house had been emptied of our father's possessions and quite a few other things, like pictures and ornaments, and he was gone.

The two biggest shocks from my father's diary were that Mum wasn't the heroine she always made herself out to be, and she didn't seem to like me very much. I only became the favourite through circumstance, because I was all she had left, not because I was a lovely person and a good daughter. Is that why I thought up The Favourite Theory after she died? Did my unconscious remember things that I didn't?

38 As soon as the pit-bull solution surfaced in my brain I shoved a finger into each of Pascale's nostrils and burrowed into her nasal cavities. She was foolish to let me do that. She must have wanted to hurt me very badly not to pull away. As soon as my fingers were in as far as they'd go, I curled them into hooks – they were strong from guitar playing – and yanked upwards. I intended to tear her nose off her face, that's what I envisioned. Her jaws sprang open and I was released. I leapt away from the bed, half crying, half shouting, 'We hate each other! We hate each other!' Mum lay perfectly still with her eyes closed. Mia pressed her back against the door, trying to disappear. The walls, the sheets, my shirt looked like abstract paintings, as if Joan Mitchell* had smeared and daubed them with a giant, red-soaked paintbrush.

But worse than all of that, I'd failed.

* Joan Mitchell (1925–92), abstract impressionist

Radio On

while from my mother's
Room the radio purls: it plays all night she leaves
it on to hear
The midnight news then sleeps and dozes
until day which now it is . . .

James Schuyler, 'The Morning of the Poem', 1980*

Whenever I wanted to talk about our family's past or asked
Mum, 'What year did Lucien leave home?' or 'When did we
move from Woodland Gardens to Woodberry Crescent?' she
would become hostile. 'What do you want to know that for?'
she'd say. Or, 'I don't know! How am I supposed to remember all
that time ago? I suppose whatever's gone wrong in your life is all
my fault now.' Two years before she died she bought a shredding
machine, pulled all her papers out of the drawers and cupboards
and shredded them. Mum had more paperwork than furniture.
She owned a few bits and pieces that she'd bought along the way.
The old lady next door left her a table and four chairs, and her
armchair was given to her by Aunty Phil. The TV was Mum's
most expensive possession and the radio her most used. She
was from the generation that called the radio 'the wireless' and
she listened to it every day. The radio was so much a part of my
environment when I was a child that I hardly noticed it. I can
just about conjure up the brown cloth with red and green threads
running through it that covered the speaker and the polished

* I was led to the poems of James Schuyler by Olivia Laing, *The Lonely City*, 2016

dark-brown veneer casing. Big it was. As she aged, Mum began to loathe the 'entitled male voices' on the BBC and tuned in to LBC Talk Radio instead ('the first sign of senility', said my friend Maura, who's found herself doing the same recently). For decades Mum slept with the radio right beside her head all night. I couldn't imagine what she was drowning out. *What does an elderly, retired woman with nothing to do all day have to worry about?* I thought for years. *Why doesn't she want to hear her thoughts?*

When I moved to Hastings and started making ceramics, building things out of clay whilst my marriage was disintegrating, Mum gave me a shiny black Roberts radio to keep me company. It was the perfect present for those lonely times.

Vida was seven years old when we left London to live by the sea. Our departure was such a terrible shock and wrench for her that she had some kind of nervous collapse and developed shingles. Two months later, I showed her round the studio I was renting in the middle of Hastings, two rooms at the top of a tall white Regency building that used to be an art gallery. The day she visited, sunshine streamed in through the full-length windows, seagulls squawked and dived outside and the old oak floorboards glistened like dark honey. Mum wandered around the room admiring the white plaster cornicing, the ceiling rose and the black wrought-iron balcony (not safe to step onto) and surprised me by saying, 'I'm so jealous. I'd have loved this, to come here every day and work.' This bright, high-ceilinged room appealed to her, tugged at something lying dormant within. Something she didn't know she wanted until she saw it. The expression on her face was numinous, as if she'd stepped into a church and was overcome with a vision of a higher calling.

Much as she supported and admired me when I was in a band, making records, playing gigs, touring, or going to film school and directing, those lives didn't tweak at her the way this studio did. This was a world, a room, that had she been born into a different time, she would have loved to have spent her days in.

39

All that effort, all the grappling and grabbing, tearing and bleeding, was for nothing. Pascale was still on the bed. I couldn't think of what else to do. I was racking my brains for a plan when Mia came into focus, walking towards me, unsmiling. I thought, *She's going to chuck me out of the room.* I wasn't going to go quietly. I remembered being told that a person's hearing is the last sense to go when they're dying, so I quickly leaned down, put my mouth right up close to Mum's ear and said in a loud clear voice, 'Mum, Pascale's being a bitch.' It was my last chance to wound Pascale before I was ejected, to ruin Mum's death for her like she'd ruined it for me. I wanted to show her that I could overstep the mark and ignore Mum's feelings in order to hurt my sister too. Mia rushed at me and corralled me into a corner. I let her do it, no way I was going to fight her. Once she had me trapped, she began hopping from foot to foot with her arms outstretched, like a schoolgirl defending goal in a netball match, making sure I stayed put. But on one of her hops she jumped too far to the left and a little gap opened up. I darted through the space and wiped my bloody, spurting thumb down the front of Pascale's new blue-and-white-striped T-shirt. Marked her. It was her best top, she wore it for my book launch. I was wearing my best shirt too. Both ruined.

The Green Bag

Even though she had lived there for over thirty years I couldn't
feel Mum's presence anywhere when I packed up her flat after
she died. Not until I stood at her bedroom window, pressed
my face against the worn yellow satin curtains tied up with
mismatching ribbons and looked out at the London plane tree
with its mottled grey and brown trunk and flat three-fingered
leaves did I feel something. Mum fought with the council every
year to make sure the tree wasn't pollarded too viciously. She
recognised the pigeons that nested there and told Vida stories
about them. That's where she stood to wave me goodbye every
time I left her flat, even when I told her not to. 'Let me do it,'
she'd say. 'I like to.' I'd stop at the gate and glance up at her third-
floor window to catch a glimpse of her thin, drawn face peering
down through the trembling leaves, hand fluttering. It was as if
every time I left her she thought she'd never see me again. That's
when I cried, standing at the window in her bedroom, really
sobbed. Then I got on with emptying the flat. It wasn't quite as
chaotic as Lucien's, but there was nearly a hundred years of past
to plough through.

All Mum's trinkets: a tiny wooden hedgehog, two miniature
glass cats, a spotty dog from the 1930s, a Victorian marcasite
brooch and a Bible she won in a school spelling competition,
things like that, I put into the 'To Keep' box.

Rummaging through her chest of drawers, I discovered she'd
kept all the drawings and little notes I used to leave on the
kitchen table for her when we lived together during one of my
many homeless periods. She also kept the letters we wrote to

each other when I was staying at the Iroquois and Gramercy Park
Hotels in New York (both dives back then) while on tour with
the Slits in the seventies. I was excited to be in America for the
first time but even though I was twenty-two and surrounded
by the band and roadies and people were always coming up and
wanting to speak to me after shows, I was lonely. I missed Mum.
I sent her my itinerary so she could write ahead. I looked forward
to being handed a letter full of everyday chat when I arrived in a
new city, illustrated with stick-figure drawings of Mum rushing
off to work or carrying her shopping home.

Sorting through her paltry possessions and stacking up the
furniture – ready for a house-clearance crook to take away in
a van and charge me a fortune for – I came across her stash
of damask napkins and had another little cry. I bet every old
lady has a bit of damask tucked away in a drawer. My mother's
damask wasn't inherited, she bought it from charity shops.
Couldn't pass up a piece of clean, thick, pressed damask – what
woman of that age could? I kept the four heavy, ironed and
folded silk squares and the tablecloth. There was something so
old-fashioned about the fabric and Mum's respect for hand-

crafted work. I remember how excited she was when she bought them, turning the pieces over in her knobbly hands and marvelling that they were 'As good as new, and such quality, and with hand-sewn edges too.'

Nestled between the layers of damask I found a red, heart-shaped leather purse. Inside was a photograph of David, Mum's child by her previous marriage. A soft-focus, black-and-white picture of a two-year-old boy smiled out of the circular frame inset with tiny pearls.

I sat back on my heels. I wasn't shocked; I knew about David's existence, and had met him a few times when I was young, but no more than that. My first thought was, *It's a plant. Mum put the picture in the heart-shaped purse on purpose and left it in her drawer to be found by me and given to David* (even though she never saw him and I didn't know now if he was dead or alive) *to atone for the life they didn't have together.* 'I don't feel like I have three children. When people ask I always say I have two,' she said to me once. Why then did she keep David's photo in a little heart-shaped purse tucked up in the damask all these years? I tried to track David down to give him the picture – it was obviously what Mum wanted – but I couldn't find any trace of him.

I put the purse and the photograph in the 'To Keep' box and continued clearing the flat, wondering, as I emptied drawers and wrapped cracked vases and mismatched china in sheets of newspaper, why I had such a suspicious nature. But after years of dealing with her secretiveness I knew that what Mum said didn't necessarily tally with what she did. My outspoken and forthright mother wasn't as honest as she appeared.

Late on the second afternoon, still working through the clutter in Mum's bedroom, I climbed onto a chair and peered over the top of her wardrobe. Sitting up there all on its own was a small shamrock-green Aer Lingus zip-up flight bag, hand-luggage size, with cracked white piping running along the seams. It looked like it was from the 1960s. This was a poverty-stricken person's bag, bought for pennies from a charity shop or found on the street. Mum had loads of suitcases and bags stuffed with woollen blankets, straw hats, pegs and photographs in her flat. She even had two smart, fireproof aluminium cases for important documents like her bank details, will and passport. But no case or bag she owned was as downtrodden and pitiful-looking as this droopy green receptacle. I grasped the yellowing, fake-ivory plastic handle – it looked like it was moulded from melted-down old people's teeth – and pulled the case towards me. A cloud of dust mushroomed into my face, settling on my hair and eyelashes. Shabby as the bag was, it somehow didn't look insignificant. As I lifted it down I noticed that scrawled across the front in thick, white Tippex letters was the instruction:

'To Throw Away – UNOPENED.'

Mum wasn't daft, she knew Pascale and me: that we're disobedient, inquisitive and never do what we're told. (I've asked

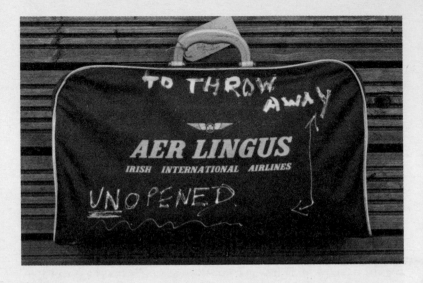

lots of people if they would have opened a parent's bag if this was written on the front, and they've all said yes.) Mum left that bag to be found. She'd have shredded the contents with all her other paperwork if she didn't want us to see them. The little green case, like the little red purse, was a plant. *Well, if they read it, it's their own fault. I left instructions for it to be thrown away.* I sat cross-legged on the brown carpet. Another dead parent, another empty flat, another dodgy bag.

40 I plotted from the corner. *How can I get past Mia, antagonise Pascale and get her away from the bed?* Nothing else mattered. But all I could think of doing was to call her names. Mum taught us never to call each other names, especially regarding our physical appearance – a very good rule to teach siblings, I think. 'Personal comments can never

be taken back,' she used to say. I never broke the rule, not until that night. Pascale did. She said my teeth were like the rocks in Nanny's garden. Nanny had a rockery. (I got braces when I was in my forties and sorted them out.) I contemplated breaking Mum's rule. What were rules now anyway? Pascale had already broken the rules, loads of them: how to treat your sister and niece at your mother's deathbed, and not swearing over your dying mother, for a start. And I'd broken the rules by starting a fight and calling her a bitch. I launched into a stream of insults. Anything I could think of that would lacerate. I said things only a sister knows will pierce. Mum must have heard it all. Mia told me later that I didn't look human when I was hissing insults at Pascale: 'Your face was unrecognisable and your eyes went black like an animal.' I went against my code of living, crossed the line. 'You're mad,' said Pascale. She was right. I was mad. Completely insane. A deranged, murderous, certifiable, raging lunatic.

Diary of a Mad Housewife*

I opened Mum's green bag. Inside, a bundle of tissuey yellowed papers covered in rows of faded grey type, held together with a rusted dressmaker's pin, lay as crisp and undisturbed as a shroud, exactly like my father's diary. Mum's diary was also written between 1965 and 1967, recounted the last two years of their marriage and was to be used as evidence in the divorce. Pinned to

* A 1970 film starring Jane Fonda, based on Sue Kaufman's 1967 book of the same name

the first page were two letters, one from her solicitor, Mr Shirley, to the county court, outlining my father's character:

Mr Shirley   Throughout the said marriage the petitioner, who is a man of selfish, jealous and quarrelsome disposition, has failed and neglected to show any affection or consideration for the respondent but has continually sought to dominate her and has succeeded in so doing. That at outset of said marriage the petitioner unreasonably refused to allow the child, David, of the respondent (by her previous marriage) to be a child of the family or to live with them and he thereby caused the respondent the utmost distress.

In the second letter, from my mother to Mr Shirley, she responded to his request for a detailed account of her marriage. He gave instructions to include 'full particulars of the date, approximate time, and place of every occasion of sexual intercourse relied upon'.

Kathleen   Dear Mr Shirley, I am going to write down the happenings of my marriage as you have asked me to – I am sorry I took so long but it all seemed so unreal. We had only moved into the new house less than three months when without my knowledge Lucien was applying to the council to sell it. I have been sent a letter from the solicitors saying he wants a divorce and it seems he has been planning it for this past year and not a word about it to me. During this time he and I were still having intercourse. It seems incredible. I can't believe it.

    We have been married 19 years.

Please, you must get me custody of the children.
Nothing else matters – please help me – and them. I
wouldn't have a peaceful night if he had custody of them.

It wasn't the house Mum wanted. Lucien was wrong about that.
She wanted her children. She wanted us. I was pleased to read
that. And how humiliating, having sex with your husband and
later discovering that all the time he was plotting to divorce you.
I'd stop speaking to a man who did that – although Mum said
in her account that Lucien stopped speaking to *her* because she
wouldn't sign her £150 annuity over to him. (Again I've added
some comments in italics to the diary excerpts.)

Kathleen   During the war Lucien was transferred to the Free French
             Navy at the collapse of France. He rejected the authority
             of the Free French and after an awful lot of trouble he
             was jailed for a year in England during the war. He was
             demobbed in England at his own request as he would not
             go back to France. We met at the end of 1944 and married
             in 1949.

In June 1940, a year into the Second World War, France was
defeated by Germany and divided into two zones, one half
governed by the Nazis, the other half by the Vichy regime, an
alliance between France and Germany. The British called this
the 'fall' or 'collapse' of France. On 3 July 1940, the Royal Navy
bombed a flotilla of French ships at Mers-el-Kébir (Operation
Catapult) to prevent the French surrendering or loaning any
of their fleet to the Germans. (The French had promised they
wouldn't give up their ships, but Churchill was not convinced.)

The attack resulted in 1,297 deaths and 350 casualties among French servicemen, destroyed the fleet and aroused a deep hatred for the British within the French navy.

Two years later, in 1942, German forces attempted to seize a large fleet of French warships that were docked in the port of Toulon (Operation Lila). My father grew up in Toulon and was a sailor on a submarine during this attack. As they had promised the Allies, the French navy scuttled seventy-seven of its own ships to avoid them falling into German hands. The hulls burned on the sea for weeks. Lucien's submarine ignored orders to scuttle and escaped, probably to Algiers. He told me that he ran up to the captain and screamed at him that they were all going to die. He was only a *matelot breveté*, the lowest rank of sailor; he probably got a slap. When the submarine was found the crew were offered the choice of going to jail in England or joining the Free French Navy and fighting the Germans under the leadership of General Charles de Gaulle. Because of the anti-British sentiment among French sailors, and because he was always one to harbour a grudge, Lucien refused to join de Gaulle and spent a year of the war in a British jail. He later reversed his decision and was released to join the Free French. By the end of the war he'd completely changed his mind and fallen in love with England. He desperately wanted to be perceived as English – he wouldn't speak French at home so that his English improved – and became such an Anglophile that whenever he went back to France he annoyed his family by praising England all the time and denigrating France.

Kathleen   We went to France to see Lucien's family in 1963 [*I was nine, Pascale was seven*] as his mother hadn't ever seen the children and was feeling old. Lucien would not tell the children it was their own grandmother, uncles and aunts we were visiting and he told me not to let them know. It made a very unhappy state of affairs as his mother felt it and queried whether the children knew. I lied and said yes as the children couldn't speak French. He doesn't tell people his real name is Lucien (he calls himself Albert in England) or that he is French. He never even got in touch with his mother after VE day [*Victory in Europe Day, 8 May 1945*] to let her know he was alive. She found him through the Red Cross Missing People's Bureau.

Can you imagine going to visit your relatives and not being told they are your family? It was extremely awkward. We didn't know how familiar to be with the people we met and stayed with, or why they were so friendly and affectionate towards us. (My parents never told us our father was French either – I didn't notice he had an accent because I grew up with it.) All the lies and the fudging they must have employed to keep us in the dark.

On our journey down to the South of France we crossed Paris on a bus, transferring from the Gare du Nord station to the Gare de Lyon. We were all settled in our seats when an injured veteran with a crutch hobbled on, and an elderly woman shouted at Lucien for not giving up his seat – I think he was sitting in the seat reserved for the disabled. Instead of apologising and getting up, my father argued back. Mum told me later that he said *he* was in the Free French Navy during the war and unlike *them*, he'd done his bit for France. I remember him throwing out his arms to include everyone on the bus and shouting in English, 'You're all a bunch of bloody collaborators!' I had no idea what he meant, Mum hadn't used that word on me yet, but I could tell it was bad by the reaction. Pandemonium broke out and we dived off the bus at the next stop. Everyone was yelling, insulting us, even the driver. It was horrible. *Why can't Dad be normal? Why does he always get into trouble wherever he goes?* We scurried down a side street. I kept looking behind me, terrified that the angry passengers would follow us and beat us up. Mum must have been scared too because she suggested we duck into a patisserie.

I had never seen such beautiful cakes before. There were no flat-topped Bakewell tarts studded with gummy glacé cherries in tinfoil trays, no round brown lumps dusted in dandruffy coconut, or chunks of Battenberg with lurid pink and yellow squares here. These shelves were filled with rows of soft, whipped, miniature pink mousses garnished with real strawberries, fat powdered doughnuts puffed up with creamy yellow custard and perfectly neat little chocolate cubes crowned with delicate toffee stars. We weren't allowed any of these exciting cakes though. Mum bought us each a boring, flat, flaky brown thing instead. It looked like a large, squashed sausage roll. 'It's that or nothing,' she said. Pascale and I were upset but hungry, so we agreed. Outside the shop I bit into my pastry, even though I didn't like the look of it. To my amazement it tasted of sugar and butter and broke into flat little flakes which stuck to my lips. Inside this crispy sweet nest, a stick of hard, cool chocolate ran all the way down the middle, end to end. It was a *pain au chocolat*, the most delicious pastry I'd ever tasted. That's when I decided that French people were not to be underestimated.

The little old French lady on the bus wasn't scared of my big bullying father. She didn't stay quiet when he shouted at her, she shouted back. The other passengers didn't ignore the disturbance, turn their heads away and look out of the window like people at home would have done back then. They joined in and made their voices heard. And French cake shops, even ones hidden away down dark narrow alleyways, were filled with exquisite little cakes and ugly brown pastries hiding secret chocolate middles.

41 Trapped in the corner, penned in by Mia, aching with frustration, I still wasn't ready to give up. Any chance that came my way, I was all set to take advantage. Meanwhile, Pascale went on sitting, Mum went on sleeping and Vida went on watching. My moment came when Mia picked up a little Pyrex glass and poured some water from Mum's plastic jug into it. I was concentrating so hard on her actions, I swear I could see every molecule of H_2O as it streamed out of the spout and splashed and swirled around inside the glass. As she poured, Mia spoke to me in a soft, steady voice, but I couldn't hear what she was saying for the blood rushing inside my head. I'd had an idea. She proffered the glass with a hesitant smile. I reached for it slowly so as not to spook her. *I must not do anything to make her change her mind or doubt me in any way.* I was sure my scheme was written all over my face. I raised the glass to my lips and took a sip. Mia smiled broadly, pleased with herself. 'Thank you,' I whispered, and smiled back gratefully. Then I swivelled round and chucked

the contents of the glass in Pascale's face. She reared back, eyes wide, face white and wet. I noted that not a drop had landed on Mum.

Pussy Riot

I've had a few altercations on buses myself. I take after my father in that respect. Or did the bold Parisian woman lodge in my brain as deeply as the French cakes when I was nine years old? The first time I ever saw a woman stand up to a man was on that French bus – Mum didn't challenge my father in the early days.

Not long after moving to Hackney I went to Amnesty International in East London to hear the women from Pussy Riot discuss their experiences of protesting and prison. On the way home I was feeling militant. The bus was crowded and a man in his late twenties, about six foot two, beige corduroy jacket, floppy fringe, lounged across the last empty seat with his legs sprawled out so no one else could sit there. Lots of people were standing up, letting him get away with it, but I asked him to move his legs so I could sit down. 'Excuse me?' he said (here we go), meaning, *Why the fuck are you talking to me, you silly woman?* He was upper-class and supercilious. I asked him again to move his legs so I could sit down. 'Excuse me?' he repeated, with a wrinkled-up nose and a 'You smell of shit' expression. 'You heard,' I said in a nasty skinhead voice. That took him aback. The exchange went on like this for a while, with him not moving his legs and acting all superior as if I were so revolting and thick that he couldn't understand what I was saying. When I

called him a 'posh twat' he got out his phone and, with a snidey
smile, tried to take my picture. I wasn't having that. I wrestled
him for the phone. Bit of a risk, but I was willing to take a
punch for it. Things got quite physical. He didn't get to take the
picture.

Sometimes you mess with the wrong middle-aged woman.

He said he was going to call the police. A Saturday night in
Hackney and Mr Six Foot Two was calling the police because
a woman stood up to him. He must have been very unused to
being challenged. He jumped up from the two seats he'd been
occupying and pressed the red emergency button. I sat down.
The bus stopped in the middle of the road, holding up the traffic,
while the man dialled 999 and told the police, his voice slurred
from alcohol, that he'd been assaulted by a woman. (I didn't
hit him, just prevented him from taking my picture.) The bus
driver shouted at him to stop being a dick. The other passengers,
Hackney locals, older men and women of all ages and races, had
a go too. 'The whole bus is attacking me now,' he whined into
the phone. I couldn't believe the police stayed on the line so
long – maybe it was his posh accent. They must have told him
to piss off eventually because he hung up and the bus set off
again.

There are more and more of us women out there who won't be
pushed around and will give back a lot more than was bargained
for. You have to mean it though.

42

I could tell by her slumped posture that Pascale was beginning to weaken, but she wasn't beaten and I was running out of ideas. All I had left was the empty glass. It was my last chance, I had to make a move before it was taken off me.

My arm went up. Vida's head turned. Mia's jaw dropped. The glass flew. It hit Pascale's head and fell to the floor. I felt the vibrations travel up through my socks and into my feet. Silence. Pascale's hand flew to her face. *Here we go, a big fuss about nothing, bloody hypochondriac.* A spot of blood appeared from under her fingers. I wasn't expecting that. If I thought anything would happen, it was that one of those golfball-sized lumps would appear. More blood. I felt a twinge of remorse but checked myself. *Hold firm. Don't give in now.* A trickle of red wended its way from Pascale's hairline down to her cheek – not pouring, but definitely on the move.

Pascale looked over at Mia. 'Are you going to do something about this?'

'Yes.' Mia's voice was barely audible.

But I Lost It

O mother, mother!
What have you done?
Coriolanus to Volumnia. William
Shakespeare, *Coriolanus*, 1608

Sitting on the carpet, legs crossed, arse aching, my mother's diary balanced on my knees, I read on as the light faded and the lamp post outside her bedroom window glowed pink, then orange.

To set the scene, Mum started in 1937, when her elder sister, Ivy-Ann, introduced her to Gerry Mansfield, David's father. He threatened to commit suicide if Mum didn't marry him. She was eighteen and frightened. Mansfield was thirty-one and the first man she'd slept with. She married him and gave birth to David in 1939, when she was nineteen years old. It was the start of the Second World War. I'd always wondered what Mum did in the war, but whenever I asked her she'd intimate she was still a child. She said she refused to be evacuated and stayed at home with her parents. (She never told us her age. If we, or anyone else, ever asked, she'd say, 'Over twenty-one.' I only discovered her age a couple of years before she died, when a doctor asked when she was born and I was standing by the bed. Mum looked up at me, winced and said, '1919.') She also said she wasn't scared of the bombs and that after the first couple of attacks she didn't bother going to the air-raid shelters any more.

After reading her diary I learned the truth. During the war Mum was in her early twenties and worked as a secretary. (I was disappointed she wasn't a code-breaker at Bletchley Park. I'd always imagined that was the reason for her reticence.) She lived with her mother, her father and her baby in North London, having separated from Gerry Mansfield. It was legitimate that Mum didn't participate in active service as she had a young baby. I don't think she lied about it because she was a coward. She was ashamed of having a baby and being separated from the father at twenty-one years of age. It's probably true that she wasn't scared of the bombs and didn't go to the shelters. She was fearless and unsentimental. Or maybe she didn't care if she lived or died. You'd think having a new baby would make you nervous and concerned for his and your safety, but one of the few times we talked about David she said, 'I didn't know what to do with the baby. I was just a silly child. I dressed him up, dandled him and played with him like a toy.'

I wish she'd been honest with me about her past, at least when I was older. It's not as if I was a conventional daughter. Although, now I think about it, I also kept things about myself hidden from my daughter at the insistence of my husband – he said it would be a bad influence on her to know I'd been in a band and had lived an itinerant life, that I swore, had taken drugs and made sculptures of naked female bodies. This was fifty years after Mum's first marriage and after I'd been in the Slits. It's more difficult to make sense of why I was so cowed in the 1990s than why my mother was so secretive in the 1940s. Like her, I attempted to give the impression to Vida that I was a perfect person, had no complicated history and had never put a foot wrong in life. (What kind of a role model is that for a child?)

Divorce made an honest woman of me. Vida was eight when my marriage began to disintegrate and I couldn't bear pretending to her or anyone else any more. I was sick of trying to appear normal. Vida didn't reject me for showing my true self – that's what I imagined would happen. Far from it, we grew even closer. She especially enjoyed my swearing. (I only swore in front of her when she was older. Everything has to be revealed at an appropriate time.) A child derives a sense of safety from knowing the person who looks after them is respectful enough to be honest. Vida has never rooted around in my cupboards and drawers or turned the house upside down searching for letters and scraps of evidence to help her piece her mother together like I did. On the contrary, she knows too much. She's not fascinated by secrets because I haven't hidden anything from her, not even the ugly stuff. When I was young, as soon as Mum left the house I'd tear it apart. I didn't know what I was looking for – the truth, I suppose. *Is that where it started? This obsession with the truth?* Vida is secure in the knowledge that, good or bad, she knows it all. There won't be any shocks or nasty surprises for her when I've gone (although obviously I've made quite different mistakes).

Kathleen   I had a child, David, by a previous marriage. Lucien was so jealous of any time I spent on or with David that he even timed how long our 'goodnights' took. [*David was six years old when Mum and Lucien met.*] I used to get up early and do David's mending so Lucien couldn't see me doing it. I always bought David exactly the same kind of clothes as before so Lucien wouldn't notice they were new, yet I was working full time.

    It got to such a state that he threatened either he would go or I must send David back to his father, he said I had to choose between them. This upset me so much, I was very distraught and half my face became paralysed for years. After two years [*David was now eight*] he sent my little boy back to his father – he said life would be much happier for us. I was so very unhappy about it. Lucien said we would have David back when we had established ourselves in Australia. [*They had decided to emigrate to Australia as 'Ten Pound Poms'. Mum also wrote that the day David was sent back to live with his father, Lucien insisted they go to the cinema, and she sat there like a zombie.*]

Lucien went to Australia and I followed about six months later after selling the furniture. During this six months I wrote and told him I was trying to get David back. [*Gerry Mansfield now had custody of David and wouldn't let Mum have him back. He said she'd lost her chance.*] David was unhappy with his father and cried so when he had to go home, it was heartbreaking. Lucien was very angry when I went ahead and had a high court case to get custody of David again, but I lost it.

'But I lost it.' All the time, the anguish, the letter-writing, the appointments and interviews, all the days spent in the library looking up facts and past cases, all the waiting and the disappointment, struggles and setbacks that cannot be conveyed in those four words, *But I lost it*. Mum not only lost custody of David in 1947, she lost faith in the justice system, the Establishment, and men in general. Her attitude was unusual. Most people in 1940s Britain were deferential to authority and took it for granted that men ruled every sphere of society from health, education and justice to culture and the home.

A combination of youth, inexperience, being under the control of men and living in a restrictive society resulted in Mum becoming pregnant by the first man she slept with, coerced into marriage, bullied into sending her son away and prevented from getting him back. For fear of being washed up, alone and on the shelf at twenty-five years old (this was standard thinking at the time), she left David behind to follow her new husband to Australia. These experiences must have built up into layer after layer of anger and disappointment as solid and bitter as an aniseed ball lodged in her gullet. 'I always try not to think about the past, I find one can live on the surface and be bright, but I won't allow myself to think. Writing this is like pulling one's insides out,' she wrote in the diary. Her buried pain, guilt and resentment, like the tiny black aniseed pip secreted under layers of hardened sugar, were bound to reveal themselves some time. They surfaced with a vengeance during the disintegration of her second marriage and tainted her thoughts and actions for the rest of her life, particularly in the way she raised Pascale and me.

43

Pascale stood up, her hand clutching her head. She was off the bed. I felt my facial muscles shifting into a surprised expression but just managed to stop them. *No. Wait. You're not there yet. Don't give her any clues. If she detects any sign of weakness she will win.* I watched as she walked towards the door; it took all of my self-control to keep my mouth from dropping open as she reached the door, opened it and disappeared into the corridor. Mia followed her. As soon as the door closed behind them, the piss-heavy cloud hanging over us lifted and the room became suffused with a warm saffron glow. The change in the atmosphere was palpable, spiritual even.

Little Psychos

Six months after Lucien travelled to Australia, Mum left her son, her parents, her brothers and sisters, her work, her friends and her country, sailed over the Atlantic Ocean and the Mediterranean Sea, through the Suez Canal, across the Indian Ocean, into the Pacific and joined her husband in Sydney to start a new life. That's the sort of thing people did back then. Everyone was starting again after the war, after losing mothers and fathers, brothers and sisters, children, husbands and wives. It seems shocking now, but there wasn't such a sentimental attitude towards family or such a fear of death then as we have now. (People who live through wars often develop attachment disorders as a protection from loss.)

During the six-week sea voyage Mum met a man. They were very attracted to each other. This is the story she told us about him:

'He was Scottish with red hair. Such a nice, kind man, he liked me very much. I should have married him instead of your father.'

'But then you wouldn't have had *us*, Mummy!'

'No, but I would have had other children. With red hair.'

Almost immediately Kathleen and Lucien's new life in Australia, which had so much riding on it, began to unravel.

Kathleen   When I arrived in Sydney to join Lucien, we lived in a boarding house but life didn't run smoothly. His work partner [*my father and another man had a painting and decorating business*] was having a baby and he was furious about it. When I said, Let's have one too, he went into a terrible temper and hit me, saying I was always spoiling his chances of work.

Since we were married I very much wanted children and offered to continue work afterwards if we could have one. But it was always, 'We must get settled first' and wait until after he'd had his 'opportunities'. I never used any birth control and he used the withdrawal method as he preferred it. It wasn't until I read a medical journal saying women who had such a sex life became sterile that he agreed to give me normal intercourse. Fortunately Viviane, the eldest, was born ten months after.

I have never refused my husband intercourse except when he has demanded anal intercourse. He insisted on this, saying it was a wifely duty and threatened divorce if I would not do it. It was not until piles appeared, and were aggravated by the birth of Viviane, and I said I wanted to get a doctor's opinion because they were bleeding and painful, that he stopped. He then started the practice of releasing into my mouth. He said he could not control himself. But when I answered that he could control himself when he was using the withdrawal method so I wouldn't get pregnant, he became violent and sulked for days saying I was no good as a wife, he would have to find another woman and it was his entitlement, so I acquiesced.

I squinted through the dark at the pastel-grey print on the lemon pages, not wanting to break the spell, even though it was a bad spell, by getting up and switching on the light. I was horrified but not surprised by what my mother said about the cruelty my father exhibited towards her: hitting her when she wouldn't do what he wanted; repeatedly forcing her to have anal sex with him against her will; taunting her by saying he wanted younger women and prostitutes; staying out all night; insisting she have a backstreet abortion (abortion wasn't legal in England until 1967 and Australia in 1971) after Pascale and I were born. 'I wanted the baby very much but he insisted I couldn't have it. He organised a baby sitter and drove me there himself.' During arguments he questioned whether Pascale and I were his and erupted into violent, jealous rages whenever she interacted with men, even her brother and the milkman.

Kathleen He never spoke one word at my friend Joy's wedding because her brother talked to me.

I woke up and he was standing over me with a pan of boiling water. He stopped speaking to me and refused to answer when I spoke to him and sulked towards the children. After two weeks he admitted, 'I was upset because I dreamed you had been out sleeping with other men.'

We only go to the pictures once or twice a year, and when I asked the commissionaire the time of the main film, Lucien sulked afterwards saying I'd made a date with him.

He kept on accusing me of being a prostitute. I've only slept with him and my first husband in my whole life. These sort of senseless accusations have gone on all through our marriage.

I shifted my weight and stretched out my legs. I'd been sitting in the dusty bedroom for hours, my throat was dry and I was hungry, but I didn't stop, even though these were not easy things to read about my mother. She must be lying, I reasoned to myself. Anal sex was illegal in the late fifties and early sixties, even within marriage. If she didn't want it, she could have gone to the police. I couldn't – didn't want to – imagine my mother being hurt, or in that position, and tried to erase the mental image by naively explaining away the circumstances. And she'd never let a man hit her, I rationalised. She was so strong and always said to us, 'Never let a man hit you. If a man hits you, walk away and never look back. If he does it once, he'll do it again.' But then other assertive women came to mind who I remembered had been hit or dominated: Colette, Vivienne Westwood, Rihanna and Tina Turner . . . myself. I know how strong I appear to my daughter, friends and colleagues, and yet how badly I've been treated by some men and how long it can take to extract yourself from an abusive relationship. Those two things *can* be found together – a strong, spirited woman and a violent, domineering partner.

Kathleen   I was eight months pregnant with Viviane when Lucien bought a car without telling me, using money we'd borrowed from my mother for rent. We had a quarrel about it. I always remember this, we were talking over the kitchen table and he was annoyed because I wouldn't agree happily to him buying the car. He got in a rage, started swearing and calling me immoral things, then he picked up the ashtray which was full of ash and cigarette ends and threw it in my face. I sat there thinking of all the

times he had hit and sworn at me. I thought of the baby I
was pregnant with and said to myself, Am I giving birth
to a coward? Would he go as far as to punch me now? So
I stood up, picked up my coffee cup and threw the coffee
over him. He sat there absolutely stunned. I walked down
to the gate. After a long time I stopped trembling, went in
and went to bed. That coffee I have heard about ever since,
but I'm not sorry. [*Quite a risk to include this in her diary,
it could have been used against her in court.*]

Oh, Mum, there I am inside you, and there are my angry
beginnings (and my liquid-throwing tendencies) in your boiling
blood and your coffee-throwing. That's me all over. And don't
worry:

> No coward soul is mine.
> No trembler in the world's storm-troubled sphere.
> Emily Brontë, 'No Coward Soul Is Mine', 1846,
> *Poems by Currer, Ellis and Acton Bell*

I was timid when I was young, I was shy until my late teens,
and I've become embroiled in some negative relationships,
but that's all stopped. Now I'm alone like you were at my age.
That's the only way either of us could be sure it would never
happen again.

Mum was so intent that Pascale and I wouldn't be bullied by
men or intimidated by authority that she ingrained in us, from
the moment we were born, the need to suppress the 'flight'
response in our brains and respond to any threat with the 'fight'
response. It's easy enough to manipulate the plasticity of a child's

brain. Bit by bit, year after year, in their own ways, our mother and father endeavoured to turn my sister and me into little psychopaths.

Kathleen   He catches flies in the summer, pulls off their wings and dashes them to the ground. In the last flat, the dog next door kept coming into our garden, Lucien piled up stones and rocks and told the children to chuck them at the dog and he threw stones himself until the man next door said he would get the law on him.

Last summer there was a bird in the garden – a cat had been after it – with its wing torn right off and its little heart and insides exposed. Lucien wanted to sew it together with a large needle and cotton, with me holding it. It was cruel. I refused, the bird was in awful pain. Lucien was furious with me and stuck the bird together with sticking plaster instead. It died that night. He said, 'If that's the way you want it, you can have it. I'm sick of you always pleasing other people instead of me.' All wrapped up in a lot of swearing. I have to think, act and say what he thinks acts and says or I am abused and threatened with divorce. That same night he moved out of our bedroom and it was later that week I found out he'd secretly been planning to divorce me for months.

My sister and I harassed all our pets. We were rough with the cat, neglected our budgies and fish and treated our puppy as if she were a plaything. We even persecuted the bees. In summer they buzzed in and out of the hollyhocks in our back garden, collecting pollen. We'd pull off a hollyhock flower and clamp it

205

over the one the bee was working in, trapping it inside a pink prison. As the buzzing got louder, higher-pitched and angrier we'd realise that not only had we trapped the bee, we'd trapped ourselves. If we freed the bee, it would fly out in a rage and sting us. I'd stand beside the gangly hollyhock stem, which was as tall as I was, knees shaking, arm outstretched, pressing the flower heads together, bee whirring furiously inside, for as long as I could bear, then fling the petals to the ground and run away screaming. (As I was the oldest, I have to take responsibility for initiating this game.)

44 I heard Pascale in the corridor talking on the phone to her partner in Canada. 'Get me on the next flight home.' A little part of me was shocked that she'd walk away from Mum while she was dying. Nothing and no one could have got me out of that room. Pascale's response – to leave Mum, the care home and the country – was so swift, it occurred to me that maybe she unconsciously didn't want to be there and face Mum's death. That she'd got what she wanted – a way out.

Mia returned and told us that Pascale had taken herself off to A & E. Then she looked at me with a worried expression and said, 'Do you think she'll come back?' And that was it. I was in control of myself again. I was back in the room.

'No,' I replied. 'She won't come back.'

'But how do you know?'

'She might come back,' said Vida.

'She won't. I know her.'

The reason I was so certain that Pascale wasn't coming back was because I *did* know her. She always runs away. The way I saw it, she ran away from us to Canada. And she ran out on Mum two years ago, on her ninety-third birthday, when Mum was frail and falling over all the time and just beginning the round of trips to hospital every couple of weeks covered in cuts and bruises. Pascale arrived from Canada for a visit and they had an argument. I wasn't there but Mum hinted that it was something to do with Pascale accusing her of treating me like the favourite and Mum replying, 'So what? All parents have a favourite,' which wasn't very diplomatic of her. (I think Mum was too ashamed to tell me outright what she'd said.) I don't know how much of this sort of thing Pascale had to endure from Mum, but Mum was also saying hurtful things like that to me: 'I love Vida much more than I ever loved you'; 'If it weren't for Vida I wouldn't bother seeing you any more.' (She always apologised later.) After the argument on Mum's birthday Pascale stormed out and caught a plane home – without telling Mum. She'd been in England for less than a day. Mum spent her ninety-third birthday ringing round hotels, trying to locate her daughter to say sorry. Eventually it dawned on her that Pascale had gone. It must have been so upsetting for Pascale to hear those words after travelling all the way from Canada to see her mother. If only she'd talked to me about it, I could have assured her that it wasn't personal. Mum's mind was breaking down and she was losing control of her thoughts and speech. I could also have told Pascale that she had nothing to worry about. I wasn't the favourite at all. Not our mother's favourite anyway.

Sanatorium

Children remember things without understanding them: they are oceans of goodwill drinking in an ocean of words.
Violette Leduc, *La bâtarde*, 1964

Kathleen and Lucien left Australia in 1958 and arrived back in England with Pascale and me in tow.

Kathleen   David had for years dreamed of joining us in Australia, I had always written to him and said I hope to see him one day, and when he was older perhaps he could join us at sixteen. It was a silly thing to promise, now I can see it, but one is made of hope.

David was eighteen years old when Mum turned up in London again. He'd been expecting to go to Australia to be with her as soon as he finished his education – he was extremely bright and went to Oxford, which was even more of an achievement in those days considering he came from a poor, broken home and had gone to a state school – but instead she reappeared with two new children *that she hadn't told him about.*

I leaned over, fished around in the 'To Keep' box, pulled out the red heart purse and looked at David's picture again. As I studied his face I remembered seeing my mother cry one other time – apart from the time I left art school and when she had to eat lentils again for tea. I looked up at the window, a pain twisting in my chest. Funny how your body records important events without you knowing. I played out the scene in my head. I'm a child and I'm sitting in Nanny's living room with Mum and David – who must have been in his early twenties – drinking tea and talking. Nanny's false teeth are making a clicking noise because they're too big for her mouth and she has to keep sucking them back up to her palate. She's saying to Mum, 'You abandoned your poor little boy, *click.* Wicked, *click,* wicked, *click,* wicked.' Mum bursts into tears. She sobs and sobs and answers, 'You know that's not how it was.' I've never seen my mother in this state before. I rush to her side and put my head on her lap. She strokes my hair as she cries. After a while we leave Nanny's and Mum takes David and me to the pub – 'You're grown up enough now,' she says. I'm excited as I've never been to a pub before. We sit in the garden and Mum and David talk while I slurp at a lemonade.

That's why our grandmother didn't like Pascale and me. She resented us on David's behalf. Frieda saw how upset David was during the eight years Mum was abroad and how abandoned he felt. Her house was a second home to him. She would have often heard him crying for his mummy. They probably read Mum's letters together too, and discussed how he'd be going to Australia soon to be with her. Frieda punished us to get at Mum. Punished the children. Adults do this a lot.

Kathleen   I understood from my mother that as a child David always thought he would definitely go to Australia when he was sixteen, and when we didn't send for him, he felt lost.

Then it occurred to me that as well as not telling David about us, Mum might not have told *Frieda* she'd had more children, or her sisters either, until we came back to England. Maybe we were a big shock to everybody. The only way she could be sure that David didn't find out about us was not to tell anyone.

David was so traumatised by the appearance of his mother's new children that he had a breakdown and was admitted to a sanatorium for six months. Mum doesn't say so in her diary, but to be away for that long, I'm guessing he attempted suicide.

Kathleen   About six years ago [*in 1959*] David had a nervous breakdown and went to a hospital. I wanted to go and see him or the doctor, but my husband forbade it. He doesn't want me to let the children know David is their half-brother, or that I have been married before.

In all the months David was in the sanatorium, Mum didn't visit him. 'I've always felt I should have gone to the hospital, it would have helped,' she writes. In her defence, all mothers in the 1950s and 60s were instructed not to visit their children in hospital, whether the illness was physical or mental. But parents of those with psychological problems were especially 'encouraged to put

their children into institutions and move on with their lives'.*
Please let this be the reason Mum didn't visit David. She can't
possibly have been that cruel on purpose.

Kathleen   I remember at this time I began to feel like ending my life.
            David was in hospital, Lucien was quarrelling with my
            family, my friends never came to see me any more and I
            had changed my job.

My sister and I were only three and five years old when Mum
contemplated suicide. I always had the feeling she didn't think
much of life, had no reverence for it. She exuded the resigned
air of a person whose children have died and who is just filling
in time until she can follow them to the grave, or who's seen too
much death to take life seriously, which I used to put down to her
living through the war.

She was only ill on three occasions during our childhood, and
they were all when Pascale and I went away without her. The first
time was when we went on a camping trip with the Woodcraft
Folk. She fell downstairs at home, knocked herself out, broke her
arm and was taken to hospital. The second time she 'fell through
the window' of the dresser in the dining room and cut the insides
of both her arms to pieces, tiny little slices of red all the way
up to her armpits. I can't remember where Pascale and I were.
The third time was when Lucien took Pascale and me to France
to see our relatives, without her. She ended up in hospital with
poisoning. When we arrived back home she looked terrible, so
white. She laughed and said she'd accidentally put boracic acid

* Steve Silberman, *Neurotribes*, 2015

powder (poisonous if taken internally, we used it as an antiseptic – although it's no longer recommended) in the sugar bowl instead of sugar. She was saved because she rang her sister, Phyllis, who phoned for an ambulance. I believed Mum when she said that's what happened, but then again, I didn't. I kept thinking, *Sugar and boracic acid are such different consistencies. Boracic acid is powdery and sugar is crystals – how could she have muddled them up?* Also, she didn't take sugar with her tea or anything else, now I come to think of it. And we didn't have a phone.

When I was a child I often used to ask Mum if she'd ever thought about suicide. 'Yes,' she'd say, and she'd tell me about the time she knelt down in front of the cooker, turned the gas on and stuck her head in the oven. As my face fell she'd brighten up and tell me not to worry: after a while she realised how ridiculous she must look with her bum stuck in the air and it made her laugh, so she got up, switched the gas off and opened the windows. Sylvia Plath committed suicide that way. There's a police photograph of her at the scene of her death looking just as Mum described, head in oven, bum in air, legs splayed, cotton dress. The story must have been in all the papers at the time, especially our local paper, as Sylvia Plath also lived in North London. Plath gassed herself in 1963, when her daughter Frieda was two years old. Two years later another interesting local woman, Hannah Gavron,* also committed suicide by gassing herself in an oven. It wasn't unheard of amongst intelligent women in North London. I don't know if Mum really did go through the motions of trying to kill herself or whether she appropriated the narratives of these other women's suicides; they must have resonated very strongly

---

* Jeremy Gavron, *A Woman on the Edge of Time*, 2015

with her at the time. I laughed nervously whenever she told the I-put-my-head-in-the-oven-haha story, but to know that she'd contemplated suicide, let alone tried it, was enough to implant fear and doubt in my mind about her ongoing presence in my life.

The last time I saw David we all boarded a bus together in Muswell Hill. Mum paid the fare for Pascale and me but not for David. She told him he had to pay for himself because she didn't have any more money. Her child, whom she hardly ever saw. That was the first time I glimpsed the coldness beneath her skin.

Mum not paying David's fare felt so hugely unjust to me that I thought my body would split open and spray my insides all over the bus. I prayed to God as I slumped onto the seat that when I put my hand into the pocket of my school blazer I would find tuppence hidden in the fluff so I could pay for him myself. I fished around but there was nothing there. I felt so powerless and so ashamed of Mum. I hated being a child and I hated adults. I'd never witnessed anything so callous in my life. Was it a ploy to get back at David's father and let him know how poor she was? Tuppence worth of revenge. The cost: David's mental and emotional health. If Mum really didn't have enough money for his bus fare (and that is possible), we should have walked.

The person I feel most sorry for in all this is David. I remember Mum coming into our bedroom with him when I was about nine and telling Pascale and me that this twenty-two-year-old man was our brother. He'd insisted that it was time we were told. I smiled at him, said I already sort of knew he was our brother, and we hugged. Secretly I wished he had long hair and looked like one of the Beatles, but with his short hair and black-rimmed glasses he looked more like Freddie from Freddie and the Dreamers.

45 Flaps of flesh hung off my thumb and I think I caught
a glimpse of something whitish under one of the
diamond-shaped gashes. Mia said I should go to A & E, that a
human bite is much dirtier than an animal bite. 'You could lose
your thumb,' she said. I didn't care if I lost my thumb. I didn't
care if I never played guitar again. I was not leaving my mother
while she was dying. I tied something round it, something
white. I think I went into the bathroom and tore off a length
of bog paper. Vida and I pulled up two chairs, one either side
of the bed, and sat down. I took Mum's bony, bruised, purple-
parchment hand gently in mine. Her eyes were closed – apart
from that one time they popped open at the beginning of
the fight, they'd been closed throughout the whole debacle. I
presumed she was too far into death to know what had gone on
so I acted as if nothing had happened.

But then she did the most extraordinary thing. She tickled the
palm of my hand with her index finger.

Repulsion

Kathleen When Pascale was three and Viviane was five, Lucien spent
all day Sunday making a whip with leather thongs which
he told the children he was going to use on them. He
finished it in the evening and hung it on the wall. When
he was at work on Monday I took it down and threw it
away. He was furious when he came home and it was gone.
He swore at me and gave me a forceful back-handed slap
across the face. The more I think of it all, I feel I should

have been much stronger a long time ago – but I loved him and always hoped things would get better.

Another time he threatened the children with his belt and I got in the way and said he wasn't to belt them. He said he would use it on me if I didn't get out of the way and I threatened him with the police. He said, 'Get out of my f. way the sight of you makes me sick, I'm glad I haven't got to look at you any more.'

On the 15th September 1966 he hit the children with his belt, which he took off, and said, 'You'll be getting worse next time.' He made Viviane clean up the floor, then he turned round poured some more water on the floor and said to her, 'Now clean that up.' I went to Mr Faulkner of the NSPCC and the children told him personally.

Lucien hit us with the belt, he didn't just threaten us. Our testimonies to the authorities, with dates, are proof. He lied in his diary. My memory of it isn't false.

Kathleen   Once he said, 'You should go down on your knees and thank God for a husband like me who doesn't drink and smoke.' I replied, 'Drinking and smoking aren't the worst things in the world.' He went berserk, threw aside the food with his arm, jumped up, punched me in the eye with his fist and screamed vehemently, 'I haven't hit you for a long time, have I?' I shook the iron at him and shouted, 'Bloody bully. That's the last time you'll hit me.' He uses his physical strength as a weapon. I went to the doctor and he sent me to Moorfields Eye Hospital. I felt so upset that I went to the Highgate Court and asked if I had to accept such behaviour – with the children growing up to be women I had to stop it. The court said no, I didn't have to accept it, but I didn't pursue it. I always thought he would be better when his worries were removed but now there doesn't seem anything left to hope for.

My mother never mentioned love or companionship, any of the upsides of having a family in a positive light when we were growing up – but from where she was standing, there weren't many. It didn't occur to me that it would be nice to have children until I was thirty-eight. Before then I'd always thought, *The last thing on earth I'll ever do is subject myself to the hellish suffocation, domination, anger and boredom of children and marriage.*

Kathleen   He accused me of being the worst wife and the children of being the worst behaved but he didn't realise it was because he didn't have any friends to go to, or visit their house as a comparison. He was always complaining we were stopping him doing things. 'If I didn't have the burden of you and the children, I would go to Rome and blow up the pope.' He wasn't joking. He used to say he would be the first to go to the moon if it wasn't for us stopping him (the children and I). That he would show the government how to run the country and the world, but no, they wouldn't give him a chance etc etc.

   In 1961 his naturalisation application was deferred for another four years, he became violent but when I tried to appease him, he knocked me across the room and punched the door breaking a wooden panel. 'It's your bloody fault, you've been discussing me with a neighbour and they've written to the Home Office. You bloody British, think you're Jesus Christ.'

He's not called me by my name since April 1965, it's always It, or She, or The Thing, even to the children. As they grew older, I felt I had to hide my emotions from them as they were so unhappy. But the less I got upset, the nastier my husband became.

I was repulsed by the idea of family for decades. By the time I wanted children it was too late and I couldn't conceive naturally. Stumbling through the many rounds of IVF – the drugs, the needles, the operations, the disappointments – I wondered why it had never occurred to me to have children in my twenties or early thirties like everyone else around me. I traced my attitude back to my mother and resented her for it.

Sick

You don't have favourites among your children,
but you do have allies.
   Zadie Smith, *On Beauty*, 2005

When I was four years old, Miss Benn, a plump nursery-school teacher I was fond of, gave me a hug. I didn't like it, I wasn't used to the feeling of a soft, warm, bosomy body. She wasn't like my bony, smoke-infused mother. Soft wasn't a virtue in our house. Treading the middle ground, being easy-going or an appeaser made you a betrayer in Mum's book (which is why the rigorous attitude of 'punk' resonated so strongly with me – it felt familiar). My father, on the other hand, liked that I saw both sides of an argument. It gave him an opportunity to insinuate himself into my affections. He hit and ridiculed Pascale for the attributes Mum praised her for – being single-minded and assertive. He shouted at Pascale about anything, even sitting too close to the TV. She was very short-sighted and needed glasses, but it took my parents years to realise. They blamed us for so much when they were the ones who got things wrong.

Kathleen   Pascale has a stronger character, Lucien can't intimidate her so he tries to break her with his continuous smacking, telling her she is stupid and sending her up to bed. She has no sense of security and I have to continuously tell her I love her and will always be with her. One day when he sent her to get a tool and she came back with another, she came in crying her eyes out saying Daddy said she was bloody stupid, not a brain in her head. I went out to him and said don't say that, she's too young, it upsets her. He started dancing up and down and yelling out, she's bloody stupid, she's bloody stupid, over and over again.

When I was young I found any signs of weakness, dirt or decrepitude in others nauseating. I couldn't eat for the rest of the day if we were out and I saw someone who wasn't well in some way, even if they were just limping or dribbling, any minor ailment. The elderly and babies turned my stomach. Once we went to the zoo and I saw bees making honey. It looked like they were vomiting it out of their mouths. I didn't eat honey again for ten years.

I wasn't a kind big sister. I was embarrassed, self-conscious and irritable with Pascale. Only when I was at junior school, where I felt safe, did I stand up for the weaker and bullied children. It was on the way to school one morning that Mum instructed me to tell a boy in Pascale's class to stop spitting at her. She said that because I was older – in the year above – he'd listen to me. I crossed the playground at break time, stood in front of the boy, confident that he'd listen to me like Mum said, and told him to stop picking on my sister. He punched me so hard in my (newly growing) chest that I thought he'd ruptured the skin and blood was running down the front of my shirt. Then he ran off. In front of the whole playground. *I hate you, Mum, I hate you, Pascale. Why can't you fight your own battles?*

In 1999, when I was diagnosed with cancer, I became that person I was repelled by – an ill person. A weak person who looked and acted as if they were frail and infirm. Who vomited, had diarrhoea and whose hands shook all the time – and I've never fully recovered. Having cancer may have ruined parts of my body and flayed my nerves, but it at least cured me of my fear of imperfection and sickness in others. My close encounter with death, disease and bodily fluids made me into a half-decent person. I needed to grow up.

46

Even though she couldn't speak or see or raise her arm and was as near death as any living person can possibly be, Mum somehow found the strength and compassion to send me a little message by tickling my hand. When I thought about it later, I wondered if she even knew it was me sitting there holding her hand, and not my sister or Vida, but then I worked out that somehow she did know. She didn't tickle Vida's hand (I asked), she only tickled mine. Mum must have heard and understood everything that went on after all. I recognised the gesture. She'd used it often over the last couple of months: when we were sitting together chatting on her sofa; leaning across the kitchen table after we'd had a laugh about something; holding hands in the hospital. That tickle meant reassurance and love, closeness and goodbye. It meant that she understood and everything was OK. That little tickle was all our shared history in one gesture, and what I took it to mean as I sat by her bed was, 'I understand and I forgive you. Don't carry this around with you for the rest of your life.' That's what flashed into my mind when she did it. Dear Mum, telepathic Mum, my conscience and my guide. With the tiniest amount of pressure – I was frightened I'd bruise her – I squeezed her hand back. It was nearly over. This really was goodbye.

Daydream

Kathleen   Usually Lucien gets on better with Viviane, she looks like
                    him and she always says yes to everything.

The second half of the above description of me is unrecognisable now. No one would ever describe me as saying yes to everything, quite the opposite – questioning, militant, aggressive. But acquiescent? Never. I wonder if the fact that I looked like Lucien irritated Mum. I've read that mothers can turn against a child who physically resembles an estranged or violent father.

Kathleen   His love is a possession of a person and Viviane often hasn't the courage to do anything but agree with him. Although when I was out he dragged Pascale up to her bedroom and kept hitting her (all over some triviality) saying she had to stay there the rest of the day. When he came down he said to Viviane, 'Daddy was right wasn't he?' and she answered, 'No.' He was furious, told her she was no good, she's got no brains, mocked her about the results of her 11 plus exam, told her he wasn't buying her any more sweets and slammed out of the room. He ignored her for the rest of the day. [*So I did disagree with him.*]

State schools weren't comprehensive at the time and after junior school you either went to a grammar school if you passed the 11-plus exam or a secondary modern if you failed. There was a stigma attached to secondary moderns and I felt written off after I failed the 11-plus. I wrote myself off, I thought I was thick. A year later my school merged with the neighbouring grammar school and became a comprehensive, Fortismere. I was pleased that no one would know I'd been to a secondary modern, but the damage was done. People in their sixties and seventies still confess to me in hushed tones that they failed the 11-plus and went to a secondary modern. The shame never goes away. Even if no one else knew I was too stupid to pass, I knew, and that knowledge still haunts me.

I never understood why I failed. I was above average in my class, liked by my teachers and found schoolwork fairly easy.

221

Mum mentions in her diary that she feels guilty and blames herself and Lucien for my failing. She puts it down to the stress I was living through at the time. 'Viviane had no consideration for her 11+ years,' she wrote. She doesn't mention that this was also the exact time she'd taken me to the doctor and he put me on barbiturates. I can still picture myself at eleven, eyes glazed, fixed somewhere up in the air, over the top of the teacher's head, losing my grip on learning, a perpetual daydreamer, detached, unable to concentrate, not interested in work.

From that year on I've daydreamed away countless hours of my life. I still use the techniques of reverie and obsessing over minor injustices that I developed aged eleven and twelve as strategies to 'self-soothe' and distract myself from stressful situations.

Windows

Gazing out of windows – moving windows, static windows – lying in bed awake for hours staring at the sky, watching the blurring landscape or the tracks coming together and separating through train windows, rats scurrying and men fly-tipping seen from the living-room window, the inside of other people's houses glimpsed from the pavement or the top deck of a bus. Since my childhood I've loved looking into and out of windows. When I moved in with Mum again in my late twenties, she and I used to walk around the local streets in Hampstead and Swiss Cottage most evenings after dinner. I was always amazed that the inhabitants didn't close their curtains, even when it was dark. As we peered down into the kitchens I'd marvel at how some people were so confident of what they wore and how they behaved that they didn't mind anyone walking past their house seeing them. Mum explained that in the past the families living in these big houses used to employ servants, but in the 1960s, when the middle classes couldn't afford maids any more, they transformed the basements where the staff used to work into large kitchen/dining rooms. (When I visited friends' houses, I sensed their parents thought they were being subversive by turning this *servants' room* into the main living space. It was a radical idea at the time.)

Those basement kitchens with large scrubbed pine tables, deliberately mismatched chairs, wine glasses and blue and white enamel bread bins looked like film sets to me, the people milling around inside like fantasy families. Life was not like that in our house. We dressed in shabby old clothes (put them on as soon as we got in so we didn't wear out our nice ones), our furniture was second-hand and we had to sit on the settee (later learned to call it the sofa) swaddled in blankets to watch TV in the lounge (later learned to call it the living room) because it was so cold. No way we wanted to expose neighbours and random passers-by to any of that. I had no idea back then that one day I'd be called middle-class. I'd have been so happy if I'd known. Being middle-class is a dream come true for me, even though I'm prejudiced against those born into it. I never feel I truly belong to that safe, shiny world though. I always look a bit crap when I'm at home, sloping around in old clothes, talking to myself. I only look middle-class when I'm in public, which is rather missing the point. I imagine genuine middle-class people live that polite, restrained life all the time, with the curtains open. Everyone who started out poor, like I did, half dreads and fully expects to end up peering through other people's windows again one day. No matter how close I get to financial security, I still feel nervous about the future. As if a rain cloud is constantly hovering above, waiting for a chance to pour misfortune down on me. And there I am, outside without a coat again.

Men R Idiots

Nothing becomes some women more than the prick of ambition. Love, on the contrary, may make them very dull.

Françoise Sagan, *Dans un mois, dans un an*, 1957

Like the scorned Miss Havisham in *Great Expectations* raising her ward Estella (which I thought the most beautiful name in the world when I read the book), my mother raised me to be contemptuous of men. In every way she could, she communicated to me that Men Are Mean Idiots. I'm not sure there's such a thing as a mean idiot, now I think about it. It takes a certain amount of awareness and empathy to be mean, to work out how to manipulate someone and hurt their feelings, so how can someone be mean *and* an idiot? My father didn't do much to challenge Mum's hypothesis though, he did somehow manage to be both. But Dickens's Estella secretly wanted love, and so did I. I wanted to transcend my teacher, prove her wrong and – despite her constantly telling me that romance was 'a load of old twaddle' – fall desperately and hopelessly in love. It took me decades to realise that Mum was right (as usual). The reason she didn't quite manage to put an end to my yearning for love and romance when I was young was that her teachings were constantly being undermined by popular culture. I soaked up love song after love song, performed by boys with dirty hair and leather jackets, thinking that their clothes and their snarls meant they were honest and untouched by mainstream society. I watched girls – who I thought were radical because they wore miniskirts and took the contraceptive pill – being decorative in films, selling things in magazines and on posters, and being assistants in game shows on TV. But the dirty hair and short skirts were masking the same old reality, that society had the same dreary old expectations of us girls as always: to be attractive, smile, acquiesce to men, search for romantic love and become supportive wives.

For me, love songs were the main promoters of these empty aspirations. I continually had pop lyrics chugging round my head – talk about brainwashed. I had no idea that these ditties were not a code to live by, or the constant reiteration of my inevitable and happy destiny by fellow rebels, but a potent mixture of theatre and commerce. Those songs streaming out of the radio every day were constructed to hook young female brains and hormones, to lure us into pursuing impossible goals and then convert our empty longings into money (records, clothes, make-up, magazines). Such an effective way to keep girls and women down and render us ineffective.

> . . . being attracted to that which destroys us keeps us away from power.
> Virginie Despentes, *King Kong Theory*, 2006

When I was in the Slits I met numerous managers, writers, performers and promoters who were involved in the marketing of those heartbreaking love songs, and they were shocked when

225

I asked them if they believed in the ideology they were peddling. They didn't. I still ask men who were young boys or teenagers at the time if they believed the lyrics to those songs. Most of them admit they didn't even listen to the words, and the few who did didn't fall for them. The songs weren't aimed at them. As I spent more time in the 'music business' I discovered that most of the musicians I admired when I was young were misogynists, a few even paedophiles. Almost none of them were the sensitive, vulnerable lovers and respecters of women and girls they portrayed in their songs.

Until I read my parents' diaries I couldn't understand why I bought into the whole love and romance myth so wholeheartedly. I managed to fight off the dogmas of patriarchy, organised religion, capitalism, class deference and respect for authority easily enough. How come I fell at the last fence and impaled myself on the railings of romance?

During my childhood and teenage years everyone and everything I knew was at war. My mother and father were at war; my sister and I were at war; I was at war with my atypical nature, desperately trying to fit in and be normal; even my genes were at war – the cool Swiss-German side versus the hotheaded Corsican. And warring away in the middle of all these wars was me, the believer in love songs, versus Mum, the love-and-romance-crusher. I was stressed, vulnerable and desperate for an escape from my everyday life. 'Easy meat' for grooming. I constantly fantasised about being rescued from my life by a handsome, sensitive boy, someone like Scott Walker (who is probably one of the few musicians who did live what they sang). I don't know where my upbringing would sit on a scale of dysfunctional family situations – fairly low, I should think – but even if it was slight in the eyes of an expert, I was traumatised and grew twisted because of it. My response to the tensions inside our home and the unfairness outside it was to fill my mind with the kind of music that whipped up dreams of romance. I needed something nice to think about, *all the time.* It didn't help that I wasn't being told any stories to counteract my fantasies, that I had no alternative visions or role models, no rebellious, artistic or guitar-playing working-class women to follow. Mum alerted me to the fact that patriarchy and the romance narrative were wrong, but she didn't have any suggestions for another path. She didn't know of any.

Where's the advert on TV telling you to call a freefone number if you've been mis-sold, not a pension, but a belief system? My religion turned out to be bogus. I'm still unpicking those decades of conditioning that were stitched, or rather, sung into my brain.

Kathleen   Already I notice Lucien gets moody when Viviane raves over the pop stars she likes and I can foresee what will happen when the time for boyfriends starts. I can't let her go through all I have been through with his jealous rages.

And he will keep going into the bathroom when she is bathing, she doesn't like it a bit now that she has a chest and puberty hair. He won't let her lock the bathroom door. I started putting both the children together in the bath to help her as she is too afraid to speak up. I cannot say anything unless it is too bad because of the scenes. This weekend [*March 1965 – I was eleven*] when he rushed in, she asked him, 'Please don't keep coming in, it embarrasses me.' He became angry and shouted at her.

Mum told me to say those words. Our bathroom was big
and cold, and surrounding the tub were dark-green tiles
with shimmering oil-spill rainbows reflected in the crackled
glaze. They were ugly and I'd spend most of my time in the
bath redecorating the room in my head. I thought Mum was
imagining things or stirring up friction between me and Lucien
when she said he shouldn't keep coming into the bathroom. *She's
just trying to put him down, place him in the wrong as usual.* I
didn't mind him coming in that much, he was just Dad. But after
she mentioned it I became more aware of his presence, and one
day I locked the bathroom door while I took a bath. He banged on
it and shouted at me, demanding I get out of the bath and let him
in. The more he insisted, the more suspicious I got. I never left
the door unlocked again.

Kathleen   Once I couldn't understand why Viviane's new birthday
            skirt was torn and when I asked her, I found out that it
            was Lucien's practice if the children took too long to take
            off their clothes for bed, to tear their clothes off himself,
            bend them over the bed and hit them. I was angry. I went
            straight to him and told him he mustn't do that, that it
            was too humiliating. He went to strike me but I threatened
            him with the police if he touched me. He said he wouldn't
            foul his hands on me.

I remember this too. Mum asked me what had happened to my
new skirt. She was surprised it was torn because I was very
careful with my clothes. I told her that Dad had torn it when he
pulled it off me. She asked why he was pulling my skirt off. I said
because I was too slow getting undressed for bed, and added that

he often pulled my clothes off and told me to lie on the bed so he could hit me. I knew he was being horrible, but I thought that was what all fathers did – tear off your clothes, put you over the bed and smack you – to children who were too slow getting ready for bed.

After Mum found out that Lucien was secretly divorcing her she moved a single bed into the corner of my bedroom and slept in there with me. My sister had her own room and there was another spare room in the house that Mum could have slept in, but she chose to put her bed in my room. 'It's still your room,' she said. 'I won't make any noise or bring my things in, I'll just slip in at night and go to bed.' But I heard her and saw her sneak in every night and it irritated me. I'd lie in the dark pretending to be asleep, appalled and transfixed by her silhouette wriggling into a nightdress and disappearing under the blankets. I hated her sleeping there and hated myself for seeing her as a trespasser. I thought she was weak (weren't we supposed not to be weak?) for needing me, that she was doing it because she was lonely. I wanted the room to myself, with my posters and my things; she spoiled my domain by being there. A group of friends visited me one Saturday morning, and when they pointed at the extra bed and asked, 'Whose bed is that?' I answered, 'Mum's.' I could tell from their shocked expressions that I'd said something wrong. As they prowled around my room, examining my trinkets on the mantelpiece, picking things up, turning them over and putting them down again, I felt invaded, as if they were lifting up flaps of my skin and peering into my body. I screamed at them all to go home, but as soon as they left I felt stupid. I didn't know why I'd done it.

Kathleen	His interest in Viviane is different from his attitude to Pascale and I am not always in agreement. When I moved out of our bedroom he started taking Viviane into bed with him all night – he only has a single bed. After three nights I stopped it by telling Viviane she doesn't get her proper rest, that it wasn't right. I said it in front of him and in such a serious tone that he knew it was for a different reason.

The first night my parents gave up sharing a bedroom Lucien asked me to sleep in his bed – he said he was cold or lonely or something, with a sad puppy-dog look. He didn't abuse me during those three nights but I was uncomfortable and didn't know how to stop the situation without upsetting him. If my father and I had continued sleeping in the same bed, who knows what might have happened – he wasn't the best of men. I was relieved when Mum said it had to stop. I didn't know until she intervened how awkward I felt about it. It's often not until after a decision is made that you know whether you've made the right choice. The relief tells you.

Now I realise Mum moved into my bedroom not because she was weak or lonely, but to protect me from sexual abuse. It's so obvious fifty years later. You think you know it all when you're a child.

47 Mia left Vida and me alone in the room. She must have trusted that nothing more could go wrong. We held Mum's hands and talked to her in low voices, recalling the fun times we'd had together: the field of daffodils in Regent's

Park on Mother's Day; our trip to the South of France two years ago and the terrace she smoked on at night, me tipping her up in the wheelchair as we raced around the boulevards. She smiled and laughed. It wasn't really a laugh, more of a phlegmy chortle. We sat beside her for hours. Sometimes Vida and I reminisced quietly between ourselves so Mum could listen and not have to respond. Vida thanked her grandma for believing in her and said she loved her. Then two nurses hustled in to change the blood-spattered bedding. They didn't smile or look at me. The edges of their mouths were pulled down and their eyebrows drawn together. They must've heard what had happened and disapproved. I didn't care; they didn't know the whole story. Vida and I sat on the floor outside in the corridor while they worked, leaning our backs against the wall. We consoled each other by saying that Mum was looking better, the blue had gone from her face and she couldn't be too ill if she could still laugh. 'You've said everything you needed to say, that's important,' I said. Vida was almost happy. There was no tension in her body any more, her face was relaxed, and I thought, *Maybe I was right to fight.*

Guilt Trip

I finished emptying Mum's flat in a stunned, robotic daze. It took months for me to be able to think about her diary without feeling sick, but gradually I began to assimilate the information and make some sense of the way she had behaved throughout her life.

When I was going through my own divorce I couldn't spend as much time with Vida as I used to. I had to get myself into a position where I could earn money to support us (having not worked for nine years) and sort out a home and a school in a new city. I hated not being with her all the time but it was more important that I secure our future. I got through those times by telling myself over and over again that I'd make it up to her and soon we'd be together all the time like we were before. While things were terrible with Lucien and she was trying to get us out, no doubt Mum was also thinking, *I'll make it up to them. I just have to get us out of this situation, then it'll all be OK again.* I think the reason she went so far with the aggression was to try and look powerful and claw back control from a man she'd been dominated by for nineteen years. She also may not have understood the lasting emotional impact of her behaviour on us. Or maybe she loved us very much and feared we'd end up with our cruel, abusive father if she didn't fight dirty, so the risks to our mental health were worth taking. Or perhaps she was just spiteful and deranged. I don't know, but I don't think so, she wasn't cruel when it was all over. I do know she'd been hit or bullied by the only two men she'd been emotionally involved with, men who were less intelligent than her but who talked down to her, double-crossed her and dominated her. As Virginia Woolf observed in *Mrs Dalloway* (1925), despite possessing 'twice his wits, she had to see things through his eyes – one of the tragedies of married life'.

The thing is, I didn't think much of my father. I'd never have chosen to live with him, so was there really any need for Mum's brainwashing and manipulation? She thought so. Not only had she been stung once before, she knew that children can be coerced by suggestions and sad expressions from adults – my father had already got me into his bed with this method. And it was possible the judge in the divorce case might have tried to influence us into changing our minds. He might have favoured Lucien; they were patriarchal times. No: to be certain of the outcome, Mum believed she had to make us hate our father – it's not like she was making us hate a nice, kind man – and instruct us on how to behave at the hearing, otherwise she risked losing us to a violent and potentially sexually abusive man. (When the divorce was eventually heard, Lucien behaved so unpredictably and with such belligerence throughout the proceedings that he was discredited. His counsel dropped him and he had to represent himself.)

As soon as my father left home the whole atmosphere changed. Mum spoiled us, not with money and presents – we were too poor for that – but with her time and attention. I'm ashamed to say I sensed her guilt and exploited it, took everything she offered and asked her to do even more. I presumed she was feeling guilty about the divorce. Not many people I knew had divorced parents (I was the only child in junior and secondary school who could wire a plug and change a fuse), but now I think she felt guilty about her behaviour during those years.

48 At four in the morning Vida's eyes kept closing, so I made her a bed on the floor by pushing three cushions together and covering her with coats. While we were bustling around I switched the TV on and turned the sound down low so that Mum would know we were still there. Vida and I had quite

an animated discussion, conducted in hissing whispers, about which channel Mum would prefer. I can't remember what we settled on. After tucking Vida in I dragged my chair over to sit by Mum's bed again. Funny how you know it when you see it. She was in exactly the same position as a moment before, mouth open, eyes closed, arms by her side. It's the stillness that tells you.

Broken Baubles

When Vida was nine years old I told her that Mummy and Daddy were going to divorce. We were on our way to buy a Christmas tree at the time. I'd planned to tell her after Christmas but she asked me point blank as we were walking, hand in hand, to the garden centre. She looked up at me and said, 'Are you and Daddy going to divorce?' I only had a second to decide whether to lie and stick to the plan, or risk spoiling her Christmas and tell the truth. I thought, *If I lie now, at such a crucial time, a time she will think back on and remember all her life, she will never trust me again*, so I said, 'Yes, we are.' After I'd explained as gently and simply as possible why we were separating, Vida thought for a moment and said, 'Can you please not say "Your mother" or "Your father" when you talk about each other?' I promised her I wouldn't, and I never have (not as easy as I thought). She didn't cry, make a fuss or ask for anything apart from that one thing. I understood what she meant when she asked me to be mindful of how I spoke to her about her dad. Every time Mum put Lucien down I'd think, *Half my genes are his. You're putting half of me down too.*

The first Christmas after Mum died I was reluctant to buy a real tree – I didn't want the nuisance of pine needles all over the floor for months afterwards – so I asked Vida whether she minded if we got a fake tree that year. Mum always bought a real Christmas tree when we were young and tried to make Christmas enjoyable for us by saving all year with the Co-op. Lots of poor people did that in the 1960s. You'd start buying pale-blue Co-op savings stamps in January, stick them in a little booklet every week and by December every page had morphed from white to blue. Then you'd go with the full book of stamps to the shop, and in return they'd give you a Christmas hamper with a packet of loose tea, chocolate biscuits, fresh dates, a bottle of R. White's lemonade and a round fruit cake with a layer of thick yellow marzipan on top (no icing, the only part I liked). All this came in a cardboard box with wood shavings and shredded paper tucked around the cartons and jars. Mum iced the cake herself and stuck two chipped plaster robins, two fawns, a

Christmas tree with hard white blobs on its green bristles and a Santa on top.

The Christmas after losing her grandmother Vida very much wanted a real tree, so in the end I agreed to get one. We put old gloves on and carried it home together. I grumbled a bit because I took most of the weight. I'm glad I gave in about the tree because lots of little things I did wrong when Vida was young still haunt me. I wish I hadn't shouted at her when she sneezed all over the (just unwrapped) chocolate log one Christmas – she was only seven. And why not let her wear a mermaid dress on her fifth birthday – so what if the theme was fairies? I also regret insisting she do her homework every night when she was in junior school and crying with tiredness. That's the sort of regret I have. Then there's the bigger stuff, like her seeing me lying on the floor, sobbing and banging my fists after a water pipe broke, flooded the ground floor and ruined my archive of photos and music memorabilia. Mum's archive was so different to mine: labels from practical school uniform – Clarks shoes, Viyella tunics and Lyle and Scott and Dannimac raincoats; receipts for ballet lessons, sewing machine parts, aluminium pots and pans and a Morphy Richards iron – everything bought for her children or because it was functional and long-lasting.

Once Vida witnessed me throw a chair (Ercol) across the room in a temper about I-can't-remember-what a couple of weeks after Mum died. It broke. I can still hear her shouting, 'Mummy! Mummy!' in a terrified voice. I've sworn at her a couple of times too and I shouted at her for getting her hair cut too short when she was sixteen. Every time I've been angry with Vida I've actually been upset about something else, nothing to do with her at all. Especially with the haircut. I'd just looked in a

well-lit mirror at the hairdresser's and seen my neck.

On our first Christmas without Mum, Vida and I decorated the reluctantly bought tree lavishly, smothering it in pink, purple, green, silver and red balls, candy canes, robins and icicles. After she went to bed I sat on the sofa and stared at it, mesmerised by the flickering lights. I was still gazing at the tree in a hypnotic trance an hour later when it pitched forward off its little table and landed face down on the floor. A whooshing sound accompanied its descent, followed by the delicate tinkling of breaking glass. It looked like every ornament was broken. I wondered if Mum was sending me a sign. *I've only been dead six months and you can't do anything right without me.* They weren't expensive ornaments, but a lot of them were Mum's and I'd seen them every year since I could remember. She used to wrap all the decorations in tissue paper and pack them in a battered biscuit tin which had a printed background of fake brown hessian embroidered with cross-stitched sayings like 'Be to her virtues very kind, be to her faults a little blind' and 'I oft have heard defended, least said is soonest mended'. Years of memories were attached to those glass shards.

Distressed by the sight of the tree prostrate at my feet, I was tempted for a second to run into Vida's bedroom, wake her up and tell her what had happened. Now Mum was dead I had nobody to tell my troubles to. I remembered just in time that I was in charge and Vida was a child and stopped myself. *You're on your own now. Just sort it out.* I heaved the whole thing back onto the table. Some of the balls were still attached to the branches but they were sharp and jagged, lethal, not cheerful. I swept up the debris, unhooked the ornaments and chucked everything into the bin. We went out the next day and bought new decorations. What a relief it was not to make a fuss, to just start again. *Remember the year the tree did a face plant? Haha. And we went to buy new decorations but the shops had sold out of almost everything, and that nice girl in Paperchase at Westfield went into the storeroom and pulled out all the stuff they'd put away for the sales when she heard our tale of woe? That's where these sparkly little robots came from, and the pink and green frosted pine cones.*

49 No scrabbling for air, no gasping for breath. No warning that she was going to die, like the medic said there would be. I was upset that I'd missed the moment. I wanted to be holding her hand when she went. (Although I've heard that it's quite common for people to slip away while nobody's looking.) 'She's gone,' I said to Vida. It was important I showed her I was OK, that a beloved grandparent's death wasn't the end of the world. So I stroked Mum's hair and told her she was beautiful. We really have to broaden our ideas about beauty. They're so narrow. My ninety-five-year-old mother *was* beautiful. 'You're so beautiful, Mum,' I said again. How can someone who's stood by you your whole life – who helped you empty the contents of the kitchen bin onto the floor when you were seventeen because you accidentally threw away a piece of hash the size of a cocoa nib, or who accompanied you, when she was eighty years old, to the Southbank Cinema on Mother's Day to watch hardcore gay and lesbian sex films because no one else would go with you (ditto a Sparks concert at the Royal Festival Hall) – how can that person, who you've been through so much with and who is now lying in front of you with snow-white hair, pale-grey eyes, soft pink skin and worry lines, not be beautiful?

Imperfect, Tense

Two days after Mum died I was invited to the George Tavern in Hackney for a wedding celebration. Vida wanted us to go. I wouldn't have bothered but I wanted to appear strong, so I said yes. Pushing the swing door open and stepping into the room I was overwhelmed. *Too many people.* I didn't know if I'd be able to cope. We headed towards the bar. I tried to relax but my legs stiffened and I stalked across the floor like a wind-up doll. It was an easy enough room to be in – distressed plaster walls, bare floorboards, scrubbed wooden tables, wild flowers in glass jam jars – but I felt as if I was swimming my first length at school and might not make it to the other end. When we reached the bar I grabbed hold of it, twisted round and looked around the room. Eryk was lounging on a banquette in the corner, long thin legs kicked out in front of him, arm stretched along the back of the seat, shaved head, high cheekbones, serious expression.

Adrenalin flushed through me, my head grew hot, I started shaking. I hadn't seen Eryk for a year, not since I'd thrown beer and vodka over him and run off down the tunnel.

Until I was about fifty, nothing agitated me as much as really liking a man. But it wasn't about the man. It's not that I thought, *Here is such a special and extraordinary person that I'm quivering with admiration.* I've met enough men, through school, art school, film, television, the music industry, writers, actors, lawyers, plumbers, builders, to know that it's not the actual man I get excited about. And I wasn't motivated by sex, so why did I get so flustered? It must have been the thought that I might have come across someone at last who would make me feel less alone. That was what made me giddy.

Vida was chatting to a friend, so I slipped into the seat opposite Eryk and smiled. He smiled back. We went outside, leaned against the windowsill and confessed we still had feelings for each other. Then we walked to the off-licence so he could buy some cigarettes. On the way to the shop he put his arm around me. I needed that arm around me so badly, it felt so good, so necessary.

Never mind that he can't talk about his feelings, doesn't contact
me regularly, is a workaholic, tells lies and wants to go to the
pub and drink all night more than he wants to see me. Right
now all that is worth it, just to walk beside him with his arm
around me. To feel connected to another human being. Was this
far-from-ideal man reappearing in my life two days after Mum's
death a way of her saying, *Here you are, Vivvy. Now that I've*
gone, you can accept the imperfect.

Eryk let me talk about emotions and feelings for quite a
while and did his best to join in, until he felt he was in danger of
getting it wrong and upsetting me, at which point he smacked his
hand to his head and said, 'I don't know! I'm no good at this. I've
been up since six this morning.' I felt sorry for him and changed
the subject to films and buildings.

Dungeness

Not long after we got back together, Eryk and I went to the
coast for the weekend. The morning after we got back from the
trip I woke up at 7.15 and made Vida breakfast – a sliced Pink
Lady apple without the skin (I know, but I couldn't be bothered
to wash it), a ginger and honey yoghurt, a vitamin pill, a fish-
oil capsule, a glass of water, scrambled eggs and baked beans
on wholemeal toast with melted grated cheddar cheese on top
– gave her £5 for her lunch, which left her with a bit to give to
the girls at school who were raising money for charity, waved
her off from the front door and went back to bed. I don't know
if I was so tired because I was depressed (don't think so), getting
old (fifty-nine), suffering from an accumulation of stress from

the last five years – divorce, packing up and selling a home, moving four times, acting in a feature film, recording an EP and an album, writing a book, raising a teenager, looking after my mother, my mother dying, travelling around Britain talking about such an intimate book – or because of what had happened with Eryk the night before.

We'd booked a hotel in Rye, East Sussex, and stopped off in Dungeness on the way there for fish and chips at the Pilot. As we sat down I remembered my friend Magnus (art GCSE, neighbour, crabs) telling me that last time he was in the Pilot he'd said the word 'rabbit' during a conversation and an elderly man had reprimanded him, 'Never say the word "rabbit" to a fisherman. It's bad luck, they won't fish that day if you say that.' Not that I intended to talk about rabbits, but you know how it is, once you've been told not to say something, it pops out of your mouth. (It didn't.) I could tell the fish was fresh by the way it flaked out of its crispy orange body bag. I don't eat batter but I ate all the chips, a huge mound of carbohydrate. I also ate all the peas and drank a glass of white wine, which didn't get me drunk even though I hardly ever drink. The alcohol must have been soaked up by all the carbs. I used to drink occasionally when I was with Eryk. It made our time together dreamlike – sometimes life needs a bit of a nudge to live up to our expectations. After lunch we walked across the beach. As we crunched over the shingle I could feel the muscles in my calves and thighs working and was glad I was fit. The first building we saw was the award-winning Black Rubber Beach House, matt and low, a stealth house, followed by two new black houses built since I had last been there. The image of the three sharp-edged black blocks set against a thick sweep of golden shingle, thin ribbon of green sea and wide band of cloudless blue sky almost hurt me. I felt a pain in my chest. The complementary colours and the proportions of the land, sea and sky stacked on top of each other were so satisfying and so unobtainable it was painful.

The two new houses were clad in narrow strips of low-grade timber battened onto a frame painted matt black, with a shadow gap between each one. Their exteriors echoed the net-drying huts that used to be dotted around the beach when this was a thriving fishing community. The windows were frameless and abutted the timber. We tramped across the shingle to have a closer look. Eryk worked out that the windows did have frames but the wood cladding was taken right up to the glass so they appeared frameless from a distance. I checked the name of the manufacturer on the doors and windows. They were made by Schuco, the same company as my sliding doors at home and most of the doors and windows of the local shops and restaurants in Hackney.

After the houses, we came across an abandoned fisherman's hut, its corrugated-iron roof draped in a tangerine and green fishing net. The net fell in delicate folds and fanned out over the

shingle like the lace train of a wedding gown, as pretty as any dress by Rodarte. As we stared, we rocked our heels up and down on the oily black sleepers of a miniature-gauge railway line that stretched down to the sea. In the past a train must have chugged backwards and forwards on the track, loaded up with fish and molluscs. On the way back to the car park I noticed Eryk was more out of breath than me. Must be all that sitting in the van.

50 Even though Mum was dead and couldn't hear me, I thought maybe she could, so I told her how wonderful all our years together had been and thanked her over and over again and said goodbye, and suggested Vida say goodbye again too. I was trying to teach Vida something about death, how to handle it – not the fighting part, that was bad, but you never know, she may have to fight for something one day that needs that level of commitment; it was more that I was trying to demonstrate how to handle my death. That was the only chance I'd ever get to show her how to carry herself when faced with the death of her mother. I wanted her to see that I wasn't going to fall apart when my mother died, and neither would she when the time came. I wanted to show her what to do, that she should talk to me, hold my hand and, when I've gone, say goodbye all over again. I wanted her to know that she was safe, I was strong and all was right with the world. Everything was in its place. We'd had our time together and now we had to let go and move on.

Nipples and Knuckles

After Dungeness Eryk and I checked into the hotel in Rye and ordered a winter Pimm's each. It was delicious, warm and musky with hints of cinnamon and cloves, but after two sips I felt sick, so Eryk finished mine. Our room had a high white ceiling with black beams, a contemporary four-poster bed and a teal-green wood-panelled bathroom which looked like the interior of a fancy beach hut. Expensive REN products were lined up along the edge of the tub. I ran a bath but accidentally made squelchy noises against the enamel as I climbed in so rubbed my butt against the sides a few more times to let Eryk know I wasn't breaking wind. I left the bathroom door ajar so I could hear the music playing from my Boom speaker.

I'd brought much more stuff with me than Eryk. He only had his laptop, a toothbrush with splayed-out bristles, a travel-sized tube of toothpaste and a spare pair of underpants with him. I bet his preparation for the trip consisted of a wash, a shave, maybe a bit of hair trimming here and there, and a coffee on the way to pick me up. My preparation, on the other hand, consisted of, first of all, timing. I made an appointment with my hairdresser to get my roots done two days before the trip, followed by a blow-dry on the morning we left. I tried to book a session with my favourite beautician, Lin, at the Vietnamese beauty salon around the corner for the day of the trip, to have the hair ripped out of every part of my body, my upper lip threaded and a pedicure (red, but not too vampiric, muted), but she was away that day, so I went in the day before. This was OK because at least the redness would've gone down by the morning, and the blobs of wax left here and there after leg-hair removal, which turn into little grey grollies in places I can't see, would have dropped off or been washed away by a couple of showers by the time Eryk and I met. The downside of not waxing the day before a date is that my hair grows so quickly I sometimes have to shave my knees beforehand (which I did – and plucked a few stray hairs from the backs of my fingers). Then I packed: a portable speaker and two leads so we'd have music in the hotel room and the atmosphere would be less awkward if we got physical; *SCUM Manifesto* by Valerie Solanas for us to read out loud to each other because it's true and funny and I thought Eryk was secure enough to get it – it would at least be a topic of conversation; a spare pair of jeans, a black rain jacket and two tops (a black crepe shirt with see-through chiffon sleeves and my old staple, a 1990s Gucci seventies-inspired shirt, so I had a choice of what to wear for dinner). I wore block-heeled ankle boots from Acne for the journey and nicked my daughter's dark-red New Balance trainers for walking in Dungeness. My make-up bag bulged with mascara, mushroom-coloured eye shadow (Estée Lauder, a freebie from Selfridges when I bought cleanser), eye-shadow brush, lipstick (Charlotte Tilbury, 'Walk of Shame'), eyebrow powder (Guerlain) and brush, black kohl pencil (Mac), BB cream with SPF 30 (YSL, it's brilliant), loose Chanel face powder, deodorant, hand cream, toothbrush, toothpaste (Janina, full-sized tube), pills (HRT and Thyroxene), magnifying mirror and dental tape. My bag weighed a ton. I arrived at our meeting point waxed, plucked, painted, blow-dried (but still looking natural due to all the money I'd spent and skill, and also that's what men think natural looks like) and sweating from carrying my bag. I also had a shoulder purse with glasses, sunglasses, packet of tissues, hand wipes, butt wipes, lip pencil, eye pencil, hand mirror, phone, debit card, loose change, lip salve, hand cream, pen, travel pass, keys, asthma inhaler and Tic Tacs.

Are you still with me? I'm barely with myself.

I don't know how I can still think of myself as a rebel after doing all that for a date, but I do. I also tried to look conventionally attractive when I was in the Slits, but kicked against it at the same time. It's a painful position to be in, having a side, but being inexorably drawn to the other side too. The Slits' singer, Ari, had a more extreme personality than me. She wasn't torn by sides, she knew who she was and suffered much abuse for being so unapologetically herself. Girls like Ari are precious and rare. They stand out for going against the norm and take a lot of flack for refusing to conform to female stereotypes.

After the bath I put on my new underwired, black net bra and looked in the mirror. My nipples, squashed flat and poked sideways by the tight mesh, made my breasts look like two milky jellyfish trawled up from Dungeness beach. The bra was a designer brand, Myla or Agent Provocateur (can't remember now, never wore it again, chucked it). I had also bought matching mesh knickers but took them back to the shop because I thought wearing the whole outfit implied I was expecting a raunchy performance from Eryk, which would be daunting for him. I'm not up to giving the performance such attire requires myself. I wore a pair of plain black pants from Gap instead. All this effort and preparation was an attempt to boost my confidence and to attract the listless Eryk.

I jumped into bed first. On top of the net bra and Gap pants I wore a loose, worn-out grey T-shirt, and on top of that the hotel's white waffle robe tied at the waist. I was trying to untangle the belt of the robe, which was caught under my back, when Eryk joined me. He was also wearing a hotel robe but underneath he had a bath towel wrapped tightly around his nether regions. Eryk stroked and touched me. He knew I like being fingered so he did that too. As I got worked up, I tugged at what I thought was a thick blanket caught between us, but Eryk stopped me with his hand. I mentally came back into the room and looked down to see that it wasn't a blanket but the bath towel wrapped around his groin that I was pulling. (Both our robes and my T-shirt were off – my net bra got no comment, which made me feel foolish.)

'Is this staying on?' I asked, gesturing at the towel, trying to keep a note of impatience out of my voice.

'Yes,' he said.

'Can you put your pants on instead? It's so thick,' I suggested.

He swung into a sitting position on the edge of the bed and slipped his pants on, shielding himself with the towel like he was changing in front of the hordes on Brighton beach. We started again. Eryk's moves felt a little workmanlike and I wondered if he was getting the physical bit out of the way as fast as possible so he could relax and get on with the rest of the evening (alcohol, sleep). This upset me and I decided to talk to him about it later. I'd rather we didn't do anything physical than have him clinically try to finish me off – not that I orgasm, but he probably thought I did. Same as the last time we were dating each other, we didn't have penetrative or oral sex. I was intrigued by Eryk's behaviour. I enjoy a chase and need some mental stimulation to get me going – even frustration will do. His Dance of the Seven Veils thing was a good match for my sexual foibles. I'm happy to experiment with different ways of communicating affection and sexual desire.

We rolled around together and after a few short bursts of intense kissing, scratching and tweaking we were both out of breath, so we dozed for half an hour, then went down to the bar. I had a peppermint tea and an aubergine fritter, and Eryk had two whisky macs. We were back upstairs and in bed at 11 p.m., and there was no more touching. I didn't initiate it in case he thought I was hassling him. I tried to sleep but felt bloated from all the chips I'd eaten earlier.

Barbara Fartland*

Eryk was soon asleep. I, on the other hand, knew I could not – and must not – sleep. I must not sleep because I must not fart. I didn't know Eryk well enough to fart. I lay in bed, eyes open, butthole clenched tight all night long, drifting off for a second only to be awoken by a little squeak. *Please don't let him be awake*, I begged the ceiling. By the time morning crept round the edge of the curtains I was tetchy from lack of sleep, exhausted from butthole clenching and knew for certain I couldn't be bothered to be with a man ever again. (I once met a woman in California who said she'd given up chocolate because it gave her wind . . . Californians, eh?) I decided to end it there and then by picking a fight, but Eryk didn't take the bait, so I stopped, paid for the hotel because I'd told him the weekend was my treat and we left. I felt like a useless hooker or john. I was too befuddled to work out which.

* Chapter title thought up by my friend Trace

We arrived back in London three hours later. Eryk deposited me at Victoria Station and drove off to work. I lugged my bags down the escalator, onto the train, changed from the underground onto the overground at Highbury and Islington, caught the train to Hackney Central, then the 55 bus to the end of my road. By the time I reached my front door I was on the verge of weeping. I had half an hour to lie on my bed and stare at the wall with grit-dry, red, murderous eyes, before driving across town and picking my daughter up from school with all her end-of-term paraphernalia.

Not one man I know, have known or have dated in the last forty-five years has ever, or would ever, put the amount of effort into himself that I put into that date – just to feel comfortable. And I know for certain that if men lived in a society that expected them to put that amount of work into a date, they wouldn't bother dating. And now I feel the same. Can't be arsed.

51

I kissed Mum's forehead. Her skin was cool and I noticed she didn't have any wrinkles. Ninety-five and no wrinkles. She only ever had a few and they seemed to have lifted off her face. 'It's not fair, Mum, you don't have any wrinkles,' I whispered into her ear. She would have laughed at that. I don't know if she heard me. It doesn't matter, Vida did.

I wasn't sure what to do next. Let someone know Mum had died or sit with her for a while longer? I wanted to sit with her but was worried that after the way I'd behaved they'd think I'd murdered her if I didn't tell them straight away. My next dilemma was whether to go and find the nurse myself or send Vida to get her. I pictured Vida alone in the yellow room with her dead grandmother while I fetched a nurse and thought, *No, that would be too awful for her.* Then I pictured Vida running down corridors she didn't know very well to deliver the message of her grandmother's death to a stranger and thought, *No, that will be too much for her.* In the end I told her to keep Grandma company, I'd be back in a minute, and walked to the door. The second I was out of sight I ran. It didn't occur to me until two years later that we both could have gone to find the nurse. Leaving Mum alone when she'd just died didn't feel like an option at the time.

Mia was at her work station. 'I think she's gone,' I said. She plucked two clear rubber surgical gloves out of a cardboard box. I didn't wait for her. I ran back to Vida.

Spartacus

I love being single. It's almost like being rich.
Sue Grafton, *D Is for Deadbeat*, 1987

I let go of Eryk, even though it's rare for me to come across a man I can stand being in a room with for a long time. I don't mean a man I can work alongside – that's occasionally possible – but one I can be with all weekend, night-times too. I persevered with him for over a year but the more I saw of him, the more I realised that his persistent unreliability made a relationship untenable. I also noticed he was skipping meals so he could drink more alcohol without putting on weight – he was consuming between ten and twenty-five units when we were out, even if we were just watching a play. And he never did reveal what was in his pants. The trouble is, if you're heterosexual and there's a lack of men around, like after the war for Mum and in my fifties and sixties for me, you can kid yourself you've done well just to have found one with teeth.

I used to give a guy three dates, but now I can tell in one if there's a possibility of it going anywhere, even as a friendship. And frankly, my dear, I'd have to be a bit desperate to want to lose a big chunk of myself all over again and put up with a dominating male presence in the house. No, that's not saying it right. I *have* been desperate. I've sobbed on the sofa at night because I've been so lonely and wanted a partner so badly. More than once I've thought I would happily compromise every day for the rest of my life to make a relationship work, but a lot of the men I've dated have been incapable of even basic kindness. I can't have anyone in my life, female or male, who's unkind. I'm not mentally or emotionally robust enough for that any more. Associating with destructive people when you're lonely is tantamount to self-harm, like drinking too much alcohol or injecting drugs. Just because it's people that are inflicting the harm doesn't make it any less dangerous. I'm out. Safer on my own.

I'll be the girl and the boy, the mummy and the daddy from now on. It's me who fixes the roof, unblocks the drain and changes the plug. *I'm* Spartacus.

52 Mia lifted Mum's arm, checked her pulse and said, 'Yes, she's just gone.' She must have been able to tell from the temperature of Mum's skin. I was terrified that she'd just let go of Mum's arm and let it flop back down onto the bed, but to my relief she didn't, she placed it carefully by Mum's side.

Two men from the funeral home appeared and asked me what clothes I'd like to dress my mother in. I chose a pale-blue linen blouse, a new chunky-knit speckled blue, black and white cardigan from Marks and Spencer, smart black trousers and black socks. I knew from doing the same for my father that they don't use shoes. Then a doctor arrived and told me I had to sign the death certificate. Vida and I left Mum to be dressed and wandered off with him to find an office. I didn't dare ask for a bit more time with Mum, or whether we'd be allowed back to see her again, because of what had happened. I wanted everyone to think I was a reasonable person. I would've liked to sit with her for a while longer and let it sink in that she'd gone. I regret that I didn't ask to do that.

Legacy

I didn't see my sister again. I went round to Mum's to clear the flat two days after she died and Pascale had packed up and gone. After I'd sorted out the accounts, which took months, we were left with four hundred quid each. A year later I discovered £12,000 worth of shares among Mum's papers. She'd been squirrelling away one or two shares a month since the 1970s. I sent Pascale's half to Canada and spent my half on a new tooth and patching up my roof. Toof and rooth. Mum would have loved to have seen my face when I found the shares. She liked surprising people and upturning their expectations of her. My inheritance can't be measured in cash though. Mum's most valuable bequest was all those years of unerring faith in me. She taught me survival skills. Not how to whittle a stick, make a shelter in the woods, catch and skin a rabbit or spear a fish. Not to run like the wind or outwit a spy. Not even to cook, clean or love. But somehow, without me noticing it happening, I became someone who after every failure, rejection and mistake can pick myself up, dust myself off and start all over again. That life skill, the first one you need, came from my mother. So thanks to her, despite the rest of my upbringing and my awkward personality, I've survived. It's true I'm not very charming – unless I want something, but often not even then – and don't fit into society particularly well, and if a man tries to lord it over me or take advantage in any way, I explode. But Mum made sure that my sister and I were solvent, had a home and made it into middle age before she went.

It's true what Gloria Steinem said of herself and many women of my generation – that we lived our mothers' unlived lives, but for me that turned out to be a good thing. My mother's unlived life consisted of not being in a band, not buying her own home, not being a filmmaker or an author, not experimenting with clothes or living life the way she wanted to. My daughter has a much less exciting time ahead of her if she chooses to live my unlived life. All she'll have to look forward to is doing her homework, revising, passing exams, not smoking, staying in, saving money and preparing for her future. On the plus side there's being well educated, retaining most of her brain cells, gender fluidity and skiing.

In Bed*

I am in bed until.

Mary Robison, *Why Did I Ever*, 2001

I made one grave error when I moved to my new home: I paid
a lot of money for a bed. It's the best piece of furniture in the
house and I spend too much time in it. I even talk to it: 'See you
later,' I say, and pat it as I leave my bedroom. I smile when I see
it again at the end of the day. As a child I was always drawing
pictures of beds: flying four-posters, beds on wheels with engines,
beds you could live in and eat in and go to school in. Whole
worlds in beds, beds you never had to leave. I'd rather lie in my
bed and stare at the wall than go to a party.

My bed was handmade at SCP. It has a grey padded-wool
headboard and stubby stainless-steel poles for legs. I'm not quite
an objectophile, although I do share some traits with people who
prefer objects over humans (quite common in people who've
had some level of childhood trauma†). I'm not an objectum
sexual either (a person who fancies objects and buildings instead
of other people). I don't have sexual feelings for my bed, but
I do feel affection for it. It asks for nothing, never judges, just
holds me and is comforting through the good times and the bad.
Sometimes my bladder is the only reason I get up. Not even
hunger can shift me – the only time I can stand to be hungry
is when I'm in bed. I've discovered that if I lie still and count to

---

* Joan Didion, 'In Bed', essay in *The White Album*, 1979
† See Amy Marsh, 'Love Among the Objectum Sexuals', *Electronic Journal of Human
Sexuality* 13, 1 March 2010

about ninety, the hunger pangs go away. They're like heartbreak: you just have to acknowledge the pain and wait until it passes. One day even my bladder won't be enough to shift me. I'll just lie there in a pool of piss and waste away.

I can easily sleep for eleven or twelve hours at a time. It's not my thyroid or an iron deficiency. I've had them checked. I told my doctor how much I slept, but she wasn't interested, just said, 'Lucky you,' through gritted teeth.

I keep the Roberts radio Mum gave me wedged against the headboard. On a good night I'll fall asleep before the shipping forecast.

When I wake up I stare at the white wall and the clothes rail at the end of my bed and marvel that I have a home after all the years I've spent wangling and ducking and diving. I can't believe I've managed to pull it off, that I have a safe place for my daughter and me to come back to, and that I'm managing to pay the bills. (I do have scary periods when there's nothing in the bank and no sign of any money coming in, but so far I've managed to weather them all.) For twenty years I've had a recurring dream that I've lost my home due to carelessness or stupidity and I awake with the same dreadful feeling I used to get the morning after I'd been dumped. A sickening, slow panic seeps up from my stomach to my chest and spreads across my body like blood through a bandage. I don't get that feeling any more after I've been dumped. I feel fury for three days, hurt for two, disappointment for a week and then I'm over it. Lovely being older.

Brian Wilson went to bed for three years. Jean-Michel Basquiat would spend all day in bed. Monica Ali, Charles Bukowski, Marcel Proust, Elizabeth Barrett Browning, Tracey

Emin, Emily Dickinson, Edith Sitwell, Frida Kahlo, William Wordsworth, René Descartes, Mark Twain, Henri Matisse, Kathy Acker, Derek Jarman and Patti Smith all worked or work from bed and they're productive people. (Am I protesting too much?) Humans take to their beds for all sorts of reasons: because they're overwhelmed by life, need to rest, think, recover from illness and trauma, because they're cold, lonely, scared, depressed – sometimes I lie in bed for weeks with a puddle of depression in my sternum – to work, even to protest (Emily Dickinson, John and Yoko). Polar bears spend six months of the year sleeping, dormice too. Half their lives are spent asleep, no one calls them lazy. There's a region in the South of France, near the Alps, where whole villages used to sleep through the seven months of winter – I might be descended from them. And in 1900, it was recorded that peasants from Pskov in northwest Russia would fall into a deep winter sleep called *lotska* for half the year: 'for six whole months out of the twelve to be in the state of Nirvana longed for by Eastern sages, free from the stress of life, from the need to labour, from the multitudinous burdens, anxieties, and vexations of existence'.*

Even when I'm well I like to lie in bed and think. It's as if I haven't heard my thoughts for years and am getting to know them all over again. I let my mind drift where it wants to go – religion, food, teenagers, any old thing – and see what I come up with. During the day I crave silence. I enjoy outside noise – children playing, the train going over the bridge, sirens, shouts from the street – but I don't want structured sound with strict rhythms and choruses, repetitive lyrics, familiar chords and

* 'Human Hibernation', *British Medical Journal*, 2000; 320:1245

rhymes cluttering up my brain. I want to experience the aural world directly now, not block it out.

The longest I ever spent in bed was following a stint working as a runner on films, straight after graduating from film school. I was thirty-three years old and sleeping on floors seven days a week so I could be on set or location by five o'clock in the morning. The lack of sleep took its toll. I went to bed after a year and a half of this, thinking, *I won't take any more work for a while and I'll get up when I'm not tired any more.* I emerged three months later. I didn't eat very much or change the sheets or my shorts the whole time, just slept and slept and slept. My shorts were so cosy and soft, but one day I noticed a thick white curd building up in the gusset and was jolted back to life. I got up, had a bath, washed the sheets and the shorts, wrote a film script and sold it for ten grand. Three months though.

53 When he saw my name on the death certificate the doctor told me he was a Slits fan. He was young and friendly and I liked that he was connected to me in a convoluted way. After we'd chatted for a while he asked for my autograph on a scrap of paper. I showed him my thumb and described the scene with my sister. He was very understanding, which made it all seem less grotesque. He also told me to go to A & E, said the same as Mia, that a human bite is more dangerous than an animal bite. I found that fact comforting. It made what had happened more serious somehow, bigger than just two silly sisters scrapping. I signed the papers even though I didn't know what they said. Halfway through writing my name I looked

up and saw the undertakers wheeling a trolley past the office window. It was Mum. She looked tiny. Her face was covered by a sheet. I'd always planned to look at her in the mortuary, same as I did with Lucien, but at that moment I decided not to. I knew I'd never see her again, that my last memory of her would be no wrinkles, peaceful, beautiful, the tickle on my hand, the three of us together. I looked away so as not to alert Vida to Mum's passage, but she sensed it and turned her head. The lift doors opened, the men trundled Mum in, Vida's face crumpled, the lift doors closed. You can't protect them from everything.

Meadow

It's all I have to bring to-day,
This, and my heart beside,
This, and my heart, and all the fields,
And all the meadows wide.

Emily Dickinson, 'It's All I Have to Bring To-day',
c.1858

Whenever I need to clear my head I turn left out of my house and walk up to London Fields. Everyone in London Fields dresses in muted colours. Male and female are almost indistinguishable, no girls or women wear heels. When I reach the middle of the Fields I stop, tilt my head back and look up at the sky and imagine I'm standing at the bottom of the sea or a massive fish tank: the grass is the seaweed, the trees are coral and the sky is the surface of the water.

I like to pick up fallen branches from the horse chestnut trees. Little things make me feel good since Mum's death, like finding a branch on the ground with the leaves still attached. I found a brown and gold leather headband on the grass once, and a Mac lipstick. I've learned to recognise the song of the blackbird, thrush, crow, magpie, starling and, best of all, parakeet from running round the fields (it's one mile all the way round; I do two). There are three acid-green long-tailed parakeets nesting in the trees. I recognise their cry immediately, like a bad-tempered child stamping on a squeaky bath toy. In autumn I take a plastic bag and pick up conkers. Mum told me that storing conkers in your drawers – not your underwear – keeps moths away. I like that I know a bit of folklore, old-fashioned stuff, because she told me about it. Now I can pass those tips on to Vida.

The row of pine trees along the outside edge of London Fields reminds me of the first time I ever saw one. (I'd probably seen them before but they hadn't registered.) It was when I was eleven years old and visiting my father's relatives in the South of France for the second time, when Mum was back in London swallowing boracic acid. Growing up in Muswell Hill, near Highgate Woods – there's a mile-long muddy mound all along the edge, a 'plague pit' where the victims of the epidemic were buried – I learned to identify oak, cherry, horse chestnut, poplar, plane, copper and silver birch. Silver birch was my favourite because of the pretty bark, until I saw the French pines. They were leaning out of the fine white sand on L'Etalon beach (that's what the locals called it, because white stallions ran along the sand), in the Camargue. I couldn't imagine how a fir tree could grow through sand just a couple of metres away from the bluest, clearest salty sea. Lucien, Pascale, our uncle Jerome and I stayed on the beach all day. Uncle Jerome cooked hot-dog sausages in their brine by balancing the tin can they came in over a handmade fire. We poked holes into crusty fresh baguettes with our fingers, pushed the sausages inside, squashed the whole thing flat – you can only do this with authentic French baguettes as they are so light – and sat munching our hot dogs. Pine cones rolled down the dunes into the sea and bobbed about in the surf. Pine trees, sand, sausages and sea, they were all wonderful but they just didn't seem to go together.

On my way out of London Fields I pass the wildflower meadow sprinkled with red poppies, blue cornflowers, white clover and purple thistles. I keep my head turned to the left so I can look at it for as long as possible, even though it makes my neck ache. The scent of honey and almonds from the clover is so strong it follows you all the way to the gate. Last year there were flyers signed by the fashion designer Katharine Hamnett attached to wooden posts around the edge of the meadow explaining that the fertiliser the council used was toxic to humans and animals. I don't think the council used it again because the following summer the plants were half the height and there were lots of patches of bare earth.

Mum loved flowers but never cut in a vase. They had to be growing. She liked things to flourish in their natural habitat – flowers, animals, birds. She knew the name of every flower in Nanny's back garden – bluebell, snowdrop, snapdragon, goldenrod, hollyhock, crocus, forget-me-not, iris, laburnum, lobelia, lily of the valley, Michaelmas daisy, honeysuckle, lupin – and couldn't pass a rose hanging over the pavement without stopping and sniffing it. Wild flowers were her favourite though. We'd go to the woods or the disused train tracks in Muswell Hill most weekends when I was a child (saw a flasher a couple of times, *Just ignore him*) and pick a harebell, a wild buttercup, a sprig of cow parsley and some interesting grasses. Only one of each – she was aware it's not good to pick wild flowers. Back home we pressed the plants between two pieces of toilet paper and buried them under a pile of telephone directories. Telephone directories in the 1960s were fat and heavy, a different pastel colour for each one: A–D was pale green, E–H pale pink, and so on. They reached up as high as my knees when they were piled on top of each other. I'd forget about the pressed flowers and find them months later, perfectly preserved. Mum suggested I paste one flower onto each rough, grey, sugar-papered page in my scrapbook and write only one line of description in ink next to it, so elegant and so much wasted space. That project made a lasting impression on me. *A surface looks better with less content and lots of empty space*; it had never occurred to me before. It was a rare lesson that meant something from the world of grown-ups.

No matter how long I keep my head screwed to the left to look at the flowers when I pass the meadow, it's never long enough.

No matter how much time I had with her, how many phone calls, cups of tea and chats at the kitchen table, no matter what we did right and what we did wrong or how it ended, it wasn't enough. And if I could go back and make a choice – consciously this time – of whether to be the fettered sibling or the freewheeling independent, I'd choose to be the fettered child all over again. I'd happily live those sixty years with Mum again, and this time I'd savour every one.

And I'd be kinder.

54 We arrived back in Hackney at six o'clock in the morning. I couldn't find my keys, so we went round the back and used the spare set that I keep under a rock – a Rose de Sable made from whipped-up desert sand that we brought back from Morocco years ago. As Vida and I crossed the yard

we made footprints on the frosty paving stones. They looked like interlocking slabs of chocolate – you know, when it's gone stale and has that white powdery bloom on it. Vida kicked an abandoned yellow tennis ball. We passed four parked cars, two white, two red, before reaching the fire escape. As we climbed the stairs I collected the suspended raindrops on my fingertips by sliding my hand up the galvanised aluminium handrail. Sirens from Mare Street wailed over the roofs. No need to say a little prayer to the ambulance that morning, I knew where the two people I loved were: Mum was dead and Vida was next to me. When we reached the top of the stairs I heard chopping. The back door of the Vietnamese restaurant was open. I looked down and caught a glimpse of a white chef's hat on straight black hair.

Red-Handed

... look at me as if you had never seen a woman before
I have red, red hands and much bitterness
Judy Grahn, 'I'm Not a Girl', *Edward the Dyke and Other Poems*, 1971

I can still picture Mum's hands in perfect detail, they're much clearer to me than her face. I bet every kid can remember their mother's hands. Mum's were covered in wrinkled, translucent skin draped over snaking, raised blue veins. She had long, tapered fingers and knobbly red knuckles. Her hands were worn out from decades of washing up and peeling potatoes. She didn't have a washing machine until she was seventy and never owned a dishwasher. When we were young I'd watch her wash our clothes in a plastic bowl in the sink (sheets were washed in the bath), squeeze them through a hand-cranked mangle and hang them on the washing line in the garden to dry. We were always dropping everything at the shout of 'Rain!' and rushing out the back door to rescue knickers, vests and sheets, laughing as we pulled them roughly from the line, sending the wooden pegs flying into the mud. She used to get cross about that.

I've inherited Mum's hands. At our wedding my husband couldn't get the ring over my knuckle, he had to force it, and once on, it spun loosely on my thin, fleshless finger. Mum's fingernails were wide and only slightly curved, like spades. She didn't paint them but they were never bitten, always filed, cuticles pushed down neatly with the moons showing. Ridges ran vertically down the nail, like the effect you get on a curved wall when it's made of flat concrete posts, and white specks dotted the surface. I used to track the progress of those little white flecks, like miniature clouds, drifting from the moon at the bottom of her nail right up to the tip until finally she filed the cloud away. Mum told me the specks were a sign of calcium deficiency. I've since heard that's a fallacy; they're due to dryness. When I inspected her nails I'd wish for her to be cured of her deficiency, but there was always another cloud appearing on the horizon. That's how well I knew my mother, I knew the speed and passage of those chalky marks on her nails. She continued wearing her gold wedding band after her divorce – 'Stops people asking too many questions.' It was too tight, her flesh swelled around it like a tree trunk in the park that's grown around a railing. It looked uncomfortable. Marriage was uncomfortable for Mum. She wasn't the marrying kind.

265

Kerosene and Paraffin

Objects that remind me of my mother have become important to me lately, as if by cherishing the things she liked I'm carrying her inside me like she once carried me. And the sounds, smells and tastes she enjoyed conjure up a whole different time for me, so that I feel it's not just Mum who's died, but a whole era. Aniseed, cloves, marzipan, lavender, sugared almonds, Gorgonzola, black treacle, molasses, fruit cake, Bath buns, coffee and walnut cake, Madeira cake, Christmas pudding, rhubarb and ginger jam, gooseberries. My mother's tastes revolted me when I was young. She even ate the overripe fruit that was left over, whereas I wouldn't touch anything with a speck of brown on it. Black jelly beans, black jelly babies, black fruit gums, black fruit pastilles, blackjacks, black wine gums, Pontefract cakes, liquorice. The only sweets she liked, apart from the strong-tasting black ones, were humbugs and cough sweets. When she was a schoolgirl with unruly dark hair and grey eyes, she used to sit in the classroom sucking camphor sweets – they were cough sweets, not allowed today, too intoxicating – and drift into a soporific stupor. I thought they looked and tasted like something you'd find under a stone in the back garden. Mum also loved the smell of road tar and kerosene and paraffin. She wanted to name my sister and me Kerosene and Paraffin, because she loved the smells and the sounds of the words – *in 1954*. Those names would have suited us too. Dripping sandwiches: 'You can have brown bread with butter or white bread with dripping,' Frieda used to say to her five children. White bread was more refined and expensive, so she paired it with the cheap meat dripping. Mum loved giraffes, elephants and hippos, said she would have joined in the riots if she was strong enough and wasn't interested in royalty or the Queen. As for the Queen Mother, 'No wonder she looks good for her age, she's never had to carry four pounds of potatoes home.'

It seems perverse, spiteful even, for me to appreciate all her idiosyncrasies now she's dead, but Mum being gone has freed up so much of my time and mental space. Now I have time to stop and admire a salmon-pink rose dangling from a garden by the bus stop. I sniffed one in Hampstead the other day. The smell of my 1950s childhood shot straight up my nostrils into my brain, and I cried. I want to hear her talk about the war and her father. I keep thinking of questions to ask her about grandmother Frieda or the early 1950s, when she lived in Australia, things she would have loved to tell me when I was young but I was in too much of a rush to listen to. She used words I don't hear any more, like 'bind' (*Oh, Vivvy, you are a bind*), 'fag' (*What a fag*, meaning 'nuisance') and 'palaver'.

Jelly beans, scented lipsticks in heavy gold cases, roast chestnuts (only smelled them once a year when we went to the West End to see a film at Christmas), the plaintive howl of ships' funnels (God knows why, the only one I ever heard was on a Steve Miller Band record; perhaps it's a memory from the ship when we sailed back to England from Australia), roast potatoes (eight, please), upside-down apple cake: these sounds and smells are an incantation, the poem of my childhood. They induce a sense of longing in me far more heart-wrenching than the memory of any girlfriend I fell out with, boy I broke up with, exam I failed or job I was fired from. Events that I thought were so important at the time have disappeared from my emotional memory and seemingly insignificant objects, tastes and impressions have taken their place.

I was formed by all those years I couldn't wait to pass. Shaped by the woman I couldn't bear to lose or wait to get away from. And now I'm turning into her. I've fought it for so long but it's happening, I'm turning into my lone, outspoken mother.

55 First thing I did when we got in was boil the kettle for a cup of tea, even though I don't drink tea. I heard myself making the same noise Mum used to make, a click of the tongue and a loud out-breath, after the first sip. Even now all I need is a McVitie's milk chocolate digestive and a cup of tea and I've conjured her back to life – we're back in our steamed-up 1970s council-flat kitchen, Mum baking rock cakes, me drawing pictures at the Formica table. After the tea Vida and I went downstairs and climbed into my bed. We didn't say anything but neither of us wanted to be alone. She fell asleep immediately. I lay beside her for about half an hour, then slipped out from under the quilt and went back upstairs to the kitchen. That's where we came in, isn't it? When I was sitting at the table writing a list of things to do, scared I wasn't feeling anything about Mum's death. Wondering whether I was in shock or a psychopath.

Reboot

I've had to rebuild myself many times during my life, after numerous shocks and failures, but Mum was always by my side, helping and advising me. Now she's dead I can build myself into anyone I want, someone new, if I like. I could stop being that judgemental and unforgiving person I was when she was alive and we'd sit at the kitchen table dismissing people who weren't perfect. Now I'm solvent there's no need to try and emulate the detached male brain (as I see it) to succeed, or to act strong and untouchable all the time to please Mum. I could undo a bit of that. I could shift from being a person who trusts objects more than people, who'd rather stay single than risk being hurt, and work towards becoming a trusting and open-hearted human being. I could learn that you don't have to hate or destroy someone or something to walk away. And do I have to keep thinking all men are idiots now Mum's gone? Perhaps a man can be right. Sometimes. (Steady on, Viv, no need to throw the baby out with the bathwater.) Is it possible I could become the kind of steady, calm and non-judgemental person I've always admired, someone who enjoys the grey areas? I railed against grey and beige when I was young. Now I enjoy them, subtle, soft, gentle, clouds, rain, clay, earth, mud.

Who am I kidding? I'm going to continue being that person who finds other people a strain, is a bit of a recluse, unforgiving, reads a lot, is secretly shy, says the wrong thing at parties, sleeps too much and is mistrustful and solitary.

One of the last things Mum said to me was, 'You can *forgive* people, you know.' I knew what she meant: now that she was on her way out, I should forgive *her*. I was shocked when she said it. *That's a joke coming from you*, I thought. *You've never forgiven anyone in your life and you've taught me to be the same. Never forgive, never forget* – that was our family motto. As she mellowed, Mum grudgingly amended it to *Forgive, but never forget*. So her saying to me, 'You can forgive people' – with an irritable tone in her voice as if I was a bit stupid for not getting it – was like she'd suddenly changed her religion after ninety-five years. (She did start saying she believed in God towards the end, even though she'd always been agnostic.) I remember sitting in our doctor's surgery in the 1960s and him quietly explaining to Mum across his desk, 'Not *everyone's* out to persecute the Albertines.' That was our default stance: everyone's against us, out to use us, do us wrong, take things from us, bleed us dry, discard us and then laugh and point at us lying in the gutter. The odd thing about our paranoia is that we didn't have anything for anyone to take, no money, no home, no clothes, no toys and no contacts (all of which I still find difficult to share). All we had was our pride, our privacy and our bodies (which for most of my life I haven't minded sharing at all).

56 When Vida woke up she said she wanted to stay in bed, so I said if she was OK with being on her own for twenty minutes I'd walk to Wilton Way and buy us a cake each for breakfast. On the way to the cake shop I kept stopping to shake the wet leaves off the soles of my brown suede Whistles boots. I bought them at Sue Ryder, the charity shop in Camden Town. Camden's great for charity shops, the golden mile down

the high street from Mornington Crescent station to the public toilets on the crossroads, then turn left up Parkway to Sue Ryder to finish off. I know how to find good clothes in those places. First scan the rails for an awkward colour, anything that jumps out as being a bit ugly, like dirty mustard, salmon pink or olive green with a bit too much brown in it. A print with an unusual combination of colours – dark green and pink, bright orange and ultramarine – is also worth checking out. If the quality of the fabric is good, pull the garment out and check the label. Well-cut clothes can look misshapen on a hanger because they're cut to look good on the body. I'll buy a good piece if it fits, even if it doesn't sometimes. Even if it's not my style or has short sleeves, or I don't like the shape or the buttons. I learn to love it. I never tire of clothes I've bought that I've had to adjust to. It's the compromise, the awkward gap that has to be bridged that makes something, someone, lovable.

Unfit Mother

You don't know worry until you've had a child.
Mum

In the care home, with just a few days left to live, Mum gave me a half-hearted smile, sighed and said, 'I suppose I've *quite* enjoyed my life.' The game was up, she couldn't pretend any more. Her pale-grey eyes were heartbroken. I knew then that my storytelling and escapades were not enough to keep back the tide of guilt and pain any longer. She must have seen my face fall because she added, 'You've been a good daughter, Vivvy,' in a gentle voice and patted my hand. 'Really, Mum?' I asked, searching her face for the truth. I didn't believe her. I don't think I was a good daughter and now it's too late to be one. Right up until the end I was hopeless. Just a few weeks before she died Mum asked me to cut her fingernails, which was an honour as she hated people doing things for her. I accidentally snipped the tip of one of her fingers off. Blood gushed out. I jammed some tissues into her hand and ran off to find someone. I was still saying sorry as the nurse bandaged up her finger, but Mum just laughed and said it didn't matter. Six heart attacks, arms and legs red and black from pooled blood and bruising, cancer in one eye, emphysema, incontinence and the tip of her finger missing, never once did Mum cry out or mention pain. Old school.

Mum admitting she'd only '*quite* enjoyed' her life makes so much more sense to me now I've read her diary. It's not that Pascale and I weren't enough to make her happy, or that we were bad children, as I always suspected we were. Mum said those words, whether she knew it or not, because of events that happened before we were born, the consequences of which were too distressing for her to live peaceably alongside. If she'd been born even fifteen years later, the difficult situations she found herself in might have been redeemable or not have happened at all.

No one comes through life clean, Mum. You did your best, you hung on in there for ninety-five years and you fought when women weren't supposed to fight. If you hadn't made those mistakes with David, you wouldn't have tried so hard with us, and if you hadn't tried so hard with us, I'm not sure we would have survived.

Love

I never came across that everlasting, romantic, mythic love with a man that I read and dreamed about as a young woman. I get the same lurching thrill now when I'm about to sit down to an egg mayonnaise sandwich and a packet of plain crisps as I used to get when I fancied someone. I've had plenty of adventures – bit fed up with adventures, to be honest, knackered – and two great loves: my mother and my daughter. My mother and I knew each other for fifty-nine years, and although our relationship was volatile, complicated and sometimes painful, it survived – and anyway, isn't all love difficult? I'm proud that we adapted to each other and stuck it out. 'Did I see Grandma enough?' I asked Vida two days after Mum's death. I knew I should keep these thoughts to myself but I didn't have anyone else to ask. 'Yes,' she replied. 'You physically couldn't have seen her any more than you did.'

Vida is so emotionally intelligent and kind, I'm going to miss her so much when she leaves home. I dread it, been dreading it since she was born. I remember when she started getting too heavy for me to carry and I had to keep putting her down – like I had to keep putting Mum down in my dream. Year by year Vida has grown further away from me. First I carried her, then we held hands. At three years old she started doing half-days at nursery and I didn't see her all day like I used to and no longer knew everything about her life. Then she didn't want to hold hands any more and confided in her friends instead of me. Now I get to wave goodbye from the front door as she strides confidently out of my sight.

And sometimes I get to stand in the audience and watch her play bass with her band, just like Mum used to watch me.

57 I turned left out of Eleanor Road onto Wilton Way with
the image of a spelt and prune scone in my head. There
are a couple of shops to pass before you reach the cake shop. First
there's J. Glinert, which has shelves sparsely dotted with odd
objects that seem to have no connection to each other: a miniature
brass watering can, old-fashioned bristle shaving brushes, spirit
levels, paperweights with real dandelion clocks suspended inside
them, a little black book to stick vintage fruit stickers in. As I
walked I chanted all the fruit sticker names I could remember

from my childhood in time with my footsteps: Del Monte, Jaffa,
Outspan, Sunkist, Fyffes (which I pronounced 'Fiffees' as a child),
Cape. Del Monte, Jaffa, Outspan, Sunkist, Fyffes, Cape. Del
Monte, Jaffa, Outspan, Sunkist, Fyffes, Cape. Fruit labels were
important when I was a teenager; we boycotted the South African
ones because of apartheid. The next shop along, Momosan, is
owned by a young Japanese woman. I often catch a glimpse of
her through the open door, sweeping the floor with a broom
made from rushes bound together with red-and-white-striped

string. Her window is peppered with tiny earthenware tea pots, cups without handles and pointy grey felt slippers that look as if they're from a Brothers Grimm fairy tale. Next there's a steamed-up cafe, but I find their cakes too exotic, red fruit and whipped cream oozing out from between wedges of yellow sponge. All I wanted that morning was plain brown cake. Not even chocolate cake would do. I needed penance cake. Punishment cake. Cake for someone who'd caused a scene at her mother's deathbed.

Lonelady*

Whatever I do today has to be done right because I don't have time to do it over again.

Betty Soskin, ninety-five-year-old park ranger, Richmond, California

I've felt absolutely alone – not lonely, I feel that all the time – once before: when I had cancer and it looked like I wasn't going to make it. I feel it again now. It's not so terrible a feeling, aloneness, or it's so terrible it's mind-blowing. I've never felt so present as I do now, every second on the brink of life and death. No sense of space or scale. I picture myself as a tiny person teetering on the rim of a glass of milk. (I don't know why milk, I don't like milk – a drink from childhood, perhaps, when I felt powerless.) I could go either way: lose my footing, fall in and drown, or recover my balance and survive. I'm a cell expanding

---

* Musician Julie Campbell, lonelady.co.uk

and contracting, aware of my smallness and the hugeness of the universe at the same time. My world is without edges – and you know how I love edges and borders, frames, thick black outlines and enclosures. I have no cousins, aunts or uncles (they're either dead or Mum fell out with them, and I knew she would think I was being disloyal if I contacted them, so we've lost touch), my sister is out of my life, my niece lives in America and Vida is on her own path. I don't feel I belong to any country (I live in England but have no British blood). I don't believe in romantic love, gods, art, politics or rock and roll, and I don't understand science. I have no one and nothing to lean on.

And I think that's exciting.

I do have my dodgy health, my cobbled-together education and my imagination; those are the things I work hard to protect and turn to when I need to entertain myself or get out of a fix. I've explained to Vida that I don't want her to feel responsible for my happiness, and what a weight it was to have a mother who had no friends and no partner, staying in every night, her only social life hearing about her daughter's antics (oh dear, that does sound like me).

I don't fear being old and alone. I saw my mother do it, and she did it very well, lived to a ripe old age and enjoyed her independence. Also, there were lots of single older women around when I was growing up because I was born nine years after the end of the Second World War. I never got the sense from them that something was missing from their lives, or that they were weak or pathetic. They came across as strong and resilient, even intimidating.

If I wasn't doing well in my work I'd be considered a failure in this society because I don't have many friends and I stay home a lot. If I ever say, 'OK. Bit lonely,' when someone asks me how I am, they wince with embarrassment. I'm not looking for sympathy, I state it as a fact, the same way I'd say I've got a cold or backache. I consider my type of loneliness as on a par with those ailments – backache can be worse – and there's no reason to hide it. It's one of the consequences of the path I chose: to be creative in a society that didn't support female artists (it's still difficult). Loneliness is one of our last taboos – not many left now to have a laugh and irritate people with. I'm lonely, so what. Lonely, lonely, lonely. The more I say it the less power the word has. Although I'm not immune to the pressure to be seen to be doing things and having lots of friends. After a few quiet weeks, doubt creeps in and I think, *I should be going out or having people round. And photographing it.* Life in the 'advanced economies' is so much about acquiring and achieving, succeeding and being busy and popular, even when you're older. And then you die.

Last year I went to the crematorium where Mum's ashes are scattered and booked three lines for myself in the space after her entry in the Remembrance Book. 'Called to rest after a life well-lived' is her wording, the same as grandmother Frieda's entry. They're both on the same page. We'll all be in there together one day.

Gravestones were the Facebook profiles of the old days. Never believe what's written on a gravestone – 'Loving wife, mother and daughter'. Except maybe the dates, but even then . . .

When she was a teenager, my cousin Patricia ran off down a country lane in a strop very late one night after a family row. Mum, Pascale and I were visiting at the time and I remember all the grown-ups sitting around the kitchen table talking and worrying about what would happen to Patricia if they couldn't find her. Mostly I remember my Aunty Phyllis, Patricia's mother, saying, 'If anything happens to her, I'm going to write on her gravestone, "Here Lies a Bloody Silly *Cow*".' (I loved Aunty Phil, she was so funny.)

58 I said a little prayer as I crossed Navarino Road. The prayer wasn't for Mum, it was for the eight-foot wall on the corner, covered in burnt sienna flakes and shards of flaking duck-egg blue and vanilla paint. *Please, please let the owners never mend or repaint this beautiful wall.* (It was painted over with a murky red in 2017, but one corner remains unpainted.) Pale-green letters spelling 'Violet' on a whitewashed wall, two small round aluminium tables and a blackboard propped open on the pavement signalled that I'd arrived at my destination. The smell of cinnamon and vanilla hit me so hard when I pushed the door open that I wanted to snatch every cake I could see and stuff it into my mouth. Music was playing. I wondered who the woman singing was, the instrumentation was so simple and the voice so high and peculiar. I hadn't felt that intrigued by music for ages. I strained to catch the words. It was Neil Young, about 1970. I was disappointed in myself. The counter was piled high with pastries and cupcakes, chocolate, sea-salt and rye cookies, mini banana muffins, red velvet cupcakes with salted caramel icing. No spelt scone. I scanned the cakes again, anxiety mounting in my chest. *I must have missed the scones, I'm not looking properly, I'm upset about Mum.* No spelt scone would be too much to bear. Then I spotted a lumpy brown triangle at the back, 'Buckwheat and Apple

Scone' written on a white paper flag taped to a toothpick and poked into its middle. Not spelt, but it would do. I wandered home through London Fields swinging a small white paper carrier bag containing the buckwheat scone and a large banana muffin, passing the outdoor swimming pool and the hole-in-the-wall cafe where people with straggly wet hair sat at wooden tables sipping hot chocolate.

Launch

When I began to write our story down, I thought I was writing a
record of hate but somehow the hate has got mislaid and all I know
is that in spite of her mistakes and her unreliability, she was better
than most.

Graham Greene, *The End of the Affair*, 1951

I do think my mother was better than most. I think all our
family were better than most. There was something so raw about
us. I'm glad those three relationships are over though – sorry,
Mum, even you, clever and supportive as you were. I'm also glad
I read the diaries. My father's diary showed me our family from
a different perspective. I'd only ever heard my mother's point
of view before. After finishing Lucien's account I was so moved
by his sadness and confusion that I was momentarily overcome
with love and compassion, and my attitude towards him and
men in general softened. I can't have close relationships with
them any more though. Not long into any interaction with a
man I get a whiff of the oppressor and bolt. Mum's oft-repeated
exasperated cry of 'What on earth do you want a man for?'
makes perfect sense to me now, as does her fondness for ginger
and rhubarb.

Any warm feelings I still had left for my father evaporated as
I read my mother's diary. Mum's experiences resonated so deeply
they eclipsed his. I identified with this optimistic, intelligent
young woman who was thwarted, dominated and bullied by the
men she was involved with and restricted by the society she was
born into. A woman whose life was shrapnelled with so many

petty injustices that – despite her attempts to remain strong and positive – her faith in people and her mental health were damaged by their accumulation. Just before she died I asked Mum to come back and visit me if ghosts existed. She promised she would, but even as I said it I thought, *For God's sake, give her some peace.* I hope she's having a rest. I hope you're having a nice rest, Mum. (No sightings yet.)

Two days after the scene in the care home, before I'd read Mum's diary, I was sitting on the top deck of the 55 bus, staring out of the window, daydreaming, when I got a phone call from the police. The manager of the care home must have told them what transpired that night. *Now I'm for it*, I thought. The policeman asked if I wanted to press charges against my sister for GBH (grievous bodily harm). I was so surprised it wasn't me who was in trouble that I said, 'But I hit her first!' I was aware I sounded like a child. He explained that as my injury was potentially life-changing and my sister's wasn't, mine was more serious and I could prosecute her. As he talked, an idea that had been hovering at the edge of my mind for the last few months crashed to the front of my brain and became a certainty. *We were set up. That night was years in the making. It wasn't her fault*, said a voice in my head. I can't believe it took me so long to figure it out, or that it struck me for the first time on the top deck of the 55 as a policeman gave me the option to take my sister to court. Not only was Mum's Last Night not Pascale's fault, the friction between us wasn't her fault either.

The combined circumstances of Mum and Lucien both being dead and Pascale being out of my life created a place to stand and look back at my life, without the clutter of my family and their baggage blocking the view. From this new perspective I began to form the hypothesis that it wasn't only a clash of personalities that had set Pascale and me at each other for so many years, like Mum had always tried to make out. It was also our parents, their games, their mistakes, the time that they, and we, were born into, and our family's mental health status (all on the autistic spectrum).

> . . . in many cases those who trespass against you do so out of a misery that means the punishment preceded and even precipitated the crime.
>
> Rebecca Solnit, *The Faraway Nearby*, 2013

Realising it wasn't all Pascale's fault that Mum's Last Night turned ugly, or that we never got along, was not a comforting revelation. I now had nothing to shield my emotions from the doubt and shame that rose up every time I thought about my behaviour that evening. It occurred to me that I was not being a good mother that night after all, I was just being ruthless. Maybe I just wanted Mum's death all to myself.

I didn't prosecute Pascale, and my thumb healed after a few months, but I haven't played guitar since that night, not even picked it up and looked at it.

That moment of realisation on the 55 bus has helped rekindle the love I felt for Pascale when we were young children. The love I had for her, which was buried for so long under conflicts and rivalries, has resurfaced. I feel such tenderness towards her now, and I wish her well in all she does. I think she may even feel the same towards me.

Nine months after Mum's death I had another book launch to make up for the one that didn't happen. Faber organised a party at Natalie Galustian's Rare Books, a little bookshop in Cecil Court. I was happy and excited. Vida was with me, Eryk was coming, I had my hair up in a French plait. Walking down the narrow street lined with rare book shops and places selling old coins, cigarette cards and first editions (apparently the inspiration for Diagon Alley in *Harry Potter*), Vida on my arm, not sad about Mum's death, I felt reborn. The window, dressed by Theresa Boden, was piled with giant gingerbread biscuits iced with chapter titles from my book, and posters, T-shirts, Terry de Havilland shoes and roller skates from the 1970s were strewn about the store. The room became so crowded, hot and sweaty that people spilled out onto the pavement even though it was February. We all looked like we had orange socks, trousers and tights on as our legs were lit from underneath by the pavement lights.

59 I lifted two plates down from the aluminium shelf and put them on the table, wondering why all my crockery is white. I like other people's floral and patterned plates but never buy them myself. I'd rather not live in old buildings or rooms with cosy furnishings, clutter and cosy little nooks either. I need my surroundings to be simple, I want to know what's going on in the corners. The scone slid out of the bag onto the plate, unleashing an avalanche of crumbs. I ate them up later, collected them on the pad of a licked forefinger, then scooped all remaining smears of butter from the knife and sucked the whole lot off my finger. It didn't make up for the scone being gone but it was a consolation.

When I was little my balloon burst as we were walking home from a children's party one afternoon. I saw a balloon about once a year so it was a huge loss. Mum bent down, picked the flaccid piece of rubber off the pavement, stretched it tight across her lips and twisted it as she sucked in her breath. Then she tied the old piece of string tightly around the little piece of rubber dangling from her lips and pulled a miniature balloon out of her mouth. She said the balloon had had a baby, it was a baby balloon. I stopped crying and trailed it after me all the way home. A baby balloon.

I cut a small triangle off the edge of the scone, gouged a scoop of lightly salted Danish butter out of the tub and trowelled it on like a bricklayer slathering cement onto a wall. Much too much butter, almost the same quantity of butter as scone, but as Nora Ephron's mother said, 'You can never have too much butter.'* Then I placed the whole mess on my tongue, closed my eyes – tastebuds on high alert for a fleck of salt – and let the damp earthy sponge, hardly sweet at all, meld into the creamy-cool butter. An unexpected spike of cold, tart apple shocked me. I opened my eyes with a start. I'd forgotten there was apple in there.

* Nora Ephron, *I Feel Bad About My Neck*, 2006

Burn the Diaries[*]

I have my mother's mouth and
my father's eyes; on my face
they are
still together.
>   Warsan Shire, *Teaching My Mother How to Give
>   Birth*, 2011

Kathleen's little green bag and Lucien's big brown bag are in my shed now, laid to rest, side by side. The truth isn't in one bag or the other. In my head or Pascale's head. The truth isn't in one bag, one head, one heart or one mind. Truth is splintered. I'm tempted to leave the bags in the shed in case I need them again one day. I'm not going to though, for Vida's sake. I don't want her to inherit the diaries and have to decide what to do with them when I'm dead. I want to give her no choice at all. I'm the parent, I'll take responsibility and make the decision. Enough of the story is written here if she's interested.

I know, I'll burn the diaries.

NB: Get Magnus to help, he likes making fires. As soon as this book is finished. Do it.

---

[*] Moyra Davey and Alison Strayer, *Burn the Diaries*, 2014

Acknowledgements

Special thanks to Sally OJ (Orson Jones), my first reader and a constant guide and rock throughout the writing of this book. Thanks also to Trace Newton Ingham, my intelligent, loyal and inspirational friend, for the time and forbearance she puts into me, and for the many conversations she put into this book. For his patience, enthusiasm and unwavering belief in me I wish to thank my editor, Lee Brackstone. I also wish to thank Ella Griffiths, Dan Papps, Hannah Marshall, Kate Ward, Dave Watkins, Mitzi Angel, Stephen Page, the talented and patient Donna Payne, the art department and everyone who worked on this book at Faber & Faber. Thanks too to Ian Bahrami for his meticulous proofreading. Thank you to my agent Georgia Garrett for her advice and encouragement and for all the support I receive from Rogers, Coleridge and White Literary Agency. Thanks to Alice Fox, who kindly read my manuscript and offered many rigorous and insightful observations, and to Kate Murray-Browne for her suggestions.

Special thanks to Graham Rodgers at the Imperial War Museum, Duxford, for tracking down the facts about my uncle Charlie.

For their friendship and interest in this book, I also thank Oliver Curtis, Jet, Lindsay Shapero, Sinead Gleeson, Suzie Robertson and Tom Hunter.

And to my dear daughter, thank you for being you, and for showing me how to love.

All photographs are by the author, except pages 95, 184, 260 and 279, which are by Arla Albertine, and pages 16, 84 and 134 (unknown). Back cover photograph of the author by Carolina Ambida.

p. 285 'I have my mother's . . .': acknowledgement is made for permission to reprint an extract from *Teaching My Mother How to Give Birth* (2011) by Warsan Shire. © Warsan Shire, 2011. Used by permission of flipped eye publishing.